# Awaken the Master Within

## Golden Age Teachings of Saint Germain

# ALSO BY LORI TOYE

*A Teacher Appears*

*Sisters of the Flame*

*Fields of Light*

*The Ever Present Now*

*New World Wisdom Series*

*I AM America Atlas*

*Points of Perception*

*Light of Awakening*

*Divine Destiny*

*Sacred Energies*

*Temples of Consciousness*

*Building the Seamless Garment*

*Freedom Star Book*

*I AM America Map*

*Freedom Star Map*

*6-Map Scenario*

*US Golden City Map*

# Awaken the Master Within

Golden Age Teachings of Saint Germain

GOLDEN CITY SERIES
BOOK SIX

## Lori Adaile Toye

I AM AMERICA PUBLISHING & DISTRIBUTING
P.O. Box 2511, Payson, Arizona, 85547, USA.
www.iamamerica.com

© (Copyright) 2019 by Lori Adaile Toye. All rights reserved. ISBN: 978-1-880050-28-6. All rights exclusively reserved, including under the Berne Convention and the Universal Copyright Convention. No part of this book may be reproduced or translated in any language or utilized in any form or by any means, electronic or mechanical, including photocopying, recording, or by any information storage and retrieval system, without written permission from the publisher. Published in 2019 by I AM America Seventh Ray Publishing International, P.O. Box 2511, Payson, Arizona, 85547, United States of America.

I AM America Maps and Books have been marketed since 1989 by I AM America Seventh Ray Publishing and Distributing, through workshops, conferences, and numerous bookstores in the United States and internationally. If you are interested in obtaining information on available releases please write or call:
I AM America, P.O. Box 2511, Payson, Arizona, 85547, USA. (928) 978-6435, or visit:
www.iamamerica.com
www.loritoye.com

Graphic Design and Typography by Lori Toye
Host and Questions by Lenard Toye
Editing by Elaine Cardall and Betsy Robinson

*Love, in service, breathes the breath for all!*
Print On Demand Version
10 9 8 7 6 5 4 3 2 1

*"This great Divinity that lies within is indeed a sleeping Master.
It is awakened and enlivened through the knowledge of
the Great I AM."*

~ Saint Germain

# Contents

FOREWORD *by Pamela Fernsler*     xix
PREFACE     xxiii

CHAPTER ONE
## *The Hidden Planet* • 25

Master and Student Relationship .................... 25
The Collective Reality ............................. 26
Group Karma ...................................... 26
Predestination .................................... 27
Three Plus Three, Plus One ........................ 27
Parallel Universes and Déjà Vu..................... 28
Mastery of the Seven Chakras ...................... 28
Stepping Into Fourth Dimension .................... 28
Fourth Dimension.................................. 29
Duality Provides Experience ....................... 29
Ancestral Planet................................... 30
The Awakening..................................... 30
Twin Sun Obscures ................................ 30
Ancient Builder Races ............................. 31
A Red Star ....................................... 31
Protection Through Higher Consciousness ........... 32
Protective Field of the Golden Cities .............. 32
The Readied Heart................................. 33
Sound Merges Thought, Feeling, and Action ......... 33
Progenitors....................................... 34
The Eight-sided Cell of Perfection ................ 34

Meissner Field and the Oneship . . . . . . . . . . . . . . . . . . . 35
A Mighty Transmitter. . . . . . . . . . . . . . . . . . . . . . . . . . . . . 35
Beliefs Are the Core . . . . . . . . . . . . . . . . . . . . . . . . . . . . . . 36
Called by Many Names . . . . . . . . . . . . . . . . . . . . . . . . . . . 36
Small, Steady, Sure . . . . . . . . . . . . . . . . . . . . . . . . . . . . . . 37
Integrating Golden City Energies . . . . . . . . . . . . . . . . . . . 37
Humanity Determines. . . . . . . . . . . . . . . . . . . . . . . . . . . . 38
Violet Flame Prayer . . . . . . . . . . . . . . . . . . . . . . . . . . . . . . 39
Thought, Feeling, Action . . . . . . . . . . . . . . . . . . . . . . . . . 39

CHAPTER TWO
## *All Is Love* ♦ 41

The Violet Ray . . . . . . . . . . . . . . . . . . . . . . . . . . . . . . . . . .41
A Fresh Perspective. . . . . . . . . . . . . . . . . . . . . . . . . . . . . . 42
Choice and the Process of Change. . . . . . . . . . . . . . . . . . 43
Karma and the Violet Flame. . . . . . . . . . . . . . . . . . . . . . . 44
Fear and Love . . . . . . . . . . . . . . . . . . . . . . . . . . . . . . . . . . 44
Spiritual Growth through the Law of Love . . . . . . . . . . . 45
Love Drives Evolution . . . . . . . . . . . . . . . . . . . . . . . . . . . 46
Higher Love and Consciousness . . . . . . . . . . . . . . . . . . . 47
Two Suns . . . . . . . . . . . . . . . . . . . . . . . . . . . . . . . . . . . . . 48
The Ancestors . . . . . . . . . . . . . . . . . . . . . . . . . . . . . . . . . . 49
A Hidden, Guiding Planet . . . . . . . . . . . . . . . . . . . . . . . .51
The Nondual Christ Force . . . . . . . . . . . . . . . . . . . . . . . . 52
Love, Consciousness, and Prophecy. . . . . . . . . . . . . . . . . 53
Possibility and Probability. . . . . . . . . . . . . . . . . . . . . . . . 54
"A Change of Heart" . . . . . . . . . . . . . . . . . . . . . . . . . . . . 54

CHAPTER THREE
## *The Master Within* • 57

The Metaphysical Law of Reciprocity . . . . . . . . . . . . . . . . . 57
A Teacher Lifts Emotional Burden . . . . . . . . . . . . . . . . . . . 58
Gentle Leadership. . . . . . . . . . . . . . . . . . . . . . . . . . . . . . . . 59
Within the Silence . . . . . . . . . . . . . . . . . . . . . . . . . . . . . . . 59
Out-picturing Perfection . . . . . . . . . . . . . . . . . . . . . . . . . . 60
Integration, Compassion, and Enlightenment . . . . . . . . . . 60
Absolute Self-knowledge . . . . . . . . . . . . . . . . . . . . . . . . . . .61
Opening the Heart . . . . . . . . . . . . . . . . . . . . . . . . . . . . . . .61
Choosing the Thought . . . . . . . . . . . . . . . . . . . . . . . . . . . 62
Be Ready to Receive . . . . . . . . . . . . . . . . . . . . . . . . . . . . . 63
Awaken the Master Within . . . . . . . . . . . . . . . . . . . . . . . . 63
The Spiritual Paths . . . . . . . . . . . . . . . . . . . . . . . . . . . . . . 64
We Are Always ONE . . . . . . . . . . . . . . . . . . . . . . . . . . . . . 65

CHAPTER FOUR
## *The Mighty Violet Flame* • 67

Call the Flame into Activity . . . . . . . . . . . . . . . . . . . . . . . 67
The Great Change. . . . . . . . . . . . . . . . . . . . . . . . . . . . . . . 68
Justice and the Violet Flame. . . . . . . . . . . . . . . . . . . . . . . 69
Your Divinity . . . . . . . . . . . . . . . . . . . . . . . . . . . . . . . . . . .70
Use of the I AM and the Violet Flame . . . . . . . . . . . . . . . .71
Higher Vibration. . . . . . . . . . . . . . . . . . . . . . . . . . . . . . . . 72
The New Consciousness. . . . . . . . . . . . . . . . . . . . . . . . . . 73
The Earth Plane and Planet . . . . . . . . . . . . . . . . . . . . . . . 74
The Heavenly Lords . . . . . . . . . . . . . . . . . . . . . . . . . . . . . 75
A Plane of Consciousness. . . . . . . . . . . . . . . . . . . . . . . . . 75
Beyond Imagination. . . . . . . . . . . . . . . . . . . . . . . . . . . . . 76
Awakening from Darkness. . . . . . . . . . . . . . . . . . . . . . . . 77
Silicon-based Consciousness . . . . . . . . . . . . . . . . . . . . . . 77

The Gift. . . . . . . . . . . . . . . . . . . . . . . . . . . . . . . . . . . . . . . . . . . . . 78
Trust the Process. . . . . . . . . . . . . . . . . . . . . . . . . . . . . . . . . . . . 79
Interaction of the Elemental and Deva Kingdoms . . . . . . . 79
Opening the Gate. . . . . . . . . . . . . . . . . . . . . . . . . . . . . . . . . . . 80
Immersion into the Divine . . . . . . . . . . . . . . . . . . . . . . . . . .81
Violet Flame Mantra. . . . . . . . . . . . . . . . . . . . . . . . . . . . . . . . 82
Judgment Is a Trap . . . . . . . . . . . . . . . . . . . . . . . . . . . . . . . . . 82

CHAPTER FIVE
# *I AM Awareness* • 85

Vibration and Consciousness. . . . . . . . . . . . . . . . . . . . . . . . 85
You Create Your Vibration . . . . . . . . . . . . . . . . . . . . . . . . . . 87
When Life "Happens" . . . . . . . . . . . . . . . . . . . . . . . . . . . . . . 87
Balance . . . . . . . . . . . . . . . . . . . . . . . . . . . . . . . . . . . . . . . . . . . 88
Relationship of Consciousness to Spiritual Growth . . . . . . 88
The Power of the Great I AM . . . . . . . . . . . . . . . . . . . . . . . . 89
Harmony's Blessings. . . . . . . . . . . . . . . . . . . . . . . . . . . . . . . . 90
I AM Awareness . . . . . . . . . . . . . . . . . . . . . . . . . . . . . . . . . . . 90
The Interconnectivity of the I AM . . . . . . . . . . . . . . . . . . . . 91
Cultivate Tolerance and Patience. . . . . . . . . . . . . . . . . . . . . 92
Call Forth the I AM Awareness. . . . . . . . . . . . . . . . . . . . . . . 93
Divinity Exists in All Things. . . . . . . . . . . . . . . . . . . . . . . . . 94
Out-picturing, Focus, and the Universal Flow. . . . . . . . . . . 95
Pain, the Equalizer . . . . . . . . . . . . . . . . . . . . . . . . . . . . . . . . . 96

CHAPTER SIX
## *Eternal Balance* • 97

Law of Correspondence . . . . . . . . . . . . . . . . . . . . . . . . . . . . 97
The Clarity of the Teaching . . . . . . . . . . . . . . . . . . . . . . . 98
"The Difference Is Experience". . . . . . . . . . . . . . . . . . . . . . 99
Compassion and the Open Heart . . . . . . . . . . . . . . . . . . 99
Beyond "Right" or "Wrong" . . . . . . . . . . . . . . . . . . . . . . . .100
Love for All . . . . . . . . . . . . . . . . . . . . . . . . . . . . . . . . . . . .100
The Law of Forgiveness. . . . . . . . . . . . . . . . . . . . . . . . . . . 100
Spiritual Stagnation . . . . . . . . . . . . . . . . . . . . . . . . . . . . . 101
Wahanee and the Violet Flame . . . . . . . . . . . . . . . . . . . . 102
The Schools of Light. . . . . . . . . . . . . . . . . . . . . . . . . . . . . 103
The First Seven Golden Cities. . . . . . . . . . . . . . . . . . . . . . 104
Forgiveness and Perception . . . . . . . . . . . . . . . . . . . . . . 105
Golden City Activations. . . . . . . . . . . . . . . . . . . . . . . . . . 106
Divine Intervention of the Golden Cities . . . . . . . . . . . . 107

CHAPTER SEVEN
## *Golden Ray Mantra* • 109

Political Changes. . . . . . . . . . . . . . . . . . . . . . . . . . . . . . . . 109
Golden Cities and Earth's Electromagnetism. . . . . . . . . . 110
Masters of the Gateways . . . . . . . . . . . . . . . . . . . . . . . . . 110
The DAHL Universe and the Golden Ray. . . . . . . . . . . . . 110
The Group . . . . . . . . . . . . . . . . . . . . . . . . . . . . . . . . . . . . 111
Golden Ray Mantra . . . . . . . . . . . . . . . . . . . . . . . . . . . . . 112
Harmonization of Energy . . . . . . . . . . . . . . . . . . . . . . . . 112
Use of the Golden Ray Mantra . . . . . . . . . . . . . . . . . . . . 113
Activity and Use of the Eighth Light Body . . . . . . . . . . . 113
Beyond Duality . . . . . . . . . . . . . . . . . . . . . . . . . . . . . . . . 114

CHAPTER EIGHT
## *Path of Mastery* • 115

When the Student Is Ready . . . . . . . . . . . . . . . . . . . . . . . 115
Sharing Messages . . . . . . . . . . . . . . . . . . . . . . . . . . . . . . . 116
Metaphysics of the Teacher / Student Relationship . . . . . . 116
The Chela . . . . . . . . . . . . . . . . . . . . . . . . . . . . . . . . . . . . . 118
On Teaching . . . . . . . . . . . . . . . . . . . . . . . . . . . . . . . . . . . 119
Lineage of the Master Teacher . . . . . . . . . . . . . . . . . . . . . 120
Initiation in Gobean . . . . . . . . . . . . . . . . . . . . . . . . . . . . . 121
Within Your Heart . . . . . . . . . . . . . . . . . . . . . . . . . . . . . . 122
Emissary of Energy . . . . . . . . . . . . . . . . . . . . . . . . . . . . . . 122
Step-down Energies of El Morya . . . . . . . . . . . . . . . . . . . . 123
Oral Tradition . . . . . . . . . . . . . . . . . . . . . . . . . . . . . . . . . 124

CHAPTER NINE
## *Galactic Energy* • 127

Galactic Energy and Ascension . . . . . . . . . . . . . . . . . . . . . 127
The Great Golden Age . . . . . . . . . . . . . . . . . . . . . . . . . . . 128
Transcend Karmic Patterns . . . . . . . . . . . . . . . . . . . . . . . 129
Bathe in Golden Light . . . . . . . . . . . . . . . . . . . . . . . . . . . 130
Change and the Law of Balance . . . . . . . . . . . . . . . . . . . . 130
Golden City Southern Doors . . . . . . . . . . . . . . . . . . . . . . 131
Opportunity and Challenge . . . . . . . . . . . . . . . . . . . . . . . 131
United States Economy . . . . . . . . . . . . . . . . . . . . . . . . . . 132
Accelerate Your Decree . . . . . . . . . . . . . . . . . . . . . . . . . . . 133
A Decree for Ascension . . . . . . . . . . . . . . . . . . . . . . . . . . 134
Balancing Karma . . . . . . . . . . . . . . . . . . . . . . . . . . . . . . . 135
The Beloved . . . . . . . . . . . . . . . . . . . . . . . . . . . . . . . . . . . 136
Energies of the Golden Ray . . . . . . . . . . . . . . . . . . . . . . . 137
Heightening Your Vibration . . . . . . . . . . . . . . . . . . . . . . . 137

"I Give My Service" .................................. 137
Moving Forward. ..................................... 138
Energy for Energy. ................................... 139
Adjutant Point Ceremony ........................... 140
Twenty-Year Cycles. .................................. 140

CHAPTER TEN
*Six-fold Path* • 143

Shamballa Knowledge. ............................... 144
"Who Am I?" ......................................... 144
Third Dimensional Experience ..................... 144
"Is There Another Way?" ............................ 145
Principles of the Six-fold Path. ..................... 146
Prophecy Transmutes Prediction ................... 148
The Laboratory of Self. .............................. 148
Laws of Perception. .................................. 149
Love Is the Law of Understanding ................. 150
Sponsorship by a Master Teacher .................. 150
"Self-Discipline Leads to Liberation" .............. 151
Violet Flame for Difficulties ........................ 152

CHAPTER ELEVEN
*Golden City Prayer* • 155

"I AM There" ........................................ 155
Light through the Violet Flame. .................... 156
A Crossroads ........................................ 157
Mighty Love and Light. .............................. 157
The Freed Chela. .................................... 157
Service in the Southern Doors ..................... 158
Teachers of the Fourth Dimension ................. 159
Teachers of the Fifth Dimension. ................... 159

The Teachers Appear ................................ 159
Thousands Flood the Earth ......................... 160
Service of the Step-down Transformer ............... 161
"A Great Outpouring" ............................... 162
At the Adjutant Points ............................. 162
Contrast ........................................... 163
Energy Adjustment .................................. 163
Integration of Light ............................... 164
A Migratory Sequence ............................... 165
"Of Service" ....................................... 166
Follow the Joy ..................................... 167
The Waters of the Dimensions ....................... 168
A Student's Past Life .............................. 169
A Healing Process .................................. 170

CHAPTER ELEVEN

## *Time and the Violet Flame* • 173

Transmute Fear ..................................... 173
The Lighted Stance ................................. 174
Detachment ......................................... 175
Purification and Acceleration ...................... 175
Violet Flame and Vibration ......................... 176
Golden Spiral Decree ............................... 177
Light Bodies and Ascension ......................... 178
"The Veil Is Lifted" ............................... 179
Time and the Violet Flame .......................... 180
The Violet Flame Opens Doors ....................... 182
Violet Flame Decree for Healing .................... 183
Stages of the Violet Flame ......................... 183
Time Compaction: Quick and Intense ................. 184

Use at Sunrise and Sunset . . . . . . . . . . . . . . . . . . . . . . . . . 184
Removing Financial Obstacles . . . . . . . . . . . . . . . . . . . . . 186
Live with Intention and Purpose . . . . . . . . . . . . . . . . . . 186
A Consciousness Portal . . . . . . . . . . . . . . . . . . . . . . . . . . 187
Golden Cities of the Inner Earth. . . . . . . . . . . . . . . . . . . 188
Golden City Network . . . . . . . . . . . . . . . . . . . . . . . . . . . 189
"Remove the Veil of Ignorance" . . . . . . . . . . . . . . . . . . . 190
Consciousness and Catastrophe. . . . . . . . . . . . . . . . . . . .191
The Field of Protection . . . . . . . . . . . . . . . . . . . . . . . . . . 192
A Quickening. . . . . . . . . . . . . . . . . . . . . . . . . . . . . . . . . . 193
Adjustment of Earth's Vibration . . . . . . . . . . . . . . . . . . . 193
Prophecies of the White Star. . . . . . . . . . . . . . . . . . . . . . 194
The Time Is Now . . . . . . . . . . . . . . . . . . . . . . . . . . . . . . 195
Love of Living. . . . . . . . . . . . . . . . . . . . . . . . . . . . . . . . . 196

Appendix A: *Seven Chakra System* . . . . . . . . . . . . . . . . . . . . . . . . 199
Appendix B: *Golden Cities through the Dimensions* . . . . . . . . . . . . . . 201
Appendix C: *The DAHL Universe*. . . . . . . . . . . . . . . . . . . . . . . . . . 203
Appendix D: *Eight-sided Cell of Perfection within the Human Heart* . . 205
　　　　　　*The Thirteen Pyramids and Twelve Evolution Points
　　　　　　of the Eight-sided Cell of Perfection* . . . . . . . . . . . . . . . . 206
Appendix E: *The Violet Flame* . . . . . . . . . . . . . . . . . . . . . . . . . . . 207
Appendix F: *The Law of Love*. . . . . . . . . . . . . . . . . . . . . . . . . . . . 209
Appendix G: *Golden City Vortex Activation Dates* . . . . . . . . . . . . . .211
Appendix H: *Golden City Activation* . . . . . . . . . . . . . . . . . . . . . . . 213
Appendix I: *Golden City Structure*. . . . . . . . . . . . . . . . . . . . . . . . . 215
　　　　　　*Doors of a Golden City*. . . . . . . . . . . . . . . . . . . . . . . . 216
　　　　　　*Seven Adjutant Points of a Golden City Doorway* . . . . . . . 217
Appendix J: *Sananda's Sunday Peace Meditation* . . . . . . . . . . . . . . . 219
Appendix K: *The Gold Ray*. . . . . . . . . . . . . . . . . . . . . . . . . . . . . . 223
Appendix L: *Golden Ray Mantra* . . . . . . . . . . . . . . . . . . . . . . . . . 225
Appendix M: *"Why should I listen to channeled tapes?"* . . . . . . . . . . 227

Appendix N: *Saint Germain, the Holy Brother* . . . . . . . . . . . . . . . . . . 229
Appendix O: *The Twelve Jurisdictions* . . . . . . . . . . . . . . . . . . . . . . . . . 233

| | |
|---|---|
| Spiritual Lineage of the Violet Flame | 235 |
| Glossary | 237 |
| Discography | 257 |
| Index | 259 |
| About Lori & Lenard Toye | 275 |
| About I AM America | 278 |

# Foreword

A lifetime of study and experiences follow the awakening of one's own personal Master Within. This volume will bolster your awakening by focusing on the information provided by Saint Germain and other ascended beings who are dedicated to the positive evolution of the human race as we realize who we really are. The Masters reveal new mysteries which heretofore have been held back until they considered the time not only to be right, but to be best for a mass evolution.

Awakening one's own personal Master Within takes quite a bit of doing. While exercises and meditations may help us, developing your own personal Mastery takes time. Learning something from a book and practicing it once weekly doesn't make it a habit. One must make practice constant, turning it into a lifestyle. Awakening the Master Within changes your life not only once, but again and again, as new understandings open up with habitual practice. Being the Master Within requires perseverance and dedication—to yourself.

All the messages from the Ascended Masters in Lori Toye's books direct the reader to realization of one's individuated Self. In this state, one becomes one's own mentor. This evolution correlates to the fading importance of the guru, the swami, and the mystic leader.

Self-Mastery comes from knowledge of who one is. It is said that if you know who you are, you need learn nothing else from the universe. Learning this is a many lifetimes job, and one way to do it is to study the Ascended Master teachings, which come through various groups, both esoteric and exoteric. While we learn who we are, we also learn the Laws of the Universe by which we are created and exist. We learn how we humans reflect the Laws of the Universe within us, why we are alive, what the ultimate goal is not just for this life, but for the other lives we've had. Knowing who we have been does not define us, but points to our Ascension goal, toward what we are drawn to become.

Self-Mastery derives from combining the will, the desire, and the thought. This triadic combination causes action and manifestation. Therefore, Self-Mastery brings awareness that one is responsible for all thought, action, and deed. Thus Self-Mastery brings about the ability to define one's own reality, becoming pro-active instead of remaining re-active to all influences from others. It is the defining moment when a prince or princess understands what it really means to be a king or a queen. When this moment arrives, our understanding of the universe opens, and the magic and wonder of it fill our soul.

Self-Mastery doesn't mean we don't need relationships any longer, for it is necessary for all humanity to experience the Oneness in which we are all linked. It also doesn't give one the right to control another, and such a desire vanishes when Self-Mastery is attained and practiced. For Self-Mastery is the way of the heart, not the way of degrees and titles and certificates. It is something one establishes for oneself. It is our ultimate Chi.

In Mystery School teachings, the student at the portal is told to forget everything he or she has learned up to this point. This directive often leads the student to think that there's no more value to all the learning and experiences that went before, and resentment sets in. What the schools are requesting is that one prepares to go beyond those ideas and preferences and customs and beliefs, because there is more, and it is amazing.

So put behind you all your negative thoughts of yourself, your button-pushing in relationships, your daily chores, and look upon them as good only so far, but no further. They cannot take you on your wonderful journey. Think of having driven just a car until the Awakening. Now you will step onto a different mode of transportation where you will be helped in your journey—*Awaken the Master Within* will provide you with the necessary information.

Faith without truth is hollow, brittle belief.

I wish you success on your path; make it your own; use the resources to which you are attracted. Let all the *I AM America* resources help you on your beautiful journey of Light, Life and Love.

*Pamela Fernsler*

*Born with a Mars retrograde in the 9th house in Virgo, Pam has had access to the mysteries of the Earth, and considers the sciences behind them. Access to the higher realms has been her mainstream reality, from ascended being contacts to Akashic records. She has explored various mystery schools throughout her adult life, which included The Society of the Magicians, The Rosicrucian Order (AMORC), Keepers of the Flame (from Church Universal), The Rosicrucian Fellowship, and currently the I AM America mystery school. She is familiar with the Keys of Enoch, OAHSPE, Madame Blavatsky's works, and more. Pam knows their ways and can refer individuals to the organization that may best serve their esoteric path.*

*She has produced discourses and workshops for AMORC. Her lifetime of esoteric experiences inform her an understanding of the magic of the universe, which underlies her dedication to helping it along, whether as a psychic or a friend with just the right words at the right time.*

# Preface

Studies by paranormal researchers reveal that trance channels rarely, if ever, remember the contents of a channeled session. This has undoubtedly been my experience, although I might recall a memorable passage or two from the Spiritual Teachers. By the time a channeled session is transcribed and structurally edited, I finally have the pleasure, but more often the astonishing wonder, of reading the material for the first time. Of course I can always listen to the trance session and take notes, but I'm a visual learner.

Fifteen years since the original channeling of this information, I am astounded to read the material I now put in your hands. It literally sat untouched through both the Bush and Obama administrations, yet *right now* these teachings are amazingly, perfectly timed to address current events, and the accompanying questions and obvious concerns. I have no doubt that the Masters purposely prompted us to hold back this material until this moment, when worldwide events have evolved as if to prime our receptivity to listen—waited for our spiritual "eyes and ears" to be developed enough that we could thoughtfully *see* and perceptively *hear* its message.

Whether you have just picked up this book and are new to the *I AM America Teachings*, or you've been studying for years, you won't find information like this anywhere else. *Awaken the Master Within* is a manual for students and teachers alike. These teachings are designed to help you to reaffirm your innate Divinity via contact with your true self—the Master Within. According to Saint Germain, this is through the Divine Law of Reciprocity, the metaphysical economics of giving and receiving. He reiterates this simply: "Yes, I am ready to receive. Yes, I am ready to give." His statement is a mirror of the well-known esoteric passage, "As within, so without." Our lives are a divine reflection of our spiritual generosity, reception, and acceptance.

Throughout these pages Saint Germain readily gives spiritual techniques and the vital knowledge that underlies their cultivation. Yes, this book is filled with numerous noteworthy Violet Flame decrees and practices, designed to transmute karma and instigate your passage into the soul-freeing Ascension Process. But he also describes our collective movement from carbon-based consciousness to silicon-based consciousness. This is our journey from the everyday fear-based hustle, to living a compassionate, divinely inspired life. Silicon-based consciousness thrives among the psychic super senses and drives lifespans beyond a hundred years or more. Saint Germain also shares useful insight about the twenty-year cycles of Earth, their convergence with the Gold Ray, and the value of the Sixfold Path—a spiritual teaching of tolerance, forgiveness, respect, and harmony.

Unafraid of sharing prophetic forecasts, Saint Germain imparts information about Nibiru or Planet X as the "White Star." He states its appearance ushers in a memorable period of awakening and spiritual development for humanity, strengthened by the multi-dimensional *Protective Field*. This ethereal field of light is composed of energies of the Golden Cities, located both in the inner Earth as well as the outer Earth's fifty-one locations. The powerful energetic grid is also aided by the Spiritual Hierarchy, seasoned Elohim, Archangels, and Cosmic Beings. They flood the ethereal planes of Earth by the thousands and reside in the sublime Ashrams of the Golden Cities. It is an indisputable fact that at this most precarious time on Earth, our human evolution is assisted and supported by multi-dimensional light beings from our galaxy and from our parallel galaxy—the DAHL. The only glitch to obtain their invaluable assistance lies again in our application of that great Law of Reciprocity; it is time for us to *receive* their precious gift.

My suggestion is that as you read each chapter, be prepared to discover ground-breaking spiritual teaching and new methods you've never thought possible. Ground yourself in your Divine Perfection and tune in to your own Mighty Master within through the ever present power of the I AM. The *Time is Now* for your remarkable awakening.

> "The time has come for man to receive the gift."
>
> *Lori Toye*

# 1

## The Hidden Planet
*Saint Germain*

Greetings Beloved chelas in that mighty Christ. I AM Saint Germain and I stream forth on that Violet Ray of Mercy, Compassion, and ultimate Forgiveness. As usual Dear ones, Dear hearts, I request permission to come forward.

Response: *You have permission and you are most welcome.*

There is much work for us still to complete Dear ones, Dear chelas of mine. When I make this statement, it is a statement of eternal truth for indeed we are working together, are we not?

Response: *Yes, we are.*

MASTER AND STUDENT RELATIONSHIP

There may be those who do not understand the relationship of the guru and the chela. There may be those who do not understand the relationship between a student and a teacher. There may be those who may not understand the relationship between a Master and one who is aspiring to become as ONE. In our relationship, all three of these components are contained. Indeed, there is a guru and there is a chela; there is a Master and there is a student; there is indeed an Ascended Master working with the true aspirant upon the path.

## THE COLLECTIVE REALITY

Dear ones, Dear hearts, it is important to understand that at this time there is much work to be completed for the I AM America Material. There is still information that will be given about the upcoming Earth Changes. Earth Changes, indeed, presented as a prophecy but also Earth Changes that are scheduled to occur. You see Dear ones, Dear hearts, the teachings of prophecy have always been given as a warning—way ahead of time—so that different choices can be made. Let me explain.

You well understand the Co-creation process. You well understand how thought, feeling, action, and Divine Will all come together in that moment to create, shall we say, realities. We have explained some of this in the Point of Perception Discourse. It is important also to understand that parallel universes exist, altered realities, or altered outcomes, shall we say, of scenarios that exist within a given context or frame of mind. It is true that mind is the builder but will or choice will help determine the direction and focus of how a creation is to come forward. Will and choice, at all times, can come forward and change situations, circumstances. You see this in your everyday will and the thought is then always brought forward. Is it probable for this to happen in a collective reality? For you see Dear ones, Dear hearts, indeed the many thoughts, the many feelings, and the many actions are always coming forward, creating in that collective reality.

## GROUP KARMA

The collective reality is that present moment that you are experiencing, shall we say, in a broader sense. This broader sense is the political scene that you are experiencing. That broader sense is the economics that you are currently experiencing. It would, in this way, be explained more as a collective-group karma, a group of souls that are choosing to understand a given situation in a certain context. It too becomes a perception. In your own regional area, within a 200-mile radius, you are all experiencing a certain weather pattern, a certain ecosystem. This too is created through a set of circumstances that are allowing those within that collective understanding, that collective, to create a reality.

## PREDESTINATION

That mind that comes forward within that ecosystem brings forward, in its own thought body, its mental out-picturing; in its own emotional body, its emotional out-picturing; and in its own action body, its action out-picturing. These come together to form, shall we say, a total will. This will is always understood to be congruent with the Divine Plan. Yet it would seem at times that the Divine Plan operates through collective choices and yet it also works with the grand predestination. This predestination, as you have well understood, is held through the Galactic Center of the Great Central Sun and the seven rays of light and sound. But do not steer too far away from this discourse today on collective thought and collective outcome. It is important that we stay focused upon the idea again of thought, feeling, and action.

## THREE PLUS THREE, PLUS ONE

As you will note I just also gave to you another key of the out-picturing process. Each layer of the field indeed has its own out-picturing. This out-picturing is a very important aspect. So you see again, there are six congruent ideas coming together to form within the will, the everlasting paradigm or pattern of the septenary Rays coming forward again. This is an important concept to understand. Why is it so Dear ones, Dear hearts? Because the septenary qualities carry a collective harmony, carry that First Jurisdiction within their being. Three plus three plus one; three on one side and three upon the other brings a perfect balance. This may be difficult for some to understand but this is maybe the most simplistic mathematical way to begin to understand how all thoughts, feelings, and actions work together to form a collective motion.

## PARALLEL AND DÈJÀ VU EXPERIENCES

This collective motion is carried forward, yes, through a Divine Plan, through the Divine Will. But it is important also to understand that Divine Choices made, shall we say, for a higher and a greater good, can indeed effect an outcome. These Divine Choices carry with them cosmic qualities then, primarily the Law of Love. Add to this the other Jurisdictions, as you well know, Laws of Charity . . . Laws of Harmony . . . Laws of Abundance . . . Laws of Cooperation, all orchestrating a greater design. Parallel universes exist also within the creation of the septenary qualities. They enact through the overtones, again another subtle nuance to understanding the system of creation. That is why at times you may feel that sense of déjà vu. You may feel a sense of altered reality, like "I have been here before, haven't I?" For indeed Dear ones, Dear hearts, you may have traveled that path within a past life; you may have also been there within a parallel experience.

## MASTERY OF THE CHAKRA SYSTEM

How does one group all such experiences into collective consciousness? How does one bring this into the eternal memory of the self, into conscious immortality? It requires, shall we say, first a great discipline of the Kundalini. This comes through a Mastery of the Seven-Chakra System; again, three plus three plus one. Now let us speak at that neutral point, which is ONE. When I speak of ONE, the Oneship, this is now gaining greater clarity for you, is it not?[1]

Answer: *Yes it is.*

## STEPPING INTO FOURTH DIMENSION

This Oneship comes forward Dear ones, Dear hearts, within the heart. Again, it is the Eight-Sided Cell of Perfection, for the seven, when gathered, creates a total of eight and *there* is the stepping-

---

1. See Appendix A, *Seven Chakra System,* page 199.

stone for the Fourth Dimension. The Fourth Dimension, you see Dear ones, Dear hearts, functions entirely differently. As you well know the Third Dimension and its functionality, it is true that it contains parallel universes and contains time but the Fourth Dimension is as we are now, bringing in this greater understanding, working beyond time. It is that frame of reference where past, present, and future become the ever present now. Everything is seen in the Fourth Dimension in terms of the existence of time, working from this principle, having the qualities of past, present, and future. But time is seen in the context of existing as the eternal ONE.

## FOURTH DIMENSION

Embracing the Oneship is the beginning of understanding the Fourth Dimension. When the Fourth Dimension is embraced Dear ones, Dear hearts, through this total understanding of the ONE, then one begins to understand a greater Co-creation and how things can move beyond the constraints of duality.[2]

## DUALITY PROVIDES EXPERIENCE

Duality Dear ones, Dear hearts, functions upon the Law of Opposites. These Laws of Opposites provide a great understanding for those who come for education. They provide a great experience. For indeed, it is true, one does not truly know through knowledge; one truly begins to understand through experience. This greater understanding through experience leads one to recognize and understand a greater will that exists, a greater will that exists and can be defined through collective action. Now that I have laid down these simple principles again to you Dear ones, Dear hearts, let us talk about the Earth Changes.

---

*2. See Appendix B, Golden Cities through the Dimensions, page 201.*

## ANCESTRAL PLANET

It is true that there is another planet that exists behind your solar Sun. It has contained within it, the ancestry of the genetic strains that exist upon the Earth Plane and Planet. Some of this information has been recorded within your history. Some of it is correct and some of it is not. It is not, in this moment, for me to make comment on the dual aspects of this, but it is important for you to begin to understand the choices that are now in front of you.

## THE AWAKENING

It was long determined, in the period of time where the atomic bomb was developed and created again upon the Earth, that a group or series of souls must return to the Earth to teach the basis of Co-creation, to teach the basis of the collective ONE, and to bring a greater understanding of these laws to humanity. It is indeed an ancient understanding that has been upon this planet before but it is an understanding that must be awakened among the masses. It is based upon that spark within the heart, the perfection of Divinity, the heart of love, and the Oneship, but it moves in its greater understanding. As you begin to understand that three plus three equals ONE, as the Law of Balance, a greater balance can then occur.

## TWIN SUN OBSCURES

This planet that exists behind your solar Sun (I am not referring to the Great Central Sun, or the Galactic Center; I am referring to the local sun), is different from what some have spoken of as the dead Sun that exists as a twin to your solar Sun. This dead Sun exists from the birth of that planet, for the planet was thrown off by your Sun in a mighty explosion, or shall we say, cosmic birth. In the same way as moons are carried around planets, a twin, non-luminous Sun is attached to your Sun. This dead Sun hides and obscures at times the position and location of this planet.

## ANCIENT BUILDER RACES

The ancestors who came from this planet, at one time had great and deep spiritual knowledge. They understood that the Earth contained the ability to bring life streams forward into greater understanding. Many civilizations were built upon the Earth by the higher groups from this planet. Shamballa and the interaction of it within the Gobi Desert was enacted by several of the great leaders who came from this planet. But as you well know, time as it moves forward in its own sojourn and the re-entrance of Kali Yuga, brought a lessening of light to the planet, brought a darkness upon the planet. As consciousness was descending during this time, those of the higher knowledge of this planet fled, for they understood the law and that they could become trapped within the annals of history. Other planets then came forward who were greater prepared to handle such tribulation, for lack of a better word.

These other beings came from groups of planets known as the Pleiades, and several from the Dahl Universe.[3] They came forward into their outpost located upon the planet Venus and then from there, continued bringing forward the spiritual upliftment for those of humanity. Now Dear ones, Dear hearts, I hope that I have brought this into a greater understanding, into a greater perception so you can begin to understand a greater reality.

## A RED STAR

This planet circles around the Galactic Center with an elliptic type of orbit; therefore, it is almost impossible to see, hidden in that mirror-like quality, the dead sun. But there will come a time that indeed it will appear again. It will appear again in the Eastern horizon. It has been known at other times to be called a Red Star but know this, Dear ones, Dear hearts, that the Red Star comes forward to bring a greater education. It will come forward to bring a greater knowledge; for you see, as I have said Dear ones, Dear hearts, there is no mistake ever, ever, ever.

---

*3. See Appendix C, The Dahl Universe, page 203.*

## PROTECTION THROUGH HIGHER CONSCIOUSNESS

The Earth Changes Prophecies were brought, not only to tell you of the Time of Change that was coming to the planet, but also to herald and usher in a New Time of the birth of the golden consciousness. This planet comes forward, heralding a greater consciousness. Now, there are those who are concerned of its probable impact with the Earth or the trail of its moons that follow. There are some possibilities of this Dear ones, Dear hearts and that is why we have given you the instructions of consciousness . . . the instructions of working towards the Fourth Dimension . . . the instructions of working to build that greater unified field of understanding and reality. In that greater field of understanding and reality lies a greater potential of protection. Let me explain this so you can understand it.

## PROTECTIVE FIELD OF THE GOLDEN CITIES

In the body, as it breaks down into the process of dis-ease, you see a restructuring of the Chakra System; you see a restructuring of the grid system. In this instance, when there is an encounter of the Earth's energetic fields with those it is not that familiar with, again a breakdown begins to occur. There becomes a shakeup, so to speak, within the fields and within the grid patterns. This is now happening upon the Earth Plane and Planet and you are witnesses to a great birth. But know this and understand this, that within the Golden City Vortices is the power that has been directed for you to utilize.

Within the Golden City Vortices has been given all of the information to bring this into a greater alignment, into a greater convergence of harmony. For you see Dear ones, Dear hearts, as we have said so many times before, there we have implanted our consciousness at a Third Dimensional level. There you will feel the energy and the radiance of this consciousness as it interplays in leading you to the Fourth Dimension, in leading you to understanding a greater reality. In this activation of *you* as light sources . . . in *you* as light bearers . . . in *you* as stewards of consciousness, is the ability to put your own protective field about the Earth. This has been the challenge. This is the work in front of us.

## THE READIED HEART

That is why we have stated so many times by design, one heart at a time. Why is this so? Why cannot the masses be led? For you know Dear ones, Dear hearts, the masses are led only by ignorance. But the heart who is ready . . . who is humble . . . who is pure . . . who has seen through the opening of the true eyes . . . who hears the opening of the true sound and light . . . who is ready to receive . . . who is purified by all desires, is ready to enter into a greater understanding. It is true, there are other ways that this consciousness can be attained and we have worked with you to bring a greater understanding. You will now bring that greater understanding into the physical reality and I hope that you know of that which I speak. This alchemical process will bring you into the understanding of Fourth Dimensional reality. In this moment right now, in this moment of discourse, do you hear the finer energies? Do you hear the current of the River of Life?

Answer: *The flow, yes.*

## SOUND MERGES THOUGHT, FEELING, AND ACTION

This flow, as you call it, is indeed a quality of the Fourth Dimension. It manifests itself in the Third Dimension; it is understood in the Second and also the First Dimensions. But its greater reality is expressed within the Fourth Dimension. This flow or current of sound is ever important. This flow and current of sound is the existence of collective, unified understanding. It is the merging of all thoughts, feelings, and actions into a greater Oneship, into that mind that serves the greater Cause Divine. Perhaps you think I speak in cryptic tones but believe me Dear ones, Dear hearts, my words are simplistic; take them as such. Now I sense your questions.

Question: *I have always thought that you spoke directly and exactly and nothing was cryptic. It was just simple. So, within our solar system is our sun, which is luminescent, and then another part of our sun, which is not luminescent, and a planet in that general area. Is this so?*

PROGENITORS

It is so Dear ones, Dear hearts. And from this grew a great race of beings, a great race who carried out a force among this entire solar system. For indeed, they were in charge of the education, at an evolutionary and spiritual level, of those incarnated within this solar system. Do you understand?

Response and question: *Yes. Are we the genetic remnants of this race?*

It is so Dear ones, Dear hearts, but to not confuse the issue, you are not limited by your genetic background. As you well know, how could that principle be so? However, the genetic principle sets up a predisposition. It is the predisposition and the lack of knowledge therein where confusion arises.

EIGHT-SIDED CELL OF PERFECTION

Question: *The remaining genetic piece is the Eight-Sided Cell of Perfection?*

It is true Dear ones, Dear hearts, for it was deemed long ago, when this universe was created for the activity of teaching and bringing higher knowledge and understanding of the Oneship, of the Godship, of the mighty I AM, that this would always be placed within the heart. So at any time and under any circumstance or situation, the Eight-Sided Cell could be activated through the will of the individual to bring it into greater awareness and understanding. This is not to promise that one would instantly become enlightened but it was to ensure that through the proper principles, through hard work, application, and understanding, the science that exists behind the genetic codes, that one then could be set free.

## MEISSNER FIELD AND THE ONESHIP

Question: *And this one Cell is, in essence, the window to this great luminosity?*

It is indeed. It is the connection, as I have always stated, to the mind and behind all it carries within it, the Akashic Record of all that has been and ever will be within the Third Dimension. It carries within it, the force to create a greater unified Oneship. Now, when I speak of this Oneship, I am speaking of what has been called the Meissner Field; however, the identification of the Misner Field, as understood currently, is somewhat limited. So I prefer to call it the Oneship.

Response: *And so, the Oneship comes through this Cell.*

## A MIGHTY TRANSMITTER

Indeed it does Dear ones, Dear hearts. In this moment, I come through this Cell. I come through the activated Cell of you. I come through the activated Cell of the channel, the transmitter. You see, for indeed that is how it works. It works as a mighty transmitter within the body. The Eight-Sided Cell activates the cells . . . it activates the senses . . . it activates the greater Mind Divine . . . it activates the greater emotion . . . it activates the greater will.[4]

Question: *And so when you say three plus three equals ONE, you are referring to the Ray System that functions here, where all come together as ONE?*

Indeed they do Dear ones, Dear hearts. It is the way of dividing this greater Oneship and bringing it into an understanding. But

---
4. See Appendix D, *Eight-sided Cell of Perfection*, page 205.

it works in complete harmony. This harmony comes through the existence of the Fourth Dimension. This harmony comes, indeed, through the Eight-Sided Cell of Perfection.

Question: *So in essence, what you are here to preserve and sustain for humanity is not the physical form of our bodies but the flow and the cohesiveness of our consciousness. That is what is to survive; that is what is to go on?*

BELIEFS ARE THE CORE

But understand this, that your bodies are formed of the consciousness. This is the next level that must be impressed upon you. This is why I gave the example of disease; for there, you can well see how choice is involved within the healing process. That choice is not made through herbal supplements. That choice is not made through the electro-magnetic energies of the healer. That choice is not made through a miracle drug or miracle treatment. That choice is made through the individualized will. Now that is not to say that those essences or energies do not give support to the process of choice, for they work strongly and powerfully with the belief systems. You are well versed upon the placebo effect and believe me Dear ones, Dear hearts, beliefs are the core and crux of the Third Dimension. Yet beliefs are also, in their greater understanding, bringing forward the Fourth Dimension, the Oneship.

Response: *Yes, I understand what you are saying. That it is only through this consciousness that we actually can create, that we actually can focus.*

CALLED BY MANY NAMES

Consciousness is the core of creation and Co-creation. Consciousness is the I AM THAT I AM. Now how does one filter through consciousness? For you see, in the Third Dimension, consciousness is called by many names, by many levels, and by many truths. These many truths are indeed sometimes based upon beliefs, but those who have the eyes to see, the ears to hear, know that truth is based upon experience. It is indeed a time Dear ones, to bring this greater gift, to bring this greater awakening to a new understanding. Proceed.

Response: *Then, as I understand this path, it is time that we and all of our students go to the Star of Gobean.*

So Be It.

SMALL, STEADY, SURE

Response: *So Be It. As I understand this consciousness, this choice, this development, is incremental for all of us and only a choice can be made as to when one can understand or perceive.*

It is true Dear ones, Dear hearts, small steps as we have always said, but small, steady, sure steps.

*I understand and we will continue on with our other projects that you have assigned to us.*

As I have always said, there is no mistake ever, ever, ever. And now I sense that you have further questions.

Response: *Yes. I'm asking for your help and support and for the energies of those who work with you and us in our project there in the Star.*

INTEGRATING GOLDEN CITY ENERGIES

It is important Dear ones, for those that are entering into the Star, that they use, as I have instructed you, the energies of the four Doorways first. It brings a greater integration into the creation of a more sensitive mind, if you will. This is the only way that I can bring this understanding to you at this time. Another way to integrate these energies is of course to travel through all four doorways and to stay for at least two nights to be able to absorb and assimilate the energies. However, as you well know, sometimes it does take some time just to settle within an energy field and an energy force. This brings, shall we say, an initiation that occurs not only within the spiritual body of the individual but also within the Kundalini System. It allows the electromagnetic system to settle in and the chakras to know and understand the energy force that they are dealing with. Then, the purification of migrating to the Star of true self-knowledge can follow. Do you understand?

Answer: *Yes, I do. That self-knowledge will only come through the experience and the absorption, as I have discovered from myself.*

Questions?

Question: *Yes. You have brought up the idea of Earth Changes again. Are we to see some in the near future?*

## HUMANITY DETERMINES

Again, all is based upon the collective choice at will. All is based upon probabilities and their manifestations. As you well know Dear ones, Dear hearts, we can only explain to you the possibility. It is up to humanity to determine the probability.

Response: *Yes. I understand what you are saying and so we have possibilities coming, but whether they become probable will depend on us collectively.*

It is true Dear ones, Dear hearts, for you well know that prayer works, even from your own personal experience Dear chela.

Response: *Yes, Dear Master. I have learned that without a doubt.*

And you have the experience of this, do you not?

Answer: *Yes, I do.*

Then share such experience in this higher light and understanding.

Response: *It is through the application of the Violet Flame that I have watched many and much transformation.*

## VIOLET FLAME PRAYER

> May the Violet Flame come forward and give comfort to those who have fear. May the Violet Flame come forward and give peace to those who seek it.
> May the Violet Flame come forward and bring healing to those who need healing.

Dear ones, Dear hearts, the Violet Flame in its beauty, in its glory, and in its purification and great Alchemy, has been brought forward to lead one into that greater understanding of the three plus three equals ONE . . . to bring one into the greater understanding of balance . . . to bring one into the greater understanding of the birth of the Christ. Do you understand?

Answer and question: *Yes. I think the " three plus three equals ONE" may be confusing for some people. We are dealing with thought, feeling, and action. We are dealing with healing, devotion, and transmutation, all coming to that perfect purity of the ONE, are we not?*

## THOUGHT, FEELING, ACTION

It is so Dear one. It is the out-picturing of thought, feeling, and action, coming together in complete harmony and balance. This is the principle.

Response: *Yes, as I have understood this, Mastery is this balance of your thought, feeling, and action. At this time, I have no further questions.*

Then I shall take my leave from you Dear ones, Dear hearts and feel free to share this teaching generously.

Response: *Certainly and thank you.*

In that mighty Christ, may the Violet Flame come forward and serve all.

Response: *So Be It.*

# 2

## All Is Love
*Saint Germain*

Greetings Beloved chelas, students of mine, in that mighty Christ. I AM Saint Germain and I stream forth on that Violet Ray of Mercy, Compassion, and Forgiveness. As usual Dear hearts, I request permission to come forward.

Response: *Please Saint Germain, come forward. You are most welcome.*

THE VIOLET RAY

As usual Dear ones, Dear hearts, there is much work for us still to complete, much work still to be dispensed upon that Green Ray of Ministry and Service to mankind. But also, there is that work of the Violet Ray, that which I represent, the Violet Ray of Mercy, Compassion, Forgiveness, Transmutation, and Purification. The Violet Ray comes forward to give that most refreshing drink in the hour of need. It comes forward to set you at a new pace. It comes forward to give you a new perspective. It comes forward to lead you, shall we say, to a greener pasture.

Dear ones, Dear hearts, in this respect, the Violet Ray is indeed a great purveyor for adjusting perception; for in the work of the Violet Ray, when one applies it and uses it with great earnestness, one is then able to see, know, and apply with a fresh perspective what waits ahead. The fresh perspective then allows one to see with a new vision . . . to hear with new ears . . . to speak with a new voice . . . for the heart to open and truly unite with the one consciousness. The one consciousness that I speak of is indeed the consciousness of the Christ, but it is also the consciousness of unity, of Brother to Brother, Sister to Sister, Mother to Father, child to parent. It contains within it all relationships. It exists in a greater scope of understanding. It is unity, Unana, the ONE.

This energy force that exists cannot be seen in duality; for indeed, it exists beyond duality. However, it is felt, shall we say, as a great invisible rush. This rush or force of energy that you feel Dear ones, is indeed one that you feel when you invoke and use the Violet Flame. And while in this moment, I can see that Violet Flame flickering about you, you only can sense it through, shall we say, a higher awareness. Of course, there are those who have the opening of the Third Eye and see a purple light that tinges about the energy fields. But you must understand Dear ones, Dear hearts, that the consciousness that I speak of is one that does not exist within the field of duality; however, it is that next realm of consciousness where your evolution and growth lies.

A FRESH PERSPECTIVE

In the growth of this higher consciousness will come, shall we say, the "aha" of many new ways of seeing things. It is like unwrapping a new gift . . . seeing the birth of a new child for the first time . . . witnessing spring. It is a greening effect in that respect Dear ones, Dear hearts, for it is alive and comes again with a fresh perspective. Working towards this new, fresh perspective is important Dear ones, Dear chelas, Dear students, to allow yourself to see something in a different way.

Very often we get stuck in ruts. We get stuck in seeing things in just one way. We get stuck seeing things from just one perspective. But it takes only a movement, this energy movement, happening first from inside, is then expressed in its outer condition. This outer condition is then recognized as change. But the change has happened in the heart first, has it not? And then, the will is invoked and this great change that brings about a fresh perspective is known as choice.

## CHOICE AND THE PROCESS OF CHANGE

The pivotal point of choice is always important in all spiritual growth; for choice, you see, is engendered in that movement of the Violet Ray . . . in that movement of transmutation . . . in that movement of forgiveness . . . in that movement of purification . . . in that movement of Alchemy . . . and, yes, the ever-present, shall we say, hope of the magic. Now, when I say "magic," I speak indeed, not of illusion, but I speak of the magical moment of the mystic mystery. Dear ones, Dear hearts, mystery always surrounds growth. There is always, shall we say, stepping into the pool of the great unknown, always moving forward, not knowing exactly what lies in that void. But know this Dear ones, Dear hearts, trust within the heart . . . trust within the Mastery of the self . . . trust within the process of change itself.

Know this, that change is always a positive movement. Change is always for positive growth. Change moves always in that spiral of upward motion, especially for those who seek the Divine Will. Know and understand, Dear ones, Dear hearts, that change is always positive, change that happens in many arenas of life. Change has happened to the Earth, has it not? Change happens to your own children as they grow. Change happens in all of the Laws of Nature, in the seasons and in the weather. But beyond all of the change lies choice and there, choice becomes engendered with that greater Will Divine. There, choice leads the chela onward and upward on the spiritual path. There, onward and upward, one foot at a time, they are led towards the ultimate goal of spiritual liberation.

## KARMA AND THE VIOLET FLAME

The other dimensions await you Dear ones, Dear hearts. They are for you at your choosing. They are for you at your spiritual growth. The Third Dimension, as you well understand, was brought to you through the Law of Attraction; your vibratory rate would state in the Laws Divine that like can only seek like vibration. It is so, that the Laws of Cause and Effect draw one to the field of physicality, to bring balance to situations of the past. This is also why I have given you the work and the use of the Violet Flame, for the Violet Flame allows you to bring balance into many karmic situations that might hold you from your forward movement, that might keep you from your own choice toward that Divine Will, that greater alignment into seeking the experience of the ONE.[5]

## FEAR AND LOVE

Karma indeed holds man back with great fear, holds one back from understanding and expressing the true Divinity that lies within. Fear, you see Dear ones, Dear hearts, is always that energy that binds one to the physical plane, for it seeks release through its counterpoint, which is love. Love is indeed the only energy that can move the spiral forward. Stopping on the spiral always brings great pain to the chela, for they know that there is so much more that awaits them in the Temple of the Heart.

One seeks the peace and the solace that comes through the inner knowing and the inner knowing is brought to lead one further along the path . . . further along the path of change . . . further along into the unknown. Dear ones, Dear hearts, when I speak of this great unknown, is it really as such? For in your travel and sojourn in learning and understanding the levels of consciousness that await, how could

---

5. See Appendix E, *The Violet Flame*, page 207.

there be fear? How could there be any that would hold one back from this greater evolution and development. Before I proceed, are there questions?

Question: *When you speak of evolution and development and being held back on that spiral, isn't that a choice though, a choice to not go forward?*

## SPIRITUAL GROWTH THROUGH THE LAW OF LOVE

Indeed, all is choice Dear ones, Dear hearts. One is always choosing the emotions and the thoughts that create the actions. From those actions, choices are understood and expressed as the creation comes forth. So indeed, it is true Dear one, that there is a choice, even in no forward motion, but it is also understood, that in the lack of motion, especially in the field of duality, there comes that process, shall we say, of stagnation. This stagnation, lack of growth, or lack of forward motion, brings a sense of pain to the heart, for the heart expresses all in great knowing. The heart moves beyond the field of duality and understands that all comes into a greater balance; that left and right unite as ONE; male and female unite as ONE as well. All become reconciled in this sense, Dear ones. But, as it has been stated before, until you reach the destination, you must still use the map. You do not throw the map away until you have reached that destination of where you wish to go. So, do we stop reading the map along the journey? No Dear ones, Dear hearts, we return to the basic principles, based upon the ever-present Law of ONE, the Law of Love. Questions?[6]

Question: *So when one is being tested, the pathway through that test is the Law of Love, is it not?*

Always there is that most refreshing drink, is there not Dear heart? Only in love can things be seen through a greater lens of perception. Through the Violet Ray, one is able to adjust the force of the mind

---
6. See Appendix F, *The Law of Love*, page 209.

and train it to begin to see through a new lens of forgiveness, through a new lens of transmutation. This is indeed, as I spoke before, the magic of Alchemy. In that moment, you are able to see with crystal clarity. What you once thought was your lack of movement was indeed your tenuous growth. Proceed.

## LOVE DRIVES EVOLUTION

Response and Question: *It is apparent to me, that without that sense of love motivating us through these daily tests of life in this schoolhouse, we would seem to wither, shrivel up as a vine that didn't get enough nutrient. Is this so?*

The heart of love, Dear one, as you know, moves beyond the dual expression. True love, in its understanding as the true open heart, moves beyond the restrictions of duality. Its energy force moves beyond that which you know as the physical. It is indeed that grand invisible force, which many at times want to call as God . . . want to call as the savior . . . want to call as even the Master Teacher, that comes forward to give that most refreshing drink. It is an energy that exists beyond time. It exists beyond belief systems. Love is indeed the basis of the next dimension, that next evolutionary leap in consciousness. This love that I speak of is not an emotion; however, it is expressed through the human as an emotion. But understood in this context, it becomes a thought, a feeling, and an action, moving into ONE as a unified field of activity. Questions?

Question: *So, what you are saying is that love is not dual?*

Indeed it is not. Love is that healer that soothes all disease. Love gives understanding in trying situations. Love is indeed a peace that passes all understanding of those in the dual expression. Love is the one that gives hope. Love is the one that gives charity. Love is the basis of all of faith. Love contains harmony and abundance. Love is indeed a great equalizer of all forces. Dear ones, Dear hearts, love is the basis of your growth and evolution. And yet, at times, the pangs of love give such pain, do they not? Bring such stresses to the mind? Lead one into a greater arena of choice? But this forward movement, it is good. This forward movement is, indeed, leading you to a greater understanding. This level of consciousness is known as the Christ.

HIGHER LOVE AND CONSCIOUSNESS

Question: *And so, am I to understand that throughout creation, that love is the great motivator for the existence of creation and the completion of it?*

Love is indeed desire, but in its higher form. It is as a motivator. It is the great inspiration, is it not? But love cannot be categorized or catalogued as belonging to just one situation. It is an energy force that comes in and ties all together as ONE. Now throughout this whole discourse, I have given you many examples of love. I have shown you many different ways these examples are seen. Remember, the individual perception or experience of love is somewhat limited, but when I speak of love at these levels, it moves one ahead into a different understanding, a different consciousness. This new consciousness contains healing. This new consciousness moves beyond time. This new consciousness brings one to the deathless and the birthless body. For Dear ones, Dear hearts, love is one of the keys to conscious immortality. Love, you see Dear one, Dear heart, is that breath that breathes the breath for all, does it not?

Answer and question: *Yes, this is true, it does breathe the breath for all. So regardless of how trying a situation may be, when one can search for the love in yourself or in the situation, then you can walk that path through it?*

Always, Dear one, Dear heart. As Dear Sananda has often said to you, "All is love Dear heart. When all is said and done, that is the one that is remaining."

Question: *This is very true, as has been explained to me many times. Is there time to ask questions now from those who have had questions from the last discourse?*

I have come forward specifically for this purpose.

Question: *Then I have a question from someone who asks, 'Can you please expand on the ancient race of highly evolved inhabitants who contributed to the development of Earth civilizations. Who are they and are they here now?*

## TWO SUNS

All is present now, as all that has ever been and all that will ever be. All is contained, shall we say, within that mighty Law of Love, within that greater unity. Know and understand this first as the eternal law. But what is spoken of here is from the annals of another time, another frequency, for that brings a greater understanding. As I have said so many times, there is no mistake, ever, ever, ever. What this is indeed, is the statement of vibration, of like seeking its like, of water, shall we say, seeking its own level.

The Galactic Center, the Great Central Sun, has served as a pivotal point for the evolution of your solar system, streaming forth, arcing in light and sound consciousness, moving to your own Sun. This brought a birth, at one time in a different period, shall we say, of vibration. During this time, this force brought and birthed another Sun, which moved alongside the Sun, almost in equal light and intensity. This brought a greater and a higher consciousness to the Earth. But as I stated before, there was indeed another planet that came through this which is known now in your time as a dark Sun.

These beings resided very closely to both of the Suns. In fact, at one moment in that time period, the planet was located between the two dual Suns.

## THE ANCESTORS

The Sun, from your own experience, is hot and will burn away with great intensity but this was a planet of sorts that thrived from the energy of the light. The bodies that were of the beings upon this planet were not restricted through duality, instead their consciousness resided at higher levels of understanding. They took on bodies at will and dropped them at will. These beings understood completely the birthless and the deathless body. They encapsulated, if you could understand this, a greater purity and a greater harmony. They moved forward Dear ones, Dear hearts, as those entrusted, in a sense, as ancestors to this life stream. When I speak of this life stream, I speak now of life on Earth, as you now know it. As you know, life is continually evolving the same way that you are continually changing, moving, and growing. Your body reflects these changes through emotions . . . through smiles . . . through tears . . . through the expression of all feelings. You see these changes and feel these changes. As time moves on, you understand the growth process that your soul is making, do you not?

It is important to understand that this growth process is guided and directed by a greater consciousness. This is not to say that your own will is not developed, for indeed it is Dear ones, Dear hearts. And it is not to say that there are those controlling your choices, for indeed you are engendered with your own will. But there are influences Dear ones, Dear hearts, as you well know and understand; these influences known as light and sound play a part. They play a part in bringing you to the pivotal point of applying your will for greater good, of applying your will for choice made within and through the Law of Love. These beings have worked throughout the whole solar system. They reside within the frequencies of duality of light and sound. This is perhaps the easiest way for you to understand. They bring a greater guidance towards the Great Central Sun. They help to dispense karma; now when I say this, I say this not as an action of retribution. Indeed, they work in a greater arena, a greater scope, to allow dispensations of events, history if you will, to come forward to the Earth Plane and Planet. They will continue, Dear ones, Dear hearts, to be present and guide humanity, guide the schoolrooms of all of the solar system. This guidance comes forward Dear ones, Dear hearts, through that great understanding of the Law of Love. It comes forward, Dear one, Dear heart, in that great alignment to the Divine Plan, in the Divine Will.

It is true, as your Earth grows in light and sound frequencies, the presence of these greater beings will be known and understood. However, as you understand, like vibration can only understand like vibration. So there is some limitation presently, for lack of a greater explanation, for you to thoroughly know and understand that of which I speak. Questions?

Question: *So these great beings are, in essence, your teachers?*

Indeed they are Dear one, Dear heart.

Question: *And they are still here in sponsorship of you, as you are of the rest of us?*

It is so. For you see, they exist beyond a body. They exist beyond a form. They exist beyond the dual expression of time. However, if necessary, they put on a form at will, to provide whatever service may be needed.

## A HIDDEN, GUIDING PLANET

Question: *I understand. So, this planet which is hidden is still inhabited by them but not at the dimension we can perceive?*

It is true Dear one. It appears now only as an abandoned, dark planet, with no life contained at all; however, as you move through the annals of time, that which I speak of as Dvapara Yuga, you will know and understand this with greater perception.

Question: *So, you are saying that we have to be in a different time period, where there is more luminosity for us, to be able to perceive their existence?*

It is true Dear one, Dear heart. However, at times, you do sense the presence of this greater force. This was the intention of the one who asked this question. The one who is aligned to ask this question feels a greater harmony and alignment to this greater force, feels this presence, greater and divine, guiding their life. That is why this question was asked.

Question: *So, this planet is still in existence. All of the alien visitors who have come to our planet are really overseen by this great civilization.*

It is true Dear one, Dear heart. However, you must understand that all works upon these principles of frequency and vibration, of like attracting like, opposites repelling one another. Of course, I speak in such simple terms. In time, this understanding will grant enlightenment.

Question: *So those who are perceived, for example, in the so-called secret government, affecting and controlling the destiny of humanity, are they part of that Divine Plan and are overseen and guided by your teachers?*

It is obvious that they are, for they are here, are they not?

Answer: *Yes they are.*

And we have had several discussions, have we not, regarding the Laws of Cause and Effect?

Answer: *Yes, we have.*

Proceed with your questions.

Question: *We have another question by a person who asks, 'Is the hidden planet Nibiru?*

THE NONDUAL CHRIST FORCE

No. It is as I have spoken. However, this planet exists as well. I spoke of the hidden planet, so one could gain a greater insight into the timing of light and sound, to begin to Master choice. But there is indeed this planet that is spoken of and these beings have played a role in the present condition on planet Earth. That is why it was sent out long ago for the Lords of Venus to come and build Shamballa. There are those present upon this planet who have worked in cooperation with the Lords of Venus. For you see Dear ones, Dear hearts, when we enter into higher consciousness, we all work from a greater energy force, that which is known beyond the limitations of duality. This energy force, as you well know and understand, is sometimes known as Unana, sometimes called the Christ Force, but it is presently also known as a Meissner Field. This is contained individually and yet collectively. It is important to understand that at this level of understanding, adversity does not exist. A greater harmony moves in a greater spectrum of light and sound. Questions?

Response: *What you are saying then is, in the dualistic world, where these visitors have come and played a part in the alteration of our genetics, at the higher levels, their presence is not discord.*

It is true, for contained even within yourself are thoughts and feelings that are discordant and yet also contained within yourself are thoughts and feelings that have been brought into complete balance, are there not?

Answer: *This is all true, yes.*

LOVE, CONSCIOUSNESS, AND PROPHECY

This is indeed the human condition, working to bring all within balance, working to bring that reconciliation to that neutral point of which I speak. At this neutral point comes the opportunity to experience the Law of Love, to move into greater arenas of understanding, to experience beyond dual understanding. It is true that Nibiru contains a comet trail, or shall we say, an asteroid or meteor that trails towards Earth. As described in the Earth Changes Prophecies, this is very possible. However, as you well know, prophecy is brought forward to bring about change. It is the change within the heart, you see Dear ones, Dear hearts, that affects all at an electromagnetic level. It brings one into greater healing.

Now, imagine if you will, three people activating this greater change within the heart and moving it towards a collective understanding, into a greater global arena. Imagine then, one hundred people, one thousand people, ten thousand people. This I know Dear ones, Dear hearts, has always been your focus and your goal. It is important then to understand that consciousness contains the key to prophecy, contains the key to circumventing all disasters and moving into that fresh perspective. Do you understand?

Answer: *Yes.*

Questions?

## POSSIBILITY AND PROBABILITY

Question: *Yes. This person also asked, 'Is Nibiru the planet that will pass close by our own planet and if so, around what year would this occur?*

It is impossible to place a date upon such an event; for you see Dear ones, Dear hearts, time is a dual expression and the information and source of this instruction moves beyond the dual. However, as we have always stated, there will come a time where this will be a possibility. We state this as prophecy. We state this so there will be those who will move forward in their spiritual growth and understanding and be able to take these teachings and apply them into greater actions. As I have always stated before, there will be warnings that will come from the scientific community before such an event. There will be a minimum of seven years warning time given before such an event. Remember when we spoke of possibility versus probability?

Answer: *Yes.*

This is still a great possibility. Probability lies within the wills of humanity. Proceed.

Question: *Are we as a planet acting out of character within the harmony of the solar system and this is how these types of events are attracted to us?*

## "A CHANGE OF HEART"

It is one way of understanding. However, I would prefer to say that this is a planet that is moving, learning to move in greater light and sound frequencies. The Earth is not set upon a destructive path. It is set upon a path of construction and growth. Yes, there have been times upon the planet where destruction was necessary and indeed, these times may possibly come again. As I have always stated, that choice is left to each individual heart. Proceed.

Response and Question: *So, it literally is as you have said before, 'A change of heart can change the world.' It is one heart at a time, coming together in the unification of love that transitions all of us to that greater light. Is this not so?*

It is true Dear heart.

Response: *Then at this point, I have no further questions.*

I shall take my leave and return at our next appointed session. Hitaka.

Response: *Hitaka.*

# 3

## The Master Within
*Saint Germain*

Greetings Beloved chelas, students of mine, in that mighty Violet Ray. I AM Saint Germain and I stream forth on that Violet Ray of Mercy, Compassion, and Forgiveness. As usual Dear hearts, I request your permission to come forth.

Response: *Please Saint Germain you are most welcome. Come forth.*

THE METAPHYSICAL LAW OF RECIPROCITY

Dear ones, it is still important to note, for those who do not understand this, that I always ask permission to come forth. For you see Dear ones, we work together in this capacity through what is known as "Agreement." It is this reciprocal energy, you see Dear ones, Dear hearts, that allows this consciousness to stream forth. You see, you have said, "Yes, I am ready to receive" and I have also said, "Yes I am ready to give." In that same measure, you give back to what you know as me, the teacher, and I receive that energy back. You see, it works in a reciprocal approach. One often would think that they are always just giving their energy away to someone, but you see that is impossible, for all things work within a balance. Energy flows within; energy flows without. This is a Law Eternal of how this energy comes forth . . . of how this teaching comes forth . . . of how healing comes forth for all of humanity. Energy flows within; energy flows without.

Dear ones, Dear hearts, today I would like to give further insight into the relationship of the student and the teacher. For you see Dear ones, I have spoken before of this relationship. But it is important to understand this relationship, so one may gain deeper insight into the process. It is true that you and I have worked through many different lifetimes and have built an energy that was accessed in this lifetime with great ease. I have spoken of this in several past discourses to you. So it is no wonder Dear one, Dear heart, as you proceed in your own, shall we say, Mastership of taking on students to bring their learning to a greater level, that you too have had a past life relationship with those that you work with. That is why energy does flow within and it flows without.

Let us address another aspect, an element of this relationship. As this energy is built through lifetime after lifetime, it builds a reciprocity of the mental energies. That energy body that you call thought comes into a greater alignment. There is a sympathetic harmony and a sympathetic resonance that occurs within the teaching process. The teacher and the student also then receive this energy in a greater harmony and alignment to the Plan Divine. But it is also important to understand, in this sympathetic harmony or sympathetic resonance of energies, that there also exists an alignment to the emotional fields, the emotional bodies.

A TEACHER LIFTS EMOTIONAL BURDEN

As you have always understood, it is thought and then feeling that comes into this greater alignment. There is a resonance of feeling that is the emotion. Within this emotion, that comes forward for greater healing and greater release into the spiritual life, the teacher takes on any emotional fluctuations in a greater resonance. You well know, when you take a student on and begin to work with them, it requires a greater, shall we say, uplifting of burdens. In the same way, when the Master teacher takes on the student, you feel a great upliftment. In that moment, you feel a great joy, a great peace, a great inner harmony. For in that moment, all emotional burdens have been lifted from you, so the mental body can work with its greater clarity, in its greater capacity. Now, you with your own students, have you not noticed this? You lift their emotional burdens so that their thought processes can be freed to see with greater clarity?

Answer: *Yes and it is the path to do so.*

## GENTLE LEADERSHIP

It is indeed Dear one, Dear heart. It is the way that this time-honored tradition moves forward. From there, the Master teacher then withdraws the support of the emotional energy, gently, gracefully, with ease. This allows for that greater integration of thought and feeling to marry into a greater alignment of clarity; then, actions move forward. This is the way that we work, so that you may understand, in an energetic level. But it is also important to understand that, at all times, no expectation is held from the teacher to the student. No expectation is ever held at all. For you see, it is true that the Master teacher never truly tells the student what to do. Indeed, it is a gentle guidance or shall we say, leadership unto the natural laws, so the student may experience and experiment with the laboratory of the self. This you have come to know Dear ones, Dear hearts, that experimentation of the laboratory of the self.

## WITHIN THE SILENCE

As I have often said, "To do, to dare, and to be silent." Sometimes it is within that Great Silence of the self that one finds the greater challenge that lies within, that one finds the greater mountains of emotional upheaval or painful emotional wounds that are yet to be healed. In that Great Silence is where we find a greater alignment; an alignment, yes, to the greater Plan Divine, but also an alignment to the self, choosing to gain that element of self-Mastery. Self-Mastery requires a honed focus, for the honed focus then understands and realizes that one is working with a greater harmony of these energy bodies of thought, feeling, and action.

It is true that the emotional burdens of the past sometimes limit or, shall we say, set askew the perceptual sight. But it is important, Dear one, to spend time within the deep silence, to ask of the self, within that one clear honest moment, "Is this truly within the intention of myself?" "Is this truly in the alignment with the heart of my desires?" "Am I truly moving beyond desire and into my spiritual liberation and freedom?"

## OUT-PICTURING PERFECTION

Now, we know that all chelas, all students, that come unto this work are at different levels. Everyone, as you well know Dear one, Dear heart, moves and grows with a timing and intent. We cannot force a student to grow at a certain time. We cannot say at this moment, you will forget all that has happened, at this moment, you will transmute and purify and move to a new level of clarity. No Dear one, it does not happen that way. But that pure crystal out-picturing is always there, the out-picturing of perfection. Say unto yourself:

> Beloved Mighty I AM Presence,
> I out-picture pure perfection in this moment of my Divine Self moving towards the Ascension and light in the Divine Plan,
> Almighty I AM!

## INTEGRATION, COMPASSION, AND ENLIGHTENMENT

Such a statement brings a clarity and focus to the consciousness, does it not? It brings, in that moment, a greater knowing of the true self. This knowing brings an understanding of the mental body, using the mental body as a tool. Now Dear ones, Dear hearts, begin to understand thought and feeling and how they work within the human body in duality. The emotional body was brought forward from the animal consciousness. The emotional body contains within it, the instinct and intellect for survival. But as this body becomes more integrated with the heart, through the path of compassion, one then is ready to begin to understand the tutelage of knowledge. Greater understanding brings within it an enlightenment. This enlightenment brings the understanding that one may hold in their perception, or shall I say, Point of Perception, an understanding of creation.

## ABSOLUTE SELF-KNOWLEDGE

Of course, this Point of Perception is indeed, as you well know, a point of the Co-creation process. Co-creation moves one beyond animal behavior, moves one beyond the instincts and into pure knowledge. One does not have the gut feeling, but one has the absolute knowledge, for they are integrated as ONE with the Point of Perception. This is a choice indeed Dear ones, Dear hearts. It is a choice to gain such self-knowledge. But one is continually held back, shall we say, by the feelings of emotions. These emotions indeed are important, for they lead one into greater understanding of the human experience. Therefore Dear ones, Dear hearts, nothing is lost and all is gained.

## OPENING THE HEART

But it takes time, does it not? It takes time to bring a greater understanding. It takes time to have the experiences, to know the difference. All of this leads, at the emotional level, to the opening of the heart and the greater plan of perfection. For in the opening of the heart, then one is able to understand the intention behind Alchemy, the intention behind transmutation, the intention behind a purification process that leads one then to a greater honing of the choice of thought.

Now I'll introduce this concept to you Dear one, Dear heart: the choice of thoughts.

## CHOOSING THE THOUGHT

There are many thoughts to choose from in this world of Co-creation, many that come with their sets of beliefs, their sets of values, their sets of circumstances, situations, and experiences. These thoughts are played out in greater strata of harmony, in greater strata of understanding, in greater strata of feeling. These thoughts bring with them that greater experience of Co-creation, leading one then to the true perfection that exists within the Oneship. Now, as I explain these two bodies to you today, as we have talked about so many times before, it is my hope that you have gained greater insight, a greater insight in assisting your students, and a greater insight in understanding how energy flows within and energy flows without. Questions?

Response and question: *It is really choosing the thought that has a specific purpose, so then the feeling aids the specific focus. We can choose many thoughts and yet, not all thoughts and feelings serve the great desire that we might have, whether it is to accomplish something or whether it is to be free, is this not so?*

As always Dear one, Dear heart, for Mastery understands all choices that are available, but it also accepts the circumstances that follow such choice, without expectation. The expectations show self-desires that are more designed to keep one trapped within illusion. There is only but one desire that shall free you and that is the desire to know God . . . that is the desire to know perfection . . . that is the desire of the heart, the true energy of the Source. Dear one, Dear heart, I would also like to remind you that I am always with you, that I am always here for your help and assistance. I am but your call away.

## BE READY TO RECEIVE

In your weekly program that you are bringing forward, know this Dear one, that I will always be available to bring discourse to your students. I am always there at a moment's call, at a moment's notice. I offer this, as you see, for energy flows within; energy flows without. Those students who have now come forward are prepared and ready to receive a greater energy. They are prepared and readied now to receive this greater influx of energy, preparing them for that alignment to the Divine Plan. I bring this energy forward, not as a crutch; for as you see Dear one, Dear heart, even throughout your week, you too must take all into thought, feeling, and action.

## AWAKEN THE MASTER WITHIN

In this moment, yes, while your heart leaps with joy to know such union with God, there comes that moment too where the Master Teacher steps back and allows you to have your own experience. This comes with its variety of human emotions: frustrations, joys, expectations, love, hate, fear, all of these, as part of the human condition. But know this Dear one, within that desire to know God is the most refreshing drink. Know, that in that desire to be as ONE, is your true Divine Heritage. As you well know, this great Divinity that lies within is indeed a sleeping Master within. It is awakened and enlivened through the knowledge of the Great I AM.

> Beloved Mighty I AM Presence,
> come forth and awaken the Master within.
> May the voice that I speak align in thought, feeling, and action
> to the truth of God, eternal I AM.

As you see Beloved, as you see Dear heart, when you call this decree into action, this, shall we say, is the scientific formula that I have given to you. Call upon the Master within! Then indeed, the eyes open, the ears open, and a greater alignment comes forth. It is there to give you the support. It is there to give you the strength throughout your week. It is there to help you in your journey. Though small, yet baby steps, know this Dear one, Dear heart, there are larger steps waiting for you. For as you well know, as you travel this spiritual journey, the path does indeed seem narrow at times, the climb is arduous, but each step forward is monumental in gaining your freedom. For you see Dear ones, Dear hearts, you are working these days within yourself, using these laws eternal. This is how you do indeed gain your freedom. Questions?

Response: *Yes. My freedom is my greatest desire and to be with all of you as my family. In all honesty, this world many, many times does not offer me a great interest, except to bring forward what you have entrusted with us.*

## THE SPIRITUAL PATHS

There are several paths through which this is gained. You are familiar with these I am certain, but I will remind you. There is the Path of Love. There is the Path of Knowledge. There is the Path of Service, which is the strongest. Also, there is none at all. Sometimes a chela applies all three; sometimes the chela applies one that they feel a greater alignment towards. In your case, it has always been the Path of Service first. But it is important to understand, that all of these as a choice are just as important as any one individual. These paths come forward to give to the chela a broad spectrum of experience. They allow a greater alignment for their own Divine Plan.

It is true that some feel the harmony working day-by-day, helping another to rise above their own situation. It is true that some feel a greater harmony by understanding the mysteries of life, the laws eternal, and how they exist and work to bring mankind into greater healing and development. And there are those who simply love, love, love, and then, love more. For this is also a path of ultimate surrender to God. These unions bring a greater understanding of the quality of the Christ. They bring a greater understanding of the dimension that lies beyond duality, the dimension of Unana, the Oneship.

One path is not more important than the other, not one more pure or more innocent. But all of them work to bring the human, the one who desires perfection, to rise above the sorrows of the human condition . . . to see the joy that lies within . . . to express it on a daily basis. Is this not then the basis of immortality? Is this not then the basis of the true Oneship, of moving beyond the restraints of time, of left, right, good, bad, light, dark, or evil. Then one can clearly see with open eyes and open ears. Then one is ready to speak in the presence of the Master. This is indeed the heart that has been opened through compassion. Questions?

Response and question: *Love has brought me here to this place and instigated that service. Each of these paths is truly about feeling and in action, it is love. But there is much work we still have to do in the fulfillment of this path and it will be, in our time frame, a while before we are completely together. The question that I ask, is it only through the love for humanity and the world that all of this is brought forward?*

WE ARE ALWAYS ONE

There is a perception of separation Dear one, Dear heart, I realize, as you travel in the journey of duality. But know this, I am always with you. The Master resides within, but you must awaken the Master to bring it forward into its greater knowledge, its greater Work Divine. Know that I am always with you. Know that there are those who have gone before you and they too are with you Dear one, Dear heart. Know, as in that Law Eternal, energy flows within, energy flows without and this life force connects us all as ONE. For indeed, you must understand, in this context of knowledge, we are as ONE. In this moment of this transmission, the consciousness, or Point of Perception, is uniting our energy field. That is our thought force as ONE. Know this, that in that moment, at your request, we are always as ONE.

Response and question: *So Be It. It looks as though the decree you have given me is the next step?*

It is indeed Dear one. And know that I am always with you. Know that I am here for your assistance. Also, know this Dear heart, Dear chela, that there is no such thing as failure, only moving on the path, one sure step at a time. So Be It.

Response: *So Be It. I have no further questions.*

I shall return for our next meeting. Hitaka.

Response: *Hitaka.*

# 4

## The Mighty Violet Flame
*Saint Germain*

Greetings Beloveds, in that mighty Violet Ray. I AM Saint Germain and I request permission to come forward.

Response: *Please Saint Germain, come forward. You are most welcome.*

CALL THE FLAME INTO ACTIVITY

Welcome Dear students, chelas, aspirants on the path of light and self-Mastery. I AM Saint Germain. Dear ones, Dear hearts, it is always important to address that mighty Violet Flame, its purpose, its intention, and why I always place such great emphasis upon the Violet Flame. As you well know, the Violet Flame has been brought forward at this time to lessen the karmic burdens of humanity. When it is used and brought into its proper application, it has the effect to eliminate karmas that happen at very subtle levels. When you use the Violet Flame, call it forth into its immeasurable activity:

> Violet Flame I AM, come forth,
> from the ethers of the Great Divine.
> May the Violet Flame blaze in, through, and around me,
> transmuting the cause and effect, record and memory, forever,
> of karmas of the past, where I may be inhibited from my
> spiritual growth Divine.

This statement has the power to bring the Violet Flame surrounding you. Yes, just one statement will bring this Violet Flame and magnetize your electromagnetic fields. Throughout that day, the Violet Flame then will be carried in all interactions. That Violet Flame is also brought forth in the most trying of circumstance and situation.

> Mighty Violet Flame come forward
> and bring your Divine Intervention of comfort and peace
> to this situation.
> May all stream forward from the heart of the
> Great Central Divine Plan.
> So Be It.

Again, when you make such a statement and call that flame into its activity, into any situation and circumstance, one is lifted from all karmic inhibition and, there and then, its alchemizing fires bring a sense of purification . . . bring a sense of Alchemy . . . bring a sense of balance into any situation that is trying. It allows, at that time, for agreement to stream forth between any two individuals who may be in discord or disharmony. It allows for a harmony then to pursue an agreement which then can be enacted. In this Time of great Change, it is important that harmony reign supreme between those of humanity. It is important also to understand the Laws of Harmony and how they work at a much higher level to raise your consciousness and to bring you into a greater spiritual evolution.

THE GREAT CHANGE

The spiritual evolution is always important, Dear ones, Dear hearts. We have been discussing how human consciousness evolves and when I explained the Hidden Planet, I brought this discourse forward for you to begin to understand that there are those who have been engendered or entrusted with the Divine Plan of humanity. It is I, as a willing servant, who carry this Plan forward. Of course, I am also enjoined by my many Brothers and Sisters on the path of Mastery. There are also those among humanity who lift their hands and hearts in complete and total willingness, to bring this plan forward in a greater alignment to harmony, in a greater alignment to the great transitional change.

It was decided some time ago, that during the Time of the great Transition of Mother Earth, that this would give the greatest potential and the greatest possibility to also bring about a transformation in the collective heart of humanity. It has always been known that during these Times of great Transition, great Purification, and great Change, that the greatest possibility then awaits. Of course, we also must understand the Laws of Light and Sound and how the Ray Forces interact with the Great Central Sun, or the Great Galactic Center. It is important to see, in this timing and intention, how humanity is ordered and show how the universes, existing within the Solar System Divine, are all ordered in timing and intention.

JUSTICE AND THE VIOLET FLAME

But it is also important to understand the Violet Flame. The Violet Flame, you see Dear ones, Dear hearts, is that Law, yes, of Justice. Beyond that, it brings not only an equalizing effect but it opens up the potential for mercy and compassion in all situations. Of the highest of these two paths, it is always better to serve the heart, is it not Dear ones? It is always important to consider that compassion and mercy lift one into a higher vibration and order and prepare one for the consciousness of true Unana. Yes, it is good to feel that things are balanced. Yes, it is good to feel that things are in their right place and in their right order. But of all things Dear ones, Dear hearts, what have I taught you? But the path of the heart . . . the path of the Oneship . . . the path of compassion. This too is brought about through the understanding of the alchemizing fires of the Violet Flame.

Mighty Violet Flame, blaze in, through, and around this situation. May the Heart of Compassion now open and bring me peace.

This decree is to be said in any situation where you feel there has been an injustice or a miscarriage of events. This also brings balance into situations that you may not understand. The human condition is one where, at times, one is constantly asking the question, "Why has this happened? What can I do? How can this be?" Such questions often are never answered, are they Dear ones? But questions bring an evolutionary leap in consciousness, lead one onward to seek the true nature of the self, to enter into that true heart of desire. Within the heart itself and that great Eight-sided Cell of Perfection lies the true intention of the soul . . . lies that true connection to universal Oneship and the Brotherhoods and Sisterhoods of Breath, Sound, and Light.

YOUR DIVINITY

When I speak of the Master within, I also address this mighty Temple of the ONE, for this perfection is the Divinity that lies within. This perfection is your great inheritance. You see Dear ones, Dear hearts, you were not brought here to just bring balance to actions. You were also brought here with great purpose and intention to move forward and to realize great potential and possibility. But this great potential and possibility lies only in the knowledge that you are as the God I AM. This I AM blazes in, through, and around you and you can command the I AM into action when you say unto yourself:

I AM the resurrection and the life!

You encode, in that moment within that Perfect Cell, the vibration and the energy of life effervescent when you command unto yourself:

> I AM eternal life. Down with death!
> Conscious immortality arise through I AM!

In that moment, you affirm that life eternal is the essence over death and that the life eternal, the immortality, the true essence of the soul, is within your being. This perfection, you see Dear ones, Dear hearts, is commanded and demanded into its being. Why is this so? For you see again, as I have stated, you did not just come here to bring balance to situations. And why balance is, at times, demanded through that mighty Law of Nature, it is also important that you realize and understand your Divine Godship that lies within.

USE OF THE I AM AND THE VIOLET FLAME

In the last three discourses, we have been addressing elementary steps to self-Mastery. Today, we talk about the Great IAM and its integration with the Violet Flame, to bring one into a heightened area of realization of self. In the realization of the true self, one understands in that moment, their Co-creatorship. One understands in that moment, that in any given situation, through quiet and careful recollection, through quiet and careful silencing of the self, one can call forth that perfect source of the I AM. Yes indeed, I speak of the I AM as the great Eight-sided Cell of Perfection, but I also speak of the science of the Rays and how they work so masterfully together. As I have stated before, it is through the use of the I AM and the Violet Flame, that these two elements scientifically come together and bring comfort to the Ray Forces, melding them in one group effort, raising them to another level of understanding, and vibrating them to another Cause Divine.

Yes indeed, Dear ones, Dear hearts, the Violet Flame is a Divine Intervention. It is an intervention that has been brought at this specific time for a specific purpose. Use it daily in your applications and I promise you Dear ones, Dear hearts, that you shall have and imbibe that most refreshing drink. And now I ask, do you have any questions?

Question: *Yes I do. The Violet Flame, as I understand it, is here in its transformative ability for our growth and development, so that we may move on in our own evolution. Is this the most direct way to do this evolutionary process?*

It is true Dear one, for not only does it bring balance and justification to the karmic Law of Nature, to cause and effect, and to justice, as one would say, it also opens the heart to that ever evolutionary step of compassion and love.

Response: *So, at the simplest level, the Violet Flame is calling forth the Ray into action and it is our Divine Right to be able to do this.*

It is calling forth not only the Ray but a higher force, a higher vibration that is enjoined by many of those who have gone before you. For you see Dear ones, Dear hearts, the Violet Flame, while yes, identifies with certain Ray Forces, it is also a motion that has been set into the creation by a conscious force, to bring forward a greater evolution in humanity at this important time.

Question: *There is a difference though between the Violet Ray and the Violet Flame, isn't there?*

HIGHER VIBRATION

It is so Dear one, Dear heart. The Violet Ray is the Ray Force as it energizes and imbibes, shall we say, upon the Earth Plane and Planet. The Violet Flame is Mercy and Compassion in action. It is indeed a spiritual force that one may access on a much more subtle level. The Violet Flame is carried throughout that Tube of Light and indeed, it crosses, shall we say, for lack of better understanding, with the Ray

Forces and can be detected as a visible light force and as an audible sound. The Violet Flame is indeed a spiritual teaching that brings one to a higher order or vibration of consciousness. Do you understand?

Answer: *Yes.*

## THE NEW CONSCIOUSNESS

This is not to state that it is only a spiritual teaching, for it is not. It contains so much more. It contains within it, an awakening to another way of being. It contains the ability to adjust perception. It contains the ability to change circumstances and situations. Proceed.

Question: *So, the Violet Flame interacts with the Earth Plane and Planet?*

It brings a lightening of consciousness. When I speak of this lightening, I speak again of Rays of Light and Sound. But it also enters one into the threshold of the beginning stages of the new consciousness, that which I have always spoken of as Unana. This consciousness of the ONE is where all functions through the ONE and understands the ONE. Now I know in this moment, to introduce such an idea, especially for those who are still struggling even with the concept of dual consciousness, it is important to understand that as we move into this new understanding, the heart of love erupts with the most joy.

It is also important to understand that the Violet Flame comes at a time of great and intense suffering of humanity to uplift, to give hope. It also brings an evolutionary opportunity to move beyond the current situation. It allows the light bodies to integrate and adjust. It allows the creation of new light bodies to appear. It allows, shall we say, that burst of the new wine skin. Therefore indeed, it is a consciousness akin to the birth of the Christ, the new child within. It contains all hopes and possibilities . . . it contains all potentials to bring about self-Mastery. Questions?

## THE EARTH PLANE AND PLANET

Question: *Would you specifically define the difference between the Earth Plane and the Earth Planet?*

The Earth Plane is the realms of consciousness that exist. For instance Dear ones, there are many levels or forms of consciousness that exist at one given time. There are those, who in the most simplistic approach, have much fear. There are those who have much doubt. There are those who have education. There are those who have love. There are those who have compassion. Now, each of these are at varying degrees. There are states or levels of consciousness. There are indeed, as one would also begin to understand, points of perception. The Earth Plane is filled with many levels, many dimensions that exist of consciousness and the creations that ensue thereof. However, know this Dear ones, Dear hearts, that the Earth Plane, in its own evolution, is an illusion. Now, when I state this, it is an illusion brought with purpose, brought with intention. It is an illusion that is the balance of karma and purpose.

But now, let us move on to the Earth Planet. The Earth Planet is also a consciousness. In the same way that the Earth Plane contains many levels of consciousness, the Earth Planet is comprised of the Mineral, Vegetable, and Animal Kingdoms, and the humans. It also contains a greater comprised consciousness, the systems of Beloved Babajeran. The Earth Planet, Babajeran, exists in her own timing and intention, for she serves at this time as a great schoolroom, to assist and help mankind, to assist and help humanity, as we all well know. Babajeran serves the many rounds of incarnation that one may take into the Earth Plane and Planet.

The Earth Planet contains the physical body that must give to the Laws of Nature. And in Babajeran, the Mother Earth, exists the many Laws of Nature, the Deva Kingdoms, and the Elemental Kingdoms. Within the Elemental Kingdom are the sylphs, as the wind spirits; the undines, as the water spirits; the mighty salamanders, as the spirits of the fires; the little ones of the gnomes and the fairies; and all of the kingdoms that some have had the opportunity to contact and give information about. The Earth Planet serves in the mighty evolution of its own solar system. It serves for the arcing of Ray Forces to other planetary streams. It serves in its greater condition in this way, arcing vibrations of light and sound to other planets and getting, at will, a greater understanding of higher life forces.

## THE HEAVENLY LORDS

The Earth Plane and Planet, when stated together, contain this higher frequency or vibration as a higher consciousness that knows and understands the two as they work simultaneously together. This higher consciousness is where many of those, who have obtained liberation from the physical body, then move into these greater dimensional vibrations. These are known as the Heavenly Lords where they preside. At times, we speak of these as entering into the Fourth or the Fifth Dimension. These other dimensions indeed do exist and these are also comprised of the Earth Plane and Planet.

## A PLANE OF CONSCIOUSNESS

The human knows and understands very much of the Earth Plane, for there it comes to test, shall we say, the score of consciousness. There it comes to make choices, to learn about the will, thought, feeling, and action. As it travels in its many sojourns, learning through many situations and circumstances, it is awakened to the idea of the planet itself and its connection to a more vital life force. In that moment, it is awakened to the ONE process, understanding the common ground, or the universal consciousness, that affects all things. This universal consciousness is of course very important in all spiritual development, for then, one begins to understand the true meaning of the Earth Planet. What is the Earth Planet? How does the Earth Planet move and evolve? What is the science of the Earth Planet? You see, science then serves in its greater movement and understanding and brings the consciousness, or shall we say, active intelligence, to another level. Now this may also be perceived as a plane again of consciousness but it is a plane of consciousness that begins to integrate and move one into a greater understanding. Questions?

Response: *Yes. That was a very thorough explanation, thank you. And now, I ask permission to ask questions from those who have sent us emails.*

Proceed.

Question: *One person states, 'This week I saw a program on tech TV. A physicist was explaining the String Theory, something that some think is the next step to combine relativity and Quantum Theory into a Unified Field Theory. He said, "The mind of God is music resonating through ten dimensional strings." Can you share insights?'*

BEYOND IMAGINATION

This is indeed related to Unified Field Theory. However, it is suggested that this individual begin to study Hermetic Law. There they will find the complete teaching in its totality. It is true that all things within the universe are interrelated, in the same sense that the Earth Plane and the Earth Planet are as ONE. However, they exist simultaneously as two. It is important to understand cycles and rhythms, then one can more easily understand the idea of a Unified Field Theory.

Dear ones, Dear hearts, it is also important to understand this time, for this time is of great import to humanity. While this is stated over and over again in many discourses that I have brought forward to you, it is a wonderful opportunity that is being presented at this time. This too, is related to Unified Field Theory. You see, it has to do with the idea that consciousness can grow beyond what can be imagined. Now that may seem unusual for one who is commanding and demanding with intention and in purpose, but there are also laws that exist within the field of rhythm, as I have suggested, that allow the concept of momentum to overtake. This shall give this Dear one some solution.

Response: *Thank you. I have another question.*

   Proceed.

## AWAKENING FROM DARKNESS

Question: *Regarding Kali Yuga, I heard that in India, in January, many sages gathered for a week long celebration of the end of Kali Yuga. If you have seen a book called the 'Lemurian Scrolls,' it seems that Kali Yuga began to finish in around 1849, when the first light bulb was made. Is it an overlapping process, as you have mentioned?*

   Not only is it an overlapping process, it is also stated as a level of defining consciousness. Often times, when I speak of Kali Yuga in teachings, I speak of the broad based percentage of population. Now, at this time, it would seem that most of the population is still within the darkness of Kali Yuga, the time of iron, the time of lesser light that humanity has recently experienced. However, this is a great time of opportunity, awakening, and opening to greater light and consciousness.

## SILICON-BASED CONSCIOUSNESS

   The next stage of conscious growth is that of Dvapara Yuga, where we will see the opening of the mind to greater possibilities and potential. We will see the development, not only of the mind, in terms of its ability to receive new information, but growth within the Third Eye. We will see the use of telepathy to integrate with new technologies as they are developed within the next 200 years. We will see also this, as I have always stated, the silicon-based consciousness that is erupting within humanity. We will see many great changes in the medical field. In this, in particular, you will see in the next 150 years, great changes in terms of longevity. This is also one of the newer opportunities presented through the greater light spectrum of Dvapara Yuga.

It is true that in the Time of Kali, the consciousness fell and the teachings that were guarded needed to be kept from those who would misuse them and bring even greater suffering upon the ignorant masses. But it is time now for these spiritual teachings to come forward for the greater understanding of the Oneship, of Unana, to be present and applied. Dvapara Yuga now rules for those who have the eyes to see and the ears to hear. In this same respect, so does Kali Yuga. But a Golden Age, Dear ones, Dear hearts, also can exist, if you but have the eyes to see and the ears to hear. Now, this would also indicate that, at any time, consciousness can be raised to its fullest potential. That I cannot deny, for I AM THAT I AM. Questions?

THE GIFT

Question: *Are you saying that the energy that flows from within and from without, as things transition, can overlap, but that the focus the individual carries allows them to interact with either the Kali Yuga cycle, the Dvapara Yuga cycle, or the Golden Age cycle, depending on the choice of focus?*

Perception always creates reality, as I have always stated in many of the teachings. It depends on how you wish to see it. Is the glass half filled or half empty? Does the rose have thorns or a sweet smelling petal? Again Dear one, it is up to the perceiver of experience. But realistically too, in timing and intention, this is also a time where things can vastly open up for those who choose for them to open. Dear ones, Dear hearts, the awakening is at hand. As Dear Sananda has said, "The time has come for man to receive the gift." Questions?

## TRUST THE PROCESS

Question: *Another asks, 'We have received extensive information about the possibility of the dual Sun in our solar system and the race of people that have influenced our planet for hundreds of thousands of years. Is the theory possible, that a brown dwarf star is generating heat and light for a string of orbs, where at least one of these orbs is habitable?'*

It is possible indeed Dear ones, Dear hearts, and as we move into greater consciousness and light, more will be understood with this. In the next seventy-five years, there will be massive discoveries that will be made on such a theory. Now it is important to understand, indeed, as you are the progeny of perfection, your purpose is guided and directed by those elder Brothers and Sisters who have been entrusted with the Greater Plan Divine. Now we know at times, it is impossible to understand this greater consciousness and its existence. It is hard to understand that a science of predestination also fits like a glove with that of the science of the will and the development of the Master. But trust in the process, Dear ones, Dear hearts. This is my message to the one who has asked this question.

Question: *Thank you. Another asks Saint Germain about a Vortex that is in Oklahoma City, Oklahoma. 'I am inclined to think that we have an area that has developed by the events that have taken place there. It feels like a holding area, where those who have passed from this life and need to make their transition wait.' Would you comment?*

### INTERACTION OF THE ELEMENTAL AND DEVA KINGDOMS

What is being addressed is a great emotional energy that has had an effect on the collective Astral Body of the Earth. Now, we all well know how these paranormal types of situations can sometimes exist but it is important to understand the Law of Nature, the Deva and Elemental Kingdoms, and the service that they provide. Very often, when an event of this nature has taken place with a great emotional sorrow, with great anguish, then at that moment in time, the Elemental and Deva Kingdoms come in and begin to adjust the energy fields that surround such an area. This is what this person has been sensing. It is also important for this person to begin to study this interaction, to begin to understand the Earth Planet and how it works in its own interaction in assisting and helping mankind.

This is bringing about a great healing effect, not only for those who have crossed over, for know this Dear ones, that they have gone on in the greater evolution and purpose. But the suffering and anguish, as we all well know, on the Earth Plane is for those who have been left behind. That is why the Elementals and the Devas come in and bring, shall we say, a great comfort to the suffering of the many. They come forward and remind us, that again the Sun will shine . . . that again the soft rains will fall . . . and the seasons will progress in their order and majesty. Questions?

OPENING THE GATE

Question: *Thank you. This one also asks, 'I have been working in the dream state and I need to inquire about it. At night, I have been doing work with the souls that are trapped and not able to go into the light and go home. My job has been to usher them to the light and to somehow keep the gate open. I feel rushed when doing this work, as I have trouble sustaining the opening of the light gate. How can I hone my skills, so that I can be more effective, stay longer, and reach the ones that are confused?'*

Before entering into the sleep at night repeat this:

> I AM surrounded with the Light of God that Never Fails.
> Mighy Violet Flame be with me
> through my travels and journeys into the other side of life.
> Assist and guide me Great Master within,
> so that I can help in the Plan Divine, I AM.

This will bring about a sense of protection and purpose, for it is only a matter of focus. I would also suggest that during the waking hours that this Beloved one take up the meditation with a candle, as I have instructed you. It is important now that you give her this instruction to hone her focus. This will give her great assistance.

## IMMERSION INTO THE DIVINE

Question: *Thank you. Another asks, 'I discovered the Saint Germain teachings via the I AM Foundation a little over ten years ago and was turned away at a few of the I AM centers because I used illicit drugs, including LSD and other psychedelics, for a spiritual purpose. This was the foundation's strict policy. Presently, I am in my early thirties and not using drugs anymore but I would like advice from the Ascended Masters on the subject and some clarification. It was interesting to me why indigenous peoples have used these psychoactive drugs in ceremonial events, as a jump-start for their consciousness. Is this tradition one that probably continues to some degree in the present day, in even our youth festivals, with designer drugs and such? Has using mind altering substances been a sort of unwholesome shortcut or a necessary bridge between spirit and matter on the path of Ascension?'*

> May light stream forth into the hearts and minds
> of those who serve the Plan Divine, I AM.

This is a decree that you call forth at any time that you wish to use a mind-altering drug to take you into the other realms of consciousness. You see Dear ones, Dear hearts, the use of such mind-altering substances was brought forward in the time of Kali Yuga, where humanity had lost touch with the true teachings. However, at any time through the Violet Flame, one can bring about purification and alchemization within the body. This is indeed a teaching I bring forward. Now, it also important to understand the power of belief and how belief will inhibit groups, churches, individuals, and societies. Is this not true, Dear ones, Dear hearts? It is as simple as understanding that Point of Perception. But as we know, here upon the Earth Plane and Planet, many situations and circumstances are brought forward for our education, are they not? There are situations and circumstances that one may learn through these activities. One may simply shrug and say "a karmic path," but another one may say, "experience without judgment." Of course, to obtain these higher unions with God, which is what indeed the soul is seeking to obtain, is immersion into the Divine. One simply calls upon the Violet Flame:

> Violet Flame I AM,
> come forth in the name of the God I AM.

## VIOLET FLAME MANTRA

In the force of that one statement, the Violet Flame then surrounds you and brings you into a higher vibration, a higher understanding. If you are having trouble reaching the true spirit of the God Source . . . if you are feeling disconnected or discontented . . . if you feel conflict in your spiritual path, it is important to spend time in meditation and silence. Work at the silence of the mind. Then repeat silently within your mind, the mantras of the Violet Flame.

> Violet Flame I AM,
> God I AM Violet Flame.

## JUDGMENT IS A TRAP

This begins to soothe the mind. Repeat it, seven times seven. Now, it is important to understand the Laws of Surrender and Non-judgment. These I have spoken of in many past discourses. Judgment is indeed a rare trap, for one says, "I am but discerning, I am but choosing." But understand this, that one discerns and chooses for self and does not inflict or enforce what one chooses upon the other. Again, as you well know, when one asks me, "What shall I do?" I never tell another what to do, but I only reinforce the Law and to take it unto the self; then one finds, in that grand experiment, their own result. To this Dear one, I bring this suggestion again. Try this yourself. I will not tell you what to do. You must take this into your own experience. Test the waters for yourself. Have your experience. So Be It.

Response: *Thank you. I have no further questions.*

Then I shall take my leave and come forward again at the next Divine Appointment. Hitaka.

Response: *Hitaka.*

# 5

## I AM Awareness
*Saint Germain*

Greetings Beloved chelas. Shall we resume our work together?

Response: *Yes, we shall.*

I request permission to come forward?

Answer: *Please identify yourself and come forward.*

VIBRATION AND CONSCIOUSNESS

I AM Saint Germain and I stream forth on that Violet Ray of Mercy, Compassion, and ultimate Forgiveness. Dear ones, Dear hearts, what you are experiencing is the work of vibration. Did you not notice a difference in the room as I entered? Did you not notice a difference before? Vibration is very important Dear ones, Dear hearts. That is why we have given you specific guidelines regarding diet and specific guidelines regarding the use of the Violet Flame. It is very important Dear ones, for you see, vibration will determine the quality of the consciousness that you are experiencing at any given time. It is also important to understand that vibration has a predictability that is related to consciousness. The predictability of consciousness often times is misinterpreted in a dualistic manner; that is, it is judged from a Point of Perception.

It is important to understand that it is always, always important to know where one is, to know oneself, and to understand the state of consciousness that one is experiencing. But it is also important, as we have stated so many times before, to judge not, lest you be judged yourself. In judging, this is where one enters into a dualistic state of consciousness. We realize Dear ones, Dear hearts, that it is often very difficult upon the Earth Plane and Planet, very difficult indeed, for one is always judging. One is always measuring left from right, right from wrong, up from down, or asking, "Is this the right move for me? Is this the wrong move for me?" Such is the state in nature of the human condition. This indeed becomes a predictable state of consciousness. But as you well know, it is very important to see consciousness in the great out-picturing. The out-picturing of consciousness is then used to create a vibrational state. This is often used through the Violet Flame, which indeed brings your consciousness resonating to a certain vibration.

> Mighty Violet Flame stream in, through, and around
> all circumstances at this moment.
> Raise my vibration to the level of the Violet Flame.
> Release all judgments.
> So Be It.

Response: "So Be It."

As you see Dear ones, Dear hearts, in that moment, your own consciousness is then raised to a level that vibrates with the Violet Flame. You have called it forth into your consciousness. Do you understand?

## YOU CREATE YOUR VIBRATION

Response: *Yes, I do. At that moment, it is your focus.*

It is also a vibration within the focus. Yes it is true, the focus helps in the creation process but it is also important to understand vibration. We have given you many, many teachings on vibrations, but you know Dear ones, Dear hearts, it is not until you have the experience that you begin to understand that all important difference. Vibration is all around you at all times. There are different frequencies all around you at all times. But it is important for you to choose the vibrations that you will create your own Point of Perception from. Now, it is important to understand; for you see, when you begin to create your own vibration, it is almost as if you are dealing with a blank slate and you are able then to call out the qualities that you wish to use for the level and the state of consciousness. One may choose from a Point of Perception, the quality of love, along side the attributes of devotion and the qualities of cooperation. Now these come forward in that greater Co-creation, love sending its vibration, streaming forth from the heart of great intention. This vibration comes forward almost with a prophetic consequence, creating its own energy, its own vibration.

## WHEN LIFE "HAPPENS"

But in that which is the human condition, there are predictable consequences. Not choosing a level of vibration, one is always living in a vibration and accepting a vibration. Often this comes through a dualistic quality, as I have all ready explained. Life and its circumstances just seem to happen. Life and circumstances just seem to pile up, do they not, one on top of the other? And one feels as if they are chained to the predictable state of consciousness. Yes it is true, that if a person engages in anger, that there is too, a vibration then of hate. This vibration of hate leads only to more and more self doubt of the mighty I AM and the God within. One can no longer then call upon the vibrations of the Great I AM, for one doubts that even such a Source would exist within oneself.

BALANCE

Now we have just described for you two states of consciousness. One has a prophetic consequence, imaged as a Co-creator, and one has a predictable consequence. How does the state of consciousness then move beyond such duality? As we have always said, Dear ones, Dear hearts, it is through balance. It is through that state of neutrality of non-judgment. This requires surrendering of the will to the Divine Will and accepting all situations and circumstances as being in their correct place, timing, intention, and order. That is why, so often we have said to you, there is no mistake, ever, ever, and ever. This statement alone is a great affirmation of the vibration of neutrality. All states of consciousness exist, do they not? Accepting one another and allowing, with complete tolerance, without judgment, aligns to that Mighty Will in action.

RELATIONSHIP OF CONSCIOUSNESS TO SPIRITUAL GROWTH

States and levels of consciousness do indeed affect then, a Point of Perception. The way that you see things can be so changed, just by that shift in juxtaposition. This is always so important in the growth and evolution at a spiritual level. That is why the prophecies of I AM America were sent forward to humanity, not only to teach about the relationship between consciousness and Beloved Babajeran, but also to show a relationship between states and levels of human consciousness and spiritual evolution and (to) growth. This is not to say that it is bad to hate, or that it is good to love; it is rather to understand that all states of consciousness do exist simultaneously as an experience. Once aligning to that Greater Will within the experience, one begins to see that quality of choice.

## THE POWER OF THE GREAT I AM

Choice is one of the greatest teachings of the Great I AM. For would you not say, Dear ones, Dear hearts, that when you call upon the Great I AM, you begin to see all things in a different rhythm and in a different order. Through the Great I AM, one is calling forth, not only the power of the God Omni-essence, they are calling forth the energies of all of those who have gone before them. When one calls forth the power of the Great I AM, they are calling forth the energy, not only of this hierarchy of consciousness, they are also commanding and demanding the substance of universal force to cooperate in willingness with the great Eight-sided Cell of Perfection. This of course leads the consciousness to understanding that all dual states of consciousness, existing simultaneously, side by side, merge as if into ONE. All states of consciousness merge into the great consciousness of Unana.

It is true Dear ones, that the I AM is related to this state of consciousness of Unana. The I AM is the great entry point into understanding that God is indeed within. As I have always told you Dear ones, Dear hearts, believe not a word I say, but take it unto your own greater counsel. Call upon the I AM and test the law for yourself. Experience is always the key in understanding. Experience is always the key in awareness.

> Mighty I AM Presence come forth
> in the awareness of the Great I AM THAT I AM.

Even in this moment, as I call forth the awareness of the Great I AM, do you feel another shift now in vibration and energy?

Response: *Yes, there is an energetic surge in the room.*

## HARMONY'S BLESSING

It is important always to understand how any situation, at any time, can be adjusted, shifted, altered, and changed to bring about greater understanding. This of course is an elementary teaching to what I have given you before as the Principles of Harmony. When all is functioning in that greater alignment to the Divine Plan, this harmony comes forward and gives its bountiful blessings. It is the hallmark of a greater level of consciousness. For you see Dear ones, Dear hearts, as I have taught you so many times and has been brought forth in the Jurisdictions, harmony streams forth from the Heart of the Central Sun. This harmony is the bond through which the septenary qualities come forward, orchestrating at will, the Divine Plan. Do not think for one minute whether or not these Rays, streaming forth from the Great Central Sun, are resonating or vibrating at the proper level. They come forward from that point of neutrality, streaming forth from that Great Heart, in their essence of All That Is, the Great I AM.

## I AM AWARENESS

Now this is illustrative of the fact that Omni-essence is always existing. It always is as it is. Within you, the Great I AM can carry forth its great lesson within your life. The Great I AM also can help any situation, any circumstance that you wish to bring a greater solution towards, a greater understanding and increased awareness. Calling upon the I AM Awareness at all times leads you then to be able to perceive a situation from that different Point of Perception. Questions?

Question: *The I AM Presence is the presence of our consciousness or our awareness of the I AM, is it not?*

It is true Dear ones, Dear hearts. When I speak of the I AM Awareness, I speak of a joint consciousness. That is the awareness of the I AM, as I teach in this moment, and your experience of the I AM Presence. The I AM Awareness exists between all who have activated the I AM, to bring it into its greater creative ability. The I AM Awareness, while it streams forth from the I AM Presence, is a quality of the Presence of God. Now, the I AM is the individualized presence of God that resides within every person. We have spoken about this on many occasions, spoken about the I AM Presence as it has been implanted in the great Eight-sided Cell of Perfection. But the I AM Awareness is that now which we share; for you see Dear ones, Dear hearts, the I AM Awareness leads one into a greater quality of understanding, a greater unity of states or levels of consciousness, and prepares one for the path into Unana. When you call upon the I AM Awareness, it is as if a universal consciousness is then released for you to utilize. Do you understand?

Answer: *Yes, I do.*

Proceed.

Question: *In calling upon the I AM Presence to come forward into a situation, that is an acknowledgement of your personal surrender of your will to the Presence of God, is it not?*

## THE INTERCONNECTIVITY OF THE I AM

To the Presence of God and also the surrender of your will to the Greater Will, that is, the Will that recognizes the I AM Awareness, the I AM that exists in all individuals. It is as if the I AM Awareness is the energy or the interconnectivity between two individuals. Now it is always important to understand, for in the individualized Presence of God, one may think that is a separate version of God from an overall version of God. This is not so. That thought would indeed be in error, for the I AM Presence and the I AM Awareness are interconnected as if as ONE. The I AM Presence indeed is always with you Dear ones, Dear hearts, ready to serve and acknowledge the I AM Awareness. The Great I AM exists in all circumstances and situations. Have you not noticed that when you are in a trying circumstance or situation and you call upon the mighty I AM, instantly an opportunity or a solution to your problem then appears? Is this not so?

Response: *Yes, it is so.*

That is the essence and the energy of the I AM in its awareness. Now, it is almost as if it is of a prophetic consequence, is it not? For you know in that instance, that even a greater solution can come forward when the proper focus is placed upon the right state, level of consciousness, or as in the earlier part of this discourse, on vibration. Predictable levels of consciousness are those that are not tuned into, do not understand this state of higher consciousness, this state of the I AM Awareness. It is true that even animals, although they do not contain the individualized Presence of God, are also tuned in to the I AM Awareness. All that is upon the Earth Plane and Planet are all interconnected through the Great I AM Awareness. But human beings are indeed individualized through the I AM.

CULTIVATE TOLERANCE AND PATIENCE

Souls that are perfecting on their sojourn, perfecting thought, feeling, and action in this great evolution of energy, are led to understand that there are these vibrational differences that do exist. But often, the predictable human consciousness judges things through dual experience; is this good or is this bad? The I AM Awareness accepts it all, in its perfect place and in its perfect order. Very often, the perfect order is not pleasant for one. Very often, one is disappointed for one reason or another. But the cultivation of tolerance and patience, one then begins to see the harmony that truly exists in all things. Proceed.

## CALL FORTH THE I AM AWARENESS

Question: *It is true that Divinity is in all things and this Divinity is the source of creation or God?*

This Divinity could be very much compared to the I AM Awareness. But remember, as one may have the consciousness that all things have and contain God within them, Divinity within, until you command and demand the I AM Awareness to come forward and work for you, this awareness may not be able to give you the results that you require. That is why, so often when we call upon that Mighty I AM Presence, a shift of quality and vibration immediately ensues. This is collecting and calling the I AM Awareness into its greater activity. For instance, you may call upon the I AM Awareness through the I AM Presence. You do not notice that anything has immediately happened, but you notice a calming effect over circumstances, over situations. And yet, three weeks later, upon that circumstance, there is the answer. Someone else appears at the front the door, presenting to you a solution to a problem that seemed unanswered at the time. Now again, I speak in metaphors and symbols but also Dear ones, Dear hearts, there are those instances where the I AM Awareness brings complete and total balance to a situation.

> Mighty I AM THAT I AM,
> I call forth the Awareness of the Great I AM,
> to bring balance and harmony to this situation.
> So Mote It Be.

Response: *So Mote It Be.*

In that instance, you will notice a quality, a calming, a vibration. Tuning into this frequency, one then begins to have a different experience. Immediately, the clouds begin to part; the Sun begins to shine;

things are seen from a new perception again. This awareness is the gift of God. It comes forward only to serve. Questions?

DIVINITY EXISTS IN ALL THINGS

Question: *Yes. So, if Divinity is in all and the I AM Awareness, why isn't it simply within its nature to call or command the I AM Presence into action?*

The difference, Dear one, as I have always stated, is experience. It is important again, to not believe a word that I say to you. It is important only to review this lesson and to bring that mighty law into your own experience. But for simplistic matters, Divinity indeed exists in all things. It exists in the air in this room. It exists in the chair that you sit upon. It exists in the candle that you light. It exists in the food that you eat. The Awareness is that Divinity called into motion, to put forward that Great Plan of the Divine Will, bringing forward a greater alignment to circumstances and situations. Do you understand?

Question: *Yes, I do. And so, in calling upon the I AM Presence, an individual can call God action into a circumstance or situation, into a thought of healing or personal action, so that it is completely aligned with the Divine Plan and Divine Will? And this will happen in a way that the individual will understand and comprehend, is this not so?*

It is so Dear one, Dear heart. But for the chela, the student, who wishes to understand how such a situation can exist, how such a situation even would exist in the qualification of experience, this is why I give this instruction. Now Dear one, it has been some time since we have last had discourse. Are there any questions?

Response and question: *Yes. It is my experience, in the ability to manifest something, if the picture is envisioned in a very clear manner in the mind, without the use of words, and one can see it occurring and then create a model of it in an out-pictured manner, that it comes to fruition, comes into existence in this reality. And so, is the simplest method for this Co-creative process to envision without words or thoughts, just pictures?*

OUT-PICTURING, FOCUS, AND THE UNIVERSAL FLOW

Out-picturing, you know Dear one, Dear heart, is also connected, as another way of understanding the I AM Awareness. Out-picturing also Dear ones, as I have taught you, brings into a great understanding the visualization process. Now this sometimes is easier for a chela or student to begin with; for you see, the object of their desire is instantly in front of them. They are able then to see, in this manner, a materialization in their mind's eye of the result that they seek. Now there are those who are able to work with the out-picturing process in a more abstract form and manner, but it is important to understand each level within this Co-creative process and understanding that these are all keys to self-Mastery.

Out-picturing is given for the chela, so that they can begin to understand the incremental steps that are involved in the honing of the focus. As the focus becomes more and more exercised, not through belief but through experience, one begins to see the results that do occur through this process. Then one is ready to understand and activate the I AM Awareness. For in that moment, Dear ones, Dear hearts, the chela understands that there is no mistake, ever, ever, ever. All is working with a Divine Intention, in a Divine Plan, in accordance to the Divine Will. But this does not say that one just accepts conditions the way they are; no, that is not what I imply when I state this law. Beyond acceptance is tolerance and the energy of tolerance is a vibration. In this vibration, there is a greater understanding; there is a greater knowledge. This is the I AM Awareness. One then releases expectation and begins to flow into a greater vibration or energy, for lack of better word, of the universe. Does this explain?

## PAIN, THE EQUALIZER

Question: *Yes. If one is experiencing a situation that is completely uncomfortable, is that existing discomfort the Divine Plan and the choice to change it, the ability to change it, and the laws that can change it, are also within the Divine Plan?*

It is Dear one. As you well know, pain is often the greatest teacher. Pain often shows you where not to travel again. Pain often will immediately stop you from traveling down the wrong path. Pain, you see Dear ones, when it is not resisted but understood, also becomes a great equalizer. It places you with tolerance upon this path of neutrality, for one then is able to understand this higher frequency of which I speak.

Question: *So here, in our experience in this schoolhouse, the ability to choose and to continue to choose to alter circumstances and situations, is our birthright?*

It is true, Dear ones, Dear hearts, in as much as the I AM Presence is connected (to you).

# 6

**Eternal Balance**
*Saint Germain*

Greetings Beloved chelas, in that mighty Violet Flame. I AM Saint Germain and I request permission to come forward.

Response: *Please Saint Germain, you are most welcome. Come forward.*

LAW OF CORRESPONDENCE

There is still Dear ones, Dear hearts, much work for us to complete. Many changes indeed are happening upon the Earth Plane and Planet. And there are changes yet to come; these changes, known as prophecies, are also designed to shift the perception in consciousness of the Earth Plane. In the Law of Correspondence, the changes upon the Earth Plane are destined to happen. For you see Dear ones, Dear hearts, humanity and her people are sponsored by Beloved Earth, Beloved Babajeran. The Earth, in her sojourn and travels, is also going through a great change and it is no mistake, almost by Divine Appointment, that all are here.

You are here as well, experiencing this great change, for you see Dear ones, Dear hearts, this too is an evolution of your own consciousness. As the planet moves forward in her consciousness, in her vibratory rate, you too move forward in your own evolution, in your own spiritual growth. Dear ones, Dear hearts, this too is happening by Divine Order. As you so well know, there is no mistake, ever, ever, ever. Both of you have been brought together in this instance through that mighty Law of Attraction, this law always attracting like unto itself. This electromagnetic pulse, you see, cannot be denied. It is indeed a law of pushing and pulling, of attracting onto itself and repulsing onto itself. You see Dear ones, this too is another Law of Correspondence, of like seeking like, the same vibration seeking same vibration. These are laws eternal. Laws that must be paid attention to. For you see Dear ones, Dear hearts, when you pay attention to the laws eternal, then you are able to focus upon the true God-like qualities that exist in all things. That Mighty I AM Presence that is within you is also focused upon the eternal laws.

## THE CLARITY OF THE TEACHING

The temporal illusion gives many tests indeed to the soul and gives many tests to the soul in its sojourn within the Earth Plane and Planet. This indeed is a Time of Testing and we know at times that you wonder "how much more must I endure?" But as I have stated so many times Dear ones, Dear hearts, one is never tested beyond the ability that they are capable to perform. Again, this is based upon that mighty Law of Correspondence and the Law of Attraction, in the same essence, that when the student is ready, the Master appears. When the student is ready, also the test comes forward at the level that they are perfectly capable of performing. In this moment, so many lessons are being learned. And as lessons are being learned, one must then come forward in that lesson and declare the clarity of its teaching.

This clarity of its teaching comes forward when one is tested upon the content of the material of the lesson. Indeed, there are many changes that are happening now upon the Earth Plane and Planet, many of these changes orchestrating great changes within yourself but also orchestrating great testing for all levels of humanity, at many different levels of spiritual growth and evolution. At times, it may appear that things are so chaotic, that things do not make sense, that all is working with such chaos and disorder. But know Dear ones, Dear hearts, trust within that the plan assuredly shows that all is happening in a great Divine Orchestration. All is happening in a great Divine Order.

## "THE DIFFERENCE IS EXPERIENCE"

At times, one may see or think such an insidious thought, such an insidious plan, that they would wonder how such darkness could be upon this Earth Plane and Planet at this time? But know this Dear ones, Dear hearts, all play their role. All play a part in letting the true role of light supreme reign. Know this Dear ones, Dear hearts, that the Earth is a blessing brought to you, to be your schoolroom, a place where you are brought to learn many experiences. As you well know Dear ones, Dear hearts, it is not belief that moves you forward in your evolution but experience is the guide. These experiences move you forward in your own evolution. They move you forward, one step at a time. That is why Dear Sananda has always said to you, "What is the difference?" Indeed Dear ones, Dear hearts, it is the experience. For you see, only through experience are you able to grow and understand.

## COMPASSION AND THE OPEN HEART

One level to recognize growth is first the opening of the heart. Through the opening of the heart, one then is able to walk into greater levels, or shall we say, experiences of compassion. As you well know Dear ones, mercy, love, and forgiveness are always earmarks of compassion working at this level. This is one way to always gauge spiritual growth, for the chela who has grown in their own evolution, exhibits these qualities of compassion. Never is there a rush to judgment over any situation but there is the ability to discern through the Heart of Compassion, knowing that all is moving in its own timing and its own intention. All is moving forward, expressing that great and mighty love eternal. Dear ones, Dear hearts, this is always one of the first earmarks of a chela when they have experienced a level of growth.

## BEYOND "RIGHT" OR "WRONG"

Another level of growth is the development of detachment, that one does not have to have something one way or the other. That is, they are able to move beyond the dualistic perception of their own experience. They are able then to accept that both sides, of left or right, can exist simultaneously. These Laws of Detachment leave one to an understanding of the truer Laws of Neutrality. When one sees that something is neither right nor wrong, but that all sides are existing, bringing forth the great eternal balance of the ONE, growth then is achieved.

## LOVE FOR ALL

Another earmark of spiritual growth is that of love, love for all things; not only love of the fellow man but also love of nature; love of the Animal Kingdom; love of the Flower Kingdom; love of the Mineral Kingdom; love of the Elemental Kingdom. This love is always expressed and given without any expectation. Love is brought forward in this essence at an unconditional level.

## THE LAW OF FORGIVENESS

Of all of these, the most important earmark to note within spiritual growth is that of forgiveness. Forgiveness, Dear ones, Dear hearts, right now for humanity, is one of the greatest stumbling blocks that exists for all. Often we hold as humans, little injustices. These little injustices keep the Heart of Compassion from growing. These little injustices keep a level of detachment from ever forming. These little injustices limit and restrict the release of the Law of Love. Forgiving oneself first is a matter of understanding how to shift your perception. Forgiveness, at all times, is a matter of being able to see something from a whole new viewpoint, a different standing point, so to speak.

It is important always to utilize that mighty Law of Forgiveness, the Violet Flame. That is why Dear ones, Dear hearts, the Violet Flame has been brought to you. For this mighty Violet Flame is indeed a Divine Intervention, a great gift that has been brought for humanity at this time. You see, it is used almost as a fertilizer for the soul, so it can have something to feed upon to attain the next levels of growth that are essential for evolution. Now, we know these earmarks of growth always lead one to another level of understanding. That level is the level of ONE, which is the Christ. Plane. We have spoken of this in many other discourses as Unana.

SPIRITUAL STAGNATION

But not to distract us away today from this discourse, we will stay focused upon the work at hand. At times in the Times of Testing, the student, chela, or aspirant, feels as if they are moving nowhere, that they are stagnating in a pool of their own diseased thoughts, feelings, or actions. I have given these levels of understanding in this discourse today so the student may cultivate those areas which they may feel need more practice. Have we not often spoken that practice, practice, practice, always brings about a more permanent experience? This permanent experience imbeds itself within the consciousness. Then compassion, love, detachment, forgiveness, all come about with such ease and grace. The chela, the student, has practiced this so often that it becomes a simple state of consciousness. It fits as easily as a glove.

## WAHANEE AND THE VIOLET FLAME

Dear ones, Dear hearts, the Golden City of Wahanee is indeed one of the greatest Golden Cities to travel to and experience the energies of Beloved Babajeran, assisting the processes of the growth of the soul. For you see, that is where the Violet Flame is anchored firmly into the center of the Star of Wahanee. It was carried forward at a much, much earlier time and held within the spiritual grid of Mother Earth for this time. It is of no mistake that this time has come forward, Dear ones, Dear hearts, coming forward now to bring you into another level of growth, another level of experience. Wahanee, you see Dear ones, Dear hearts, is brought forward in a more cosmic sense, that is, for all at a level of Brotherhood and Sisterhood.

For those who wish to travel to Wahanee, they can receive great personal growth, great personal support, great personal instruction upon the levels of which I speak. Yes, it is true that Wahanee holds an energy to bring about a United Brotherhood and Sisterhood of the World. Now when I speak of this, do not confuse this with a one-world government of control, but it is rather, a one-world experience of love, complete Brotherhood, and peace. This that I speak of is the energy of Unana and Wahanee is very important, as it plays a continued role throughout the millennium of peace and grace, holding in continuous motion, an energy for the Dove of Peace to land upon the planet.

The ethereal schools of Wahanee are accessed, Dear ones, Dear hearts, when one travels to this Golden City Vortex and can also be experienced through meditation or the dream state, where the great instruction comes forward. Sometimes these energies are integrated just through the presence of traveling to the area, but often it is of great assistance if one is able to access the more subtler planes of energy. Know Dear ones, Dear hearts, that I am always there helping and guiding. Under my focus and direction, the energies bring about this process of compassion, the process of detachment, the process of all encompassing love eternal. Dear ones, Dear hearts, if you cannot travel to Wahanee, you can also travel in your meditation. I have given some instruction on this but before entering into the state of meditation, often it is good to meditate upon the Violet Flame. Before meditation, state this decree:

> In the name of that mighty Christ I AM,
> may the Violet Flame flow in, through, and around me.
> I AM now ONE with the Star of Wahanee.
> I AM love. I AM complete detachment.
> I AM Mercy and Forgiveness. I AM Compassion.
> So Be It.

Response: *So Be It.*

## THE SCHOOLS OF LIGHT

This statement comes forward, Dear ones, to prepare the consciousness to enter into that mighty Ray Force of the Violet Flame. The Violet Flame, as you well know, transmutes the consciousness and prepares it, in this sense, as an initiation to enter into the greater Temples of Light Supreme. These temples of consciousness, or shall we say, schools of light, lead one into a greater instruction. This is the purpose for all fifty-one Vortices upon the Earth Plane. They are brought forward at this time as a great intervention, for those who have the eyes to see and the ears to hear. It is true Dear ones, Dear heart, that when entering in to these higher schools of light, one begins to feel very differently. The first thing that they will notice is that their diet no longer works for them. They will notice that animal products seem to limit their ability to sustain the time that they enter into these schools of light. They will also notice that there is a high-pitched ring that is often vibrating within an audible sound Ray. This high vibration is indeed a shift in your consciousness.

Sometimes throughout the day, the mind begins to wander and an instant telepathic vision comes forward. One is able to see images that, at the time, may not make much sense, but when understood in the context of contact at another level, which is often known as a simultaneous reality, they are given a clearer and more lucid knowledge. For you see Dear one, when one begins to contact the School of Light, one then begins to understand that all is existing simultaneously; all is within you at once. Until these states or levels of consciousness are anchored more firmly within that permanent experience, one will feel at times a type of shaky motion, for lack of a better description, in terms of understanding their experience within these schools.

One also then begins to sustain contact, not only with the I AM, but with the I AM Awareness. As in our last discourse, the I AM Awareness is of all-importance; for you see, it is a higher consciousness frequency of relating to life eternal. That is why, when I explain relating to love, love in terms of all kingdoms of life, one is then relating through the I AM Awareness. One will also feel the presence of the Master Teacher. In this instance, if you are attending the Golden City Light Schools of Wahanee, one will feel an immediate contact or familiarity with my teachings and my tutelage.

THE FIRST SEVEN GOLDEN CITIES

Now know Dear ones, Dear hearts, if you identify with other Golden City Vortices and the teachings that they bring forward, you can use the techniques as I have described in the same manner. But I bring this teaching forward today, so you may begin to understand the importance of the Wahanee Vortex and the Golden City energies that have been placed there to serve humanity at this most important time. It is true that each Golden City Vortex is aligned to a certain continent upon the Earth. We have given some of this information in the beginning material. But now, it is important to understand that each of the Golden City Vortices, that is the first seven of them that are activated upon the Earth Plane and Planet, stabilize and help a certain continent during the great Earth Changes.[7]

---

7. *See Appendix G, Golden City Activation Dates, page 211.*

Of course, Gobean is affiliated with Gobi. It is there to stabilize the energies of Asia. Malton, you see Dear ones, is there to stabilize the energies of Europe. Wahanee is to stabilize the energies of Africa. Shalahah is there to stabilize the energies of India, even though there are those who would say that this is part of the Asian continent. At one time, this whole area was a separate continent and was related also to ancient Lemuria. Australia is also stabilized through this to some extent. It is also important to note that Klehma is there to balance North America and also South America together. The Golden Cities within Canada, Pashacino, to be exact, is there to stabilize Antarctica. [Editor's Note: The Golden City of Shalahah, (United States) is metaphysically connected to the Golden City of Sheahah, (Australia).]

The seventh Golden City, in its activation to come forward, holds an energy for the entire world. [Editor's Note: The seventh Golden City activated is Eabra in the Yukon Territory. The Master Teacher is Portia, Twin Flame to Saint Germain, holding the Violet Flame and the purpose of bringing forth joy, balance, and equality.]

So you see Dear ones, Dear hearts, this gives even a more added dimension to understanding the work of the Golden Cities and how this grid is interconnected at many, many levels. Dear ones, Dear hearts, there is much, much, more teaching that will be given upon the Golden Cities. But now, I sense your questions and open the floor.

FORGIVENESS AND PERCEPTION

Question: *Thank you. So that this is clarified, in the area of forgiveness, are you forgiving the person you sense is transgressing you or are you forgiving yourself for even perceiving a transgression and not just accepting it as an experience?*

Perhaps it is important to understand that all works simultaneously. When one has moved their perception to forgive self, one instantaneously then releases attachment to the one that they perceive a transgression has occurred with. It is most important always Dear one, to forgive the self first, for in the forgiveness of self, one then is able to see things from a whole new point of view. This indeed is that Point of Perception which is always so important.

Response: *I see. So in essence, there really isn't a transgression, you're just having an experience and if you forgive yourself for perceiving the experience as a transgression, then you will not have that sense of contention or disagreement with the other person.*

It is as simple as shifting your perception. When one moves to understand a situation or circumstance from as many perceptions as possible, then one is able to easily forgive the self. This cannot occur when one righteously assumes one level of perception and insists that is the only way that a certain situation or circumstance can be viewed. This is most important.

Question: *I understand what you're saying. The Golden Cities are activated in the planet but are they also activated through the individuals who are present there?*

They are activated through the agreement of Beloved Babajeran and the Ascended Masters.[8] Dear ones, Dear hearts, this is a work of cooperation, that is why we have stated this to be an Age of Cooperation, a New Time for peace and prosperity for the Earth and humanity.

## GOLDEN CITY ACTIVATIONS

Question: *I understand. So as more Golden Cities are activated, they will increasingly stabilize the planet. Is this at a geophysical level or is this at a spiritual level?*

---

8. *See Appendix H, Golden City Activation, page 213.*

Of course, it is at a spiritual level but, as you well know, it is that template of thought and intention that creates the physical manifestation, does it not?

Answer: *Yes, I would agree with that.*

So, as you see Dear ones, Dear hearts, this is of vast importance.

## DIVINE INTERVENTION OF THE GOLDEN CITIES

Question: *Yes, I understand what you're saying. The Golden Cities, in their sponsorship from the Ascended Masters and the planet, are they here to transmute the planet and to also transmute all of humanity?*

It is true Dear ones, it is true Dear heart. The Golden Cities have been brought forward as a great Divine Intervention, not only to bring a stabilization to the Earth at this most wondrous time, but also to bring forward the Schools of Light, so many may have access to them. This is why there were many that were given within the Earth grid, that is, in terms of their locations, so those who had the eyes to see and the ears to hear could travel to them in physical proximity. If this was not something that could be achieved, then they could also travel through working with the finer light bodies. Do you understand?

Answer and question: *Yes, I do. And so these Schools of Light are specific for each of the Rays?*

It is true Dear one. But as you so well know, it is always better to have choice, is it not?

Question: *Yes, it is. That truly helps to expand our experiences on our path of upliftment. In understanding these Schools of Light and the*

*Masters being present, is it important that actual buildings are built in the future for these schools to exist here?*

These schools exist without physical buildings. But again Dear ones, certain buildings formed with certain sacred geometrical shapes, as you well know, have the ability to intensify the result. This I have given to you in previous discourses.

Question: *Yes, you have. Just to clarify, are there specific buildings for specific Rays?*

Dear one, Dear heart, the Rays of Light and Sound exist without the formation of a building. However, if you are referring to intensifiers, that is, buildings that serve as Step-down Transformers of Ray Forces, this too can be achieved. However, this is an advanced knowledge and will be released at a later date, if you so require.

Response: *Yes, I would think these intensifiers would be very helpful to the individuals or groups who are drawn to each of these schools.*

As you well know Dear one, certain Rays of Light and Sound vibrate better to certain minerals. Substances also vibrate better to certain colors and vibrate to certain types of building materials. It is a little more detailed and a little more complicated, however, totally achievable, as it has been in past civilizations.

Question: *Yes, so in the future, if I do request, you will come forward with this detailed information for each of the Rays?*

So Be It.

# 7

## Golden Ray Mantra
*Saint Germain*

Greetings beloved Dear ones. I AM Saint Germain and I stream forth on that mighty Violet Ray of Mercy, Compassion, and ultimate Forgiveness. As usual Dear hearts, Dear ones, I request permission to come forward?

Response: *Please Saint Germain, come forward. You are most welcome.*

First let me make a finer adjustment of the energy fields.

[*He has come in with a group of angels surrounding him. They're moving about the room, adjusting energies all about.*]

POLITICAL CHANGES

I shall now proceed. Greetings and Shamballa Dear ones, Dear hearts. It is at my request that I have asked for you to be present to receive this discourse this morning. You see, there are many changes that are about to happen on the global scene of the Earth Plane and Planet; changes in political systems; changes in governments of the world; many changes also that will happen this year in the Earth Planet. But it is important for you to understand, amidst all the changes that are bound to happen in this upcoming year, to stay ever stalwart with the plan, to stay ever focused upon the work at hand, to stay close to the teachings that I have given to you Dear ones, Dear hearts.

## GOLDEN CITIES AND EARTH'S ELECTROMAGNETISM

The teachings that I have given you primarily focus upon the Prophecies of I AM America and the possibility of geophysical Earth Change. But also, it is important to keep your energies focused upon the Golden City Vortices; for indeed, as you begin to understand all of the past discourses that I have given you, you will begin to interweave each of the teachings into a greater understanding and into a greater knowledge. You see, the electromagnetism of the Earth field is changing, being assisted, not only by the five Masters who are serving the Golden City Vortices of the United States, but now also, assisted by that mighty Golden City Vortex that exists in Canada, Pashacino. Soltec is now anchoring the energies in its exact force and field, to bring forth an effect for the Canadian peoples.

## MASTERS OF THE GATEWAYS

It is important also to understand that the Golden City Vortices are interacting with the Earth Mother herself, Beloved Babajeran. This interaction is brought about as a Divine Intervention with the Master Teachers. It is also true, as I have given to you in past discourses, that there are now seven Masters who serve each of the gateways, or shall we say Doorways, of the four directions of each Golden City Vortex.[9] These Master Teachers come from many areas, not only of your galaxy but also from beyond the Pleiades. Also there are several who have volunteered to come from the Dahl Universe.

## DAHL UNIVERSE AND THE GOLDEN RAY

The Dahl Universe is an ancient universe that exists with its own separate Sun away from the Pleiades, away from your own solar system. While it feels some force from the Galactic Center, it func-

---

9. See Appendix I, *Golden City Structure, Doorways, and Adjutant Points,* page 215.

tions independently and there is, shall we say, a higher evolution of consciousness that exists in this particular galaxy. These Masters that are coming forward are those who have instructed others in times of greater light upon the Earth Plane and Planet. These new Master Teachers who are coming forward contain energies and information that have yet to be integrated into the Earth Plane and Planet but will bring a greater force and field to the work at hand.

It is important, as you begin to integrate these energies, to understand the work of the Golden Ray. For the Golden Ray Dear ones, Dear hearts, activates the Golden Thread Axis and brings the energies of the Kundalini into higher understanding and acceleration. This work, as you have known as the eighth energetic body, brings about a greater awakening. It is indeed assisted by the Sunday Meditation by Dear Beloved Sananda.[10] It is important also to utilize the energies of the Golden City Vortices to bring forth this effect. For you see Dear ones, Dear hearts, the energies that are being activated are not only those of their own solar system, but the energies of the Dahl Universe. The Pleiades is being used as a Step-down Transformer. In the same way that Jupiter, Mars, and the Sun itself are Step-down Transformers of the energy of the Great Central Sun into your own Earth, the Pleiades is used as a Step-down Transformer for this higher energy that will come in from the Dahl Universe. This will bring about a greater awakening of the forces of Unana, a greater unity of consciousness.

THE GROUP

Throughout this year, many of those who utilize the Sunday Meditation and integrate the energy within the Golden Ray, will find that they are more telepathic in their awareness, more susceptible to group contact.[11] That is why, when you enter into groups, at times you feel disturbed and disjointed. This is because of the growth of

---
10. See Appendix J, *Sananda's Sunday Peace Meditation.*, 219.
11. See Appendix K, *The Gold Ray,* page 223.

this new energy body; therefore, it is very important when you move into group contact, or group movement, that that group is keyed into a finer harmonic, into a finer tuning, if you will. For you see, the sound vibration and light vibration is very sensitive indeed. So it is important, in the creation of all harmony, that these groups are tuned together.

GOLDEN RAY MANTRA

I shall now give you vibrations of the Eighth Ray:

> Om Banandra,
> Om Banandra,
> Om Hunana,
> Om Sunana.

This is a mantra that is given for this Eighth Ray and brings forth a more balancing effect to groups. Carry forth this mantra in the group and you will see a finer tuning within the group. We have noted that you have had several meetings within your office and it is important that those who come into the central core of the working of this facility align and attune themselves to this vibrational pulse and force.[12]

HARMONIZATION OF ENERGY

You see Dear ones, Dear hearts, when you experience a disharmony, it is not because one person is out of harmony or one person is less spiritual or less divine. It is because there are certain energy force fields that are then readied to harmonize. You see, one must be readied to serve this Cause Divine. This has nothing to do with judging another or criticizing another. Indeed Dear ones, Dear hearts, it has to do with when the student is ready, the Master ap-

---
12. See Appendix L, *Golden Ray Mantra*, page 225.

pears, in this case, a Mastery of Light and Sound force fields aligning with this Eighth Ray. It is important always to visualize this vibration about the body when calling this into its group effect. For you see Dear ones, this brings about a greater activation of the Eight-Sided Cell of Perfection and the force field of Unana. This work has been present for some time upon the Earth Plane and Planet but it was just recently decided at Shamballa that you shall be given the keys, in essence, as the mantra field. Questions?

Question: *The keys as the mantra field? I do not understand.*

## USE OF THE GOLDEN RAY MANTRA

When I speak of keys as mantra fields, I speak of that of harmonics. I speak about a sound and light vibration. When you call forth the mantra of Om Hu, immediately surrounding you is a force field of Violet Light. Now when you call forth the force that I have just given you in the mantra, Om Banandra, you will then immediately feel the energy of Mother Earth and the assistance of the ancients of the Dahl Universe coming forward. This blends into, for lack of a better word, an axiotonal quality that brings about a further activation of the Kundalini and the Eight-Sided Cell of Perfection. Do you understand?

Response: *Yes I see what you are saying. Please continue.*

## ACTIVITY AND USE OF THE EIGHTH LIGHT BODY

It may not be possible for me to continue too much longer. The most important aspect and element of this discourse has been given. It is important that when you move into group activity, that this tuning of harmonics is brought about; for you see, this is why, once leading a disjointed group, one that is not tuned and in the specific harmony to bring about the larger plan at hand, one feels so disjointed and disconnected. This tuning of harmonics brings about a healing effect to the emotional body, alongside the activation of this eighth body.

You see Dear ones, Dear hearts, this eighth body has been activated for some time. However, it has yet to be put into use. It is most important in this work to understand that it is always when it is brought into activity, then it can begin to bring about the great changes within. The changes within are then the gateway to the changes without, as you well know and understand Dear ones, Dear hearts. It is important to understand that the work within the Golden City Vortices is of indeed a much subtler variety but also of great import. For you see, it allows this integration of the higher bodies to come forward in their greater intention, within their greater purpose.

## BEYOND DUALITY

The Great Central Sun, in your specific realm of understanding, meets out indeed karma and dharma. Therefore, you shall see a dual expression that comes to your universe. When one reaches the energy of beginning the Ascension process, they must then reach out to other fields or realms of understanding, expanding the consciousness into yet a greater awareness. This greater awareness brings one beyond the dual forces. When we say the words "schoolroom Earth," it is meant with great intent. It is meant then with great beneficence. Dear one, I must now take my leave, unless of course there are other questions.

Response: *I completely understand. Thank you for your time.*

I shall be with you today and give you assistance. I am at your call.

Response: *Thank You.*

# 8

## Path of Mastery
*Saint Germain*

Greetings Beloveds in that Mighty Violet Flame. I AM Saint Germain and I stream forth on that Mighty Violet Ray of Mercy, Compassion, and Forgiveness. As usual Dear hearts, Dear chelas of mine, I request permission to come forward.

Response: *Please Saint Germain, come forward. You are most welcome.*

WHEN THE STUDENT IS READY

There is much work still for us to complete in this dispensation of the Green Ray and also this Mighty Violet Ray. Dear ones, Dear hearts, as I have always stated, if you ever need my assistance, I am always there to give help, to give aid. And so for this day, I come forward to answer any questions that you may have, especially regarding the work that has been given to you. But I would also like to remind you Dear ones, Dear hearts, that there is still much work that must be completed, much work that is still to be given. All is to come forward in a timing and intent and also in a dispensation, that is, in alignment to the Divine Plan, to that Divine and mighty Will of God that Never, Never Fails. Dear ones, Dear hearts, know that always, at all times, that this work is streaming forward with a great Divine Timing and great Divine Intent. We know at times, that you work to fulfill schedules that are created in your own Earth Plane and Planet. However, you must understand that all is on that mighty Law of Vibration that is in accordance to the Divine Plan and Divine Will. Do you remember that saying, "When the student is ready, the Master then appears"?

Answer: *Oh yes, I do!*

It is important then to understand, that as you are readied as students to receive this information, it then shall be given to you. It is the same as the Cup. When the Cup is ready, the Divine Wine then is poured within it. It is then held to receive the bounty of that fruited liquid. In this instance, Dear ones, Dear hearts, when you are readied to receive certain information, then it is dispensed and given to you. It is important to understand that some of the information that we have given to you has been given to you intentionally to share with others.

SHARING MESSAGES

Now it is also important to understand that there are levels or degrees of sharing this information. Whenever we say to you Dear ones, Dear hearts, that there is information that should be kept among you, it is to be kept just between the two of you, that is, the two of you as my students, who I am preparing to bring forth this Divine Mission. When I state that you may share it with those who have the eyes to see and the ears to hear, then you may share it with those who are asking to receive this information, those who you consider to be your students, your chelas.

METAPHYSICS OF THE TEACHER / STUDENT RELATIONSHIP

Now let me explain. When a Master Teacher takes on a student, takes on a chela, one who is held close to their heart, they are then held within the Master's vibration, the Master's energy field. The Master then must be prepared to accept the karmas and the burdens of that student. In this instance, you have been plagued with a constant out breaking of sores upon your lips. This is being caused by the transmutation of energies from the students that you are now working with. We know that you have, from time to time, thought that this was something related to diet, but Dear one, it is related to a transmutation process of karmas of the students that you have taken on. It is important to understand this process and what it does to the physical body.

Now, there can be steps that you can use when this occurs. You should enter into a deep meditation and there call upon the sacred fire. Use this for approximately forty to forty-five minutes. Always, use this meditation technique as I have taught you within a salt bath. Then and only then will you be able to discard the negative karmas. This is why I have guarded you in who you do take on to be your student, for now you understand and see this has a great impact upon the body. This is also the reason for excessive weight gain of the body; as you are transmuting the karmas of these students, these chelas that you take on, you also then begin to bury a burden at a physical level, for karmas are then transmuted at a physical level.

Now, it is so important when you take on a student, that there is a daily usage of the Violet Flame; I am insistent upon a daily and a minimum of a weekly usage of the Violet Flame. For you see Dear ones, its transmuting flames then allow for a transmutation of karmas of the past. This allows then for me to enter your energy field, to come forward and actually begin to ameliorate karmas of the past, to lift you into a higher vibration and an energy that is suitable for the student and the chela relationship. Now it is my hope that you begin to understand, that when you take on a student, this is indeed what you are doing for them as well. Now I am quite certain you will have questions regarding this topic. Proceed.

Response and question: *Yes, the relationship between the teacher and student is one that is based upon love. You can see the student struggle, question, and doubt and in this process, is there a way that the Violet Flame can be used with a specific type of decree to transmute that karmic interaction between teacher and student?*

> Mighty Violet Flame, stream forth from
> the Heart of the Central Logos,
> the mighty Great Central Sun.
> Transmute the cause, the effect, the record, and memory
> of all karmas incurred upon the gross physical plane
> of all chelas and students of mine.
> Come forward in the brilliance of the light of the mighty I AM.
> Stream in through and around (*insert name of Student*),
> and bring forward a greater transmutation
> of their karmas, record, cause, and effect.
> May this mighty Light of God stream in, through,
> and around all of their activities,
> all that they bring forth throughout this day.
> I call this forth and seal it in the record of the Holy of Holies.
> Om Manaya, Pitaya, Hitaka.

Response: *Thank You. Now on the path of Mastery, as one is beginning to Master thought, feeling, action, and the physical world, there are marking points with regard to students and chelas, and more definitively chelas, those who you imbue with a part of yourself and the work that you are doing.*

THE CHELA

Dear one, Dear heart, I would like to remind you now of the difference between the student and the chela. The chela is one who is holding an ever-present energy for the teacher. The student is one who is interested in the by-product of the teaching, who reads or studies such information. But the chela is one who brings it into an activity. Do you understand?

Answer and question: *Yes, completely! As you're marking your path in your own Mastery and development of students and chelas, how does one determine how many to have or who to choose?*

ON TEACHING

It is important to understand the nature of your own physical body and your ability to transmute quickly, disease and disharmony from your own energy fields. For you see Dear ones, Dear hearts, this is why so many Master Teachers wait until they are at a stage in their life where there is enough time to bring about this transmutation for their own physical vehicle. However, it is always best when starting, to only take one at a time and work with that one student until they raise to a certain level, where their performance is at a quality that will then allow transmutation of their karmas to be held to a minimum; that is, as the light spectrum of their aura holds enough dharma, they can move forward in the breath, sound, and light of consciousness.

Now, there are always those students whom, through their own desires and their own love of the heart, that you may choose to take on. However, you should limit the quality and the quantity of this type of student. For you see Dear one, Dear heart, there will be those teachings that they will not understand and there will always be karmas and situations that will need to be dealt with. Of course, there is not one soul ever, that we turn away, is there, Dear one, Dear heart? And in this instant, you have been working with many, many different students and aspirants, from many different disciplines, who come unto this work. This was the purpose and the intention, was it not?

Answer: *You asked us to make ourselves available and we have done so.*

This you have done out of respect for your own Master Teacher and many of those who are now coming unto this energy of the

Violet Flame, unto the energy and the auspices of the Golden Cities, are now being embraced, are they not, within the quality of this work and the vibration of the New Times? This was always the purpose and the intent. It is our great hope and desire that you will continue onward with this work, for the Great White Brotherhood and Sisterhood of Breath, Sound, and Light.

Response: *I will continue on as long as is necessary. There will never be a time when I would stop, unless it was requested.*

LINEAGE OF THE MASTER TEACHER

Now you must make that decision. Should a student or chela that you have decided to take on, that you are working with, be brought under the auspice of the Brotherhood and taken into the quality of the teachings for those who have the eyes to see and the ears to hear, or would you rather hold them within your own electromagnetic vibration, where you would cradle them and hold on to them? This too is your choice.

Question: *But there is also a law that governs this type of choice, is there not?*

Before the eyes can see, they must be incapable of tears. Before the ear can hear, it must lose its sensitivity. Before the voice can speak in the presence of a Master, it must have lost the power to wound another. Before the soul can stand in the presence of the Master, the feet must be washed in the blood of the heart. This you know well, Dear one.

Response: *I know this law very well. If any member of the Spiritual Hierarchy, such as yourself, wishes to take on one of my students, that would be fine with me.*

Those who work through you Dear one, Dear heart, come through the lineage of your own Master Teacher. That is the law as well and as you understand, this is a time honored tradition.

Response: *Yes it is.*

All is also held within that realm of choice. However, there are those students who can come close to the teaching, through what you have to offer, and understand that the work that you bring forward is not only the work of the teacher, or the healer, but is also the work of the prophet. Yet, there are those times, where your work is to just give the information and that, Dear one, is enough. I am well pleased.

INITIATION IN GOBEAN

Response: *Then I suppose on this topic, we are complete for the moment. The next topic I am going to ask you about is our project in the Golden City of Gobean.*

Proceed.

Response: *In the Golden City of Gobean, things are progressing very well for the dispensation of the work of I AM America, but when moving out to the people, they seem to respond in cycles.*

It is important Dear ones, Dear hearts, as you well now know and understand, that you continue with your initiations within the Gobean Vortex. For you see Dear ones, it is true, we will bring this project under our auspices, under our blessings, and hold it with a visualization for the building of the New Times for the Golden Age. It is important however, that a greater alignment occur with Beloved El Morya. For you see Dear ones, Dear hearts, as the Master Teacher of the Gobean Vortex, he is furthering the cause and brings forth the energetic alignment between Beloved Babajeran and this Hierarchy. As this Master Teacher arcs the energy at this higher level into the realms of the Ascended Masters, we can then bring forth our assistance in a greater unity.

WITHIN YOUR HEART

It is important to understand how hierarchal light and sound works. It is very simple in its understanding but sometimes harder to embrace in its actual usage. When you go out throughout your day, carrying on your errands, you hold within your heart that mighty Eight-Sided Cell of Perfection, the energy of all works that you have brought forward in each decree session, in each prayer and meditation session, in each teaching session, in each session of discourse. Do you understand?

Answer: *Yes.*

EMISSARY OF LIGHT

This energy that you build carries with it, the emanation and the force of years and years of study, contemplation, and meditation. This indeed is a cord that ties us to you, you to us. In this moment, you are now connecting with a representative of the Great White Brotherhood and Sisterhood of Breath, Sound, and Light. As you go about your day, in the simplest of errands, you are indeed an emissary of that energy. While you may not be carrying forward a discourse with another, who is not yet ready to receive, you are still emanating that energy, that force that has been building now for the last fifteen years. Do you understand?

Answer: *Yes.*

This of course is a very simple way to understand, for we are also addressing a step-down transformation of energies. However, we shall take that body of knowledge to the side for now and work more on the hierarchal step-down. When you are working with a project such as this, one where you have made that conscious choice and intention to build a Golden Age Community within the Star of Gobean, you carry this mantle of consciousness at all times where you go. It is brought forward in your meetings with your business associates. It is brought forward in all of your contractual agreements. In that moment Dear one, Dear heart, you must understand that we are always with you. We are always sending vibration and energy in the hierarchal step-down. Does this explain?

Answer: *Yes.*

STEP-DOWN ENERGIES OF EL MORYA

Indeed as it shall be, but know and understand, in the same way that you bring forward a transmutation process for your own chelas and students, in the same way with the project, you must oversee those involved in this physical project of building a community within the Star of Gobean. At that time, you must allow a step-down hierarchal energy of El Morya to come forward within you, in your own presence. Do you see? Do you understand?

Answer and response: *Yes, then I request El Morya's presence along with yours on a daily basis.*

Hitaka!

Response: *So be it! In doing this particular project with this beautiful Wenima valley in Gobean, we are setting about to create the perfect Feng Shui design for the community. We will also be requesting more details on the types of materials to be used and the shapes and sizes of home structures.*

That will come forward from Beloved El Morya. Call upon him at any time. He shall be available for you in meditation. However, if you require discourse, that too can be arranged.

ORAL TRADITION

Response: *I thank you. At this time, we will continue on with the project of the Golden City Books, working with each of the discourses to be dispensed in a written form. It truly is a translation from the oral tradition to the written form.*

Dear one, Dear heart, in this moment, do you not feel the energy of my presence?

Response: *Yes.*

In the oral tradition, each word carries a vibration, each syllable a point of consciousness that is carried through sound vibration. This is why the oral tradition has been held at a higher vibration, a higher understanding. Also, it allows for an activation of the memory within the brain. That section of the brain that holds memory is then activated to increase the opening of the pineal gland and Third Eye activity. The more that one is able to retain in memory, the more conscious light then vibrates through the pineal gland and the entire Kundalini System. When it is translated into words, it is brought to those students who are seeking a greater alignment to understanding in their own evolutions. Yes indeed, as we have stated before, this is another form of this work. It is not the highest form, but it is another form. Proceed.

Response: *I understand what you have said. It is just my desire to maintain the accuracy of the session that has been placed in an audio file, that we are as exact as can be to that transmission.*

It is also important that it is carried forward in a form for those to understand. Remember when I have said to you, when a child enters into the feast, he is not ready yet to feast upon those heavier dishes, to digest or assimilate these. That is what I mean by another form. It may seem weaker; it may seam like pabulum to those whose ears and eyes are not yet opened, but understand this in the law supreme. Our vibration and energy will carry forward in all that is brought through. There is no mistake, ever, ever, ever. Have trust and faith Dear one, Dear heart. Know that I am there.

Response: *As you wish, we will use the tape then as the marking. I have no further questions and I thank you for your time. Unless, there is more discourse you wish to share.*

Then I shall hold you this day within the vibration of the Breath, Light, and Sound of the hierarchy. So Be It.

Response: *So Be It. And thank you eternally.*

Peace and grace I impart. Hitaka.

# 9

## Galactic Energy
*Saint Germain*

Greetings Beloved chelas, in that mighty Christ. I AM Saint Germain and I stream forth on that Violet Ray of Mercy, Compassion, and ultimate Forgiveness. As usual Dear hearts, I request permission to come forward.

Response: *Please Saint Germain, come forward. You are most welcome.*

It is with great joy and salutations that I come forward this morning. Greetings and Salutations Dear ones. Greetings and Shamballa.

Yes indeed, it has been some time since we have done our work together but it is always important to keep balance within your life. It is always important to follow the Laws of Harmony and to keep them ever present in all that you do, think, feel, and act. Dear ones, Dear hearts, I've always instructed you upon the use of the mighty Violet Flame; for you see, it is this work of the Violet Flame that comes forth in its most transmuting ability at this time for humanity.

GALACTIC ENERGY AND ASCENSION

It is true, at this moment, that there is a shifting of the guard that is occurring in the hierarchy. We are imbuing the Earth with a greater influence of the Violet Flame, so that this mighty Violet

Flame may come forward for humanity and transmute the collective karma that now the Earth Plane and Planet is reaping. You see Dear ones, Dear hearts, all realms experience cosmic cycles and right now, the Earth is experiencing an influence of energy that comes from the Galactic Center. This Galactic Energy, for lack of any other name for understanding, is being imbued upon the Earth, bringing forward an escalation of karma to humanity, in order to bring humanity into a greater understanding of its evolutionary process. Now, there are those who will see this as an escalation of war, famine, and economic hardship upon the Earth Plane and Planet. But for those who have the eyes to see and the ears to hear, it will enable them to rise to a greater understanding, a greater focus upon the Earth Ascension and ultimate spiritual liberation.

THE GREAT GOLDEN AGE

This influence from the Galactic Center also activates certain circuits within the Kundalini and many will notice at night, that their Astral Body is greater in its activation. One may have the ability to travel into the retreats, not only because of the influence of Shamballa, but because of this work of the Galactic Energy. It is true that some of this is being forwarded through the work of Saturn, but some of it also is escalated through the work of Neptune. For those who have the eyes to see and the ears to hear, this influence will at first seem as an illusion or a slight deception through the ego processes. But know Dear one, Dear heart, if you use the Violet Flame with complete and absolute vigilance, that it will bring you into a greater understanding of these energies developing the greater heart of humanity. We are moving into Bhakti, compassion for all. It also brings forward a world group of servers who will be born at this time, those who will bring the world into a greater union and understanding. This will lead and pave the pathway for the great Golden Age.

It is true Dear ones, Dear hearts, that cycles are in their great convergence right now, not only do you see the ending of one twenty-year cycle, of which we have spoken of before, but you also see the beginning of a greater ten-thousand year cycle. This ten-thousand year cycle, broken into compartments of one thousand years each, will bring a greater harmony for the Earth Planet and her people. It will bring a greater harmony in the Golden City Vortices; a greater harmony to the Mineral Kingdom; a greater harmony to the Vegetable Kingdom; a greater harmony to the Animal Kingdom. These Kingdoms come forward too in their great confluence and convergence of cycles, then rise to a higher vibration at this time.

TRANSCEND KARMIC PATTERNS

This convergence of cycles is sometimes difficult for the human to understand. If one has used that mighty Violet Flame, they can and will readily transmute the karmic cause and effect of past lives. This brings about conclusion for many people, seeing within the actions of their lives, an ending or conclusion to cycles that are now ready to close down. Cycles are ready, not to end in the sense of karmic endings, but to transmute in terms of a transcendental look at the life process and life cycles. Transcendence, Dear one, is the work of the Violet Flame. It streams forth from the heart of the Mighty Logos. It is sometimes known too as that Blue Ray. It is sometimes known too as that Pink Ray. But it is the convergence and confluence of these two Rays, working together, that brings that mighty Violet Ray forward in its greater harmony to the world, soothing the perspective of those situations and circumstances that do indeed appear to be karmic or dualistic in outlook.

When I use the word "karma" from this lesson and perspective, I am speaking of duality. It is karma, in this understanding, that brings forth a more limiting or obstacle-creating environment. Now we do know indeed that karma is only action, cause, and effect. But also, those who are in the process of releasing negative karmic patterns can now move forward with this great influence from the Galactic Energy. This will also bring a higher vibration to the Golden City Vortices and you will notice during this Shamballa activity, a greater revving of the metabolism and the ability to fast and stay away from any type of dualistic food stuffs. The body will be taking in greater light through all seven chakras, being prepared for a higher alignment, especially towards the Kundalini and the Eight-Sided Cell of Perfection.

BATHE IN GOLDEN LIGHT

This great Cell that resides within the being, as that Mighty Monad, the jiva of existence, and is also being accelerated at this time through this experience of the Galactic Energy. We ask you Dear ones, Dear hearts, in your meditation processes, to see your body bathed within this golden light, activated through the Crown Chakra, extending onward through the pineal gland, through the throat, and resting within that Heart of mighty Compassion. Dear ones, this also brings about a greater activation of Star seed groups forming, so that you can understand their greater nucleus, to be later prepared for greater work within this new twenty-year cycle.

CHANGE AND THE LAW OF BALANCE

You see Dear ones, Dear hearts, as we close down one twenty-year cycle, you will find many relationships with individuals closing and ending and new relationships with others opening up and coming to their fructification. All runs within cycles and tides upon the dualistic Earth. But how does one rise above, to reach that greater liberation beyond expectation? It comes forth through the understanding that Faith is the almighty Law. Have faith Dear ones, and hope, yes, that all will come to this greater liberation and Ascension in that mighty Light of God that Never, Never Faileth.

Now for those who would ask, "How am I to reach my Ascension when I cannot even deal with the affairs of my daily life?" It is important always to reach emotional balance through the use of the Violet Flame. This is perhaps one of the greatest uses of this mighty law. But know too Dear ones, Dear hearts, that I shall reach through that mighty flame and imbue my Ascended Master Consciousness into that great and mighty Heart of Compassion, to assist and help you to rise into a greater Law of Balance.

## GOLDEN CITY SOUTHERN DOORS

Dear ones, Dear hearts, there are also many changes that will be coming in this next year and I would like to give you great assurance at this time, that I and many other Ascended Masters will be assisting all of you who have the eyes to see and the ears to hear, to stay upon the path of spiritual development, to stay upon the path of your liberation and ultimate Ascension and freedom in that Light of God that Never, Never Faileth. It is also important to know that during this year, great accelerations will be happening in all Southern Doors of Golden City Vortices. This acceleration will be coming about through the different Masters that have been placed at the Adjutant Points. Now, you will notice this, Dear one, Dear chela, in your work, as when you were sent to the Southern Door of Gobean. Is this not true?

Answer: *Yes, it is.*

## OPPORTUNITY AND CHALLENGE

You were sent upon that mission, so that you could understand the positions and points. It also set up a frequency for Master Teachers to come forward within those specific points. These Master Teachers will now become available to assist many upon the path of healing. For you see Dear ones, Dear hearts, as the healing forces and transcendent forces upon the Earth rise in vibration and energy during this year, also there will show a like energy in dualism rise. This is the Law of Balance. Now when I say "like," I state this only in the presence of the eternal law in duality: As above, so below; for left, there is right. These hermetic statements are important to understand, for these parallels exist throughout all of creation and when the chela begins to understand this, they will then begin to understand why one may experience the best of times and the worst of times. In the greatest opportunity is also the greatest challenge.

Hold to almighty I AM Faith, Dear ones, Dear chelas of mine. Know that in this greater acceleration of the Time of Testing comes a greater opportunity for your evolution and freedom in that mighty Light of God that Never, Never Faileth. We will see many changes that will happen during this year. While there will be the possibility of Earth Changes, as you well know Dear one, this is related to how the collective emotional body of humanity responds to situations and circumstances. But now, I would like to outline for you specifically, so you can begin to understand.

UNITED STATES ECONOMY

There is a shift within the powers of darkness. For you see, they are clamoring for their last, shall we say, grasp upon the consciousness of humanity, using always, anything that vibrates to fear. You will see adjustments in the economic situation of the United States, this of course having a complete bearing upon the rest of the world markets. Now, this adjustment has its own agenda, coming from those who would like to see humanity kept in a greater prison of materiality. But know this Dear ones, Dear hearts, this knowledge will come into greater light. Now is the time for those who have the eyes to see, the ears to hear, chelas of the light, to come forward and to direct through that Mighty I AM:

Mighty Violet Flame stream forth into the economy of the United States.
Transmute and annihilate any plan, covert or otherwise, that will destroy the economic stability of the United States.
May all harmony rule supreme, I AM.

Through these mighty statements, through the I AM THAT I AM, when used on a steady basis, all economic situations within the United States can be brought into that healing balance. When one begins to understand what is happening at a greater level and, not to over simplify situations, but when one truly gives contemplation and understanding, one then can see that each single problem is really a challenge with ten-thousand solutions. This is but one decree that you may use. Gather it unto the light; gather it unto your light bodies. Project this energy from that mighty Eight-Sided Cell of Perfection by placing your left hand over your heart when you call upon this decree and project the energies outward through the palm of the right hand as I have instructed you. Questions?

Response: *Yes, we do have questions. If there is more discourse though, please continue and I will ask questions at the completion of the discourse.*

ACCELERATE YOUR DECREE

It is most important at this time to understand the peril that is upon the Earth. However, it is also important to understand that alongside such challenge is always the Light that Never, Never Faileth, Dear ones, Dear hearts of mine. Call upon this mighty Light through the I AM THAT I AM. Project it outward in all of your daily activities. As it projects outward into your daily activities, it will grow in its collective consciousness. This consciousness, as set by only one kernel through one small decree, grows and grows until it imbues an energy that fills and permeates consciousness itself. It is important to understand that all decrees that are used in the Stars of Golden City Vortices are empowered a thousand-fold. So Dear ones, for those who wish to go and help and serve those at a greater collective level, this is why the locations of Stars in the Golden City Vortices have been given.

There are many other accelerations that will happen throughout this year. It is important Dear ones, Dear hearts, that we continue with our work. And now, unless if there are other questions, I open the floor for your discussion.

Question: *With regard to the United States economy and the global economy, as we see these manipulations going on, this decree that you have just given us is for everyone and anyone who understands this?*

It is for those who feel a kinship to my work, to my vibration. I ask for you to come forward as chelas and students, knowing too that as I have given this decree, it is imbued with my Ascended Master Energy. It is imbued also with the purpose and the intention of the Spiritual Hierarchy.

A DECREE FOR ASCENSION

Response: *I understand. Thank you very much. I have a set of questions regarding specific persons, one requesting a decree for his son.*

This Beloved being has incarnated many times upon the Earth Plane and Planet and in this lifetime is seeking liberation. It is important now to use the Violet Flame to move the self forward into the spirit knowledge and understanding of liberating from worldly activity:

> Mighty Violet Flame blaze in, through,
> and around all of my light bodies.
> Blaze in, through, and around my Causal body, my Astral Body,
> and my physical body.

Transmute the cause and effect, record and memory, forever,
of karmas of the past.
Mighty Violet Flame lead me into greater union
with the mighty I AM.
Mighty Violet Flame transmute and lead me to the Ascension
in the Light of I AM THAT I AM.
So Be It.

## BALANCING KARMA

Question: *So Be It. Thank you. The next question I have is actually from Lori. Is it possible that she can do personal trance-missions for individuals? If so, how would you suggest that they are done?*

Of course, I am always ready, willing, and available for those who ask for this type of work and information. However, there must be an alignment process that occurs for those who come forward. For you see Dear ones, Dear hearts, as in this instant, you have aligned your energy, so you are receptive to the information that I bring to you. For those who have asked, it is always appropriate. For you see, it is based upon that mighty law: When the student is willing and asking, the Master then appears and gives instruction. It is important for those who ask for this type of information, that I come forward to bring that information. It is also important for you to understand the service that the channel brings. That this is part of the liberation process for the channel as well, to provide this service.
Now you, serving in your capacity as monitor, it is my request that you be present at these readings; for it is important that you are always there to provide ample protection and energy to the channel during such transmission, as you well know and understand. But know this Dear ones, Dear hearts, that there is no mistake, ever, ever, ever. And with the stream of this Galactic Energy, opening the collective heart of humanity, there will be many more now who will be asking within this year, "Who am I?" "What is my purpose?"

"How can I move into greater understanding of the spiritual life?" You see Dear one, Dear heart, this is a natural course of events.

Response and question: *I understand what you're saying. Can you also give any guidelines for the monitor and that service to Lori while she's receiving these trance-missions?*

It is important for you to understand that you are bringing your service forward to balance your karma as well. Each time you participate and assist, help the channel in service, you bring a greater balance of your karma. Also in this opportunity, you and I have an opportunity for interaction, do we not?

Answer: *Yes we do.*

This has brought a great upliftment to your soul, a greater understanding of the working of life. It also assists you in your own purpose of teaching and helping others. Is this not true?

Answer: *This is true.*

THE BELOVED

It is important that when you bring your service forward for the channel, that you bring it with purity and with detachment from expectation, that you bring it forward with a great love for the Master. Do you see Dear one, Dear heart, it is not the Master Saint Germain, it is the Master I AM that you serve, the Beloved within yourself, the Beloved within all of humanity. But, so you are not confused upon your service, you bring your service to the channel, then you bring your service to the Master Teacher. Do you understand?

Response: *Yes, I understand what you've said.*

## ENERGIES OF THE GOLDEN RAY

It is also important that you direct energy to the channel in doing this type of work. Perhaps a weekly energy balancing, as I have instructed you, would also assist in this function. Also, the use of fruits of the Golden Ray are quite good before and after the channeling. These can be juices from lemons, oranges, pineapples, and any other citrus fruits that contain within them a yellow vibration. For you see, this increases the energy of the Golden Ray for the channel and brings also a heightening of energy for those who participate within the direct teaching. You see Dear ones, Dear hearts, it is time to bring about a heightening of vibration upon the Earth Plane and Planet.

## HEIGHTENING YOUR VIBRATION

Those who come forward and are asking are indeed touched by this energy and are brought to a higher understanding. This you have known as a Step-down Transformer. When they are touched by this energy, it radiates for a minimum of fourteen days afterwards. That is why, even when listening to a tape recording of a session such as this, there is a heightening of vibration that is brought about for many days thereafter.[13] It is also my request that each of these sessions is recorded, although I shall caution you, that upon occasion, there could be problems with recording due to vibratory influences. But it is important that there is a record of what is said, so that it can be shared with all of humanity.

## "I GIVE MY SERVICE"

While I will be happy to help at a personal level to transmute personal karmas, to understand the ramification of past life experiences, I will also be moving forward in my lessons and

---

*13. See Appendix M, "Why should I listen to channeled tapes?", page 227.*

vibratory influence for humanity at large. Therefore, my world work will not be interrupted by the flow of information that will move at an individual basis. So, it is important that those who come understand the nature of this work and that we will always be seeing a forward motion. But I am always available to give assistance, especially to those who ask, Dear one, Dear heart. I AM Sanctus Germanus, the Beloved Holy Brother, and I give my service to those who are readied.[14]

MOVING FORWARD

Question: *Okay, that's fine. Can you give any suggestions or guidelines for the I AM America fellowship and our spiritual work there?*

It is important to first place an emphasis upon the Twelve Jurisdictions.[15] These Laws of Jurisprudence were outlined for humanity, for how to move forward into the New Times, beyond the influence of Kali Yuga, and into the Crystal Golden Age. This will bring consciousness to a higher point of understanding. Once there is a completion of the Twelve Jurisdictions, I will give further instruction.

Question: *And who do you wish to do the presentation of these Jurisdictions?*

It is important that a student, who is aligned to the teachings of I AM America, bring this information forward, as one who has an understanding of their innate quality.

Question: *And how do we determine that?*

---

14. *See Appendix N, Saint Germain, the Holy Brother, page 229.*
15. *See Appendix O, The Twelve Jurisdictions, page 233.*

You will know again through the process of elimination.

ENERGY FOR ENERGY

Question: *So, you're not asking Lori or I to give that presentation?*

You can, if you choose Dear one. Again, it is all a service. Remember, when you help your Brother on the path to self-Mastery, you indeed help yourself.

Response: *It is energy for energy. I understand.*

All is energy for energy. But it is also important Dear one, Dear heart, to understand that for such a fellowship to exist, that there must always be energy for energy. Therefore, it is suggested that all who participate understand this thoroughly.

*And is that also true for the personal trance-missions for individuals?*

It is always true, Dear one, Dear heart. The teachings that I give are my service to humanity. You see, it brings me great joy to lift another to an understanding beyond the worldly experience. You know and understand this Dear one, Dear heart.

Response: *Yes I do. I agree.*

But it is also important to know, that while I give my service, there is also an energy for energy. There is much that is expected of the chela, the student, to rise in their vibration and to give their sacrifice of their energy in the same way that I have sacrificed my energy within the teaching. For the channel, in this case, it is important that proper support is given. This of course is something that you may set yourself in your organization. However, if you have questions, I am always available for counsel.

Question: *In a prior transmissions several years ago, you suggested the alignment process which involves several devotional ceremonies at certain geophysical points in the Gobean Vortex. We are now preparing to complete that work. Do you have any suggestions or additional teachings or input?*

ADJUTANT POINT CEREMONY

It is most important to complete this work; for you see Dear ones, Dear hearts, this aligns your collective consciousness with the greater vibration and heart of harmony within the Gobean Vortex. It will also bring about a great assistance to your work in the Star, that is, in your project at Wenima. When you align yourself to these greater Adjutant Points within the Golden City Vortices, you also then align yourself to a greater source of Ascended Master energy. Do you understand?

Answer and question: *Yes, I do. So this is something that Lori and I should go and do together, as soon as possible.*

Yes and for all of those who are involved in the Wenima project. This will bring about a greater harmony between all of you and build the energy to a greater pivot point of understanding.

Question: *So even during this time of Shamballa, that would be an appropriate time to complete this?*

It would Dear one. Proceed.

TWENTY-YEAR CYCLES

Response and question: *Thank you very much. I have one other written question here that deals with the twenty-year cycle. It asks for information about this change of cycle that we are now experiencing on Earth, a twenty-year Feng Shui cycle. Would you comment on it?*

Indeed, these cycles vibrate from the Galactic Center. This is the alignment of two great forces, that of the Yellow and the Blue Ray, or what you know as Jupiter and Saturn within the skies from Earth. These bring about a jumbling and a tumbling effect through the Galactic Center. It often takes a two to four year cycle on the Earth for this to adjust. This adjustment now is occurring upon the Earth Plane and energies are being readied. This of course causes many changes in the way that people think. When Ray Forces work upon the human consciousness, it is as if that they are gladdened in their consciousness by this Ray Force and then express only the qualities of that force. The twenty-year cycles are very important to understand, for they set in motion, sometimes a cycle of karmic retribution, but sometimes they also set forward cycles of the transcendence of karma. This is all possible within the range of human consciousness.

Response: *I understand. There are no further questions on our sheet. I thank you very much for your time, your energy, and your patience with me. I have felt a great stress of the last several years and you know my strengths and weaknesses of karma transmuted and of karma yet to be transmuted. And I will take all that you have said into that great silence and apply it to the best of my ability. But you always have my love. You always have my devotion. I will always be available for whatever it is you or the channel need, and I want you to know that is eternal. So Be It.*

Dear one, Dear heart, my love and eternal gratitude are always given to you. So Be It.

Response: *So Be It.*

# 10

## Six-fold Path
*Saint Germain*

Greetings Beloved chelas in that Mighty Violet Flame. I AM Saint Germain and I stream forth on that Mighty Violet Ray of Mercy, Compassion, and ultimate Forgiveness. As usual Dear hearts, I request permission to come forward. Is this permission granted?

Response: *Please Saint Germain, you are most welcome. Come forward.*

[*I ask a visiting chela if she gives Saint Germain permission and she responds "Oh yes, Saint Germain has my permission."*]

Greetings Dear ones, Dear hearts, greetings and Shamballa, for you see this is a time of great feasting in all realms of experience. Many of you have wondered about the celebration and location of Shamballa and let me tell you Dear ones, Dear hearts, that even within the Third Dimension of the Earth Plane and Planet, our intention of experience comes from that Fifth Dimensional understanding. We actually do take on physical form during this time. For you see Dear ones, Dear hearts, we anchor the Unfed Flame of Love, Wisdom, and Power into the Earth Plane, so that humanity may then grow forward in its greater evolution, in its greater understanding, and in the greater application of spiritual law.

## SHAMBALLA KNOWLEDGE

Dear ones, Shamballa is a time, not only of great celebration, but a time of great joy for humanity. For you see, at this time, not only is there a great dispensation of celestial force upon the Earth Plane and Planet, there is also a great dispensation that occurs in humanity's evolution. This is of course moving forward through the Great Central Sun or Galactic Center, but also through the Divine Intervention of the Ascended Masters and the Angelic Kingdom. Dear ones, Dear hearts, at this time the Angelic Kingdom also takes a greater role in bringing forward its service during Shamballa. Many of you may have experiences in your physical world, the encounter of an angel at this time, especially during Shamballa.

## "WHO AM I?"

The Mighty I AM Presence is also empowered at a much deeper and greater level for humanity at this time. So there are many who will come into a greater understanding of the undertaking of lifetime after lifetime after lifetime. There are many upon the Earth Plane and Planet who are now evolving and asking the question, "Who Am I?" "Where do I come from?" "Why is life the way it is?" "Is there a much bigger picture?" During this Shamballa, we will be imbuing the Earth at a Third Dimensional level to bring forth an activation of the Galactic Energy, so many past lives can be revealed to those who have asked this question of themselves, to those who are saying, "Is there much, much more to this life than I have upon the Earth Plane and Planet?"

## THIRD DIMENSIONAL EXPERIENCE

Dear ones, Dear hearts, know that each lifetime is connected to every other lifetime. There is not one lifetime that does not have significance or purpose. Every lifetime allows the soul to move forward in its evolution and purpose and allows the soul then, to develop greater aspects and energies that are held inherently within it. Now, we all know that there is Divine Perfection within the self, but in the human experience, one is always striving to obtain greater levels of perfection, greater levels of spiritual understanding. This is the purpose, you see Dear ones, Dear hearts, to gain an education through the Third Dimensional experience, so one, in their already perfected state, is then perfecting at will, the Third Dimensional experience. Shamballa is also a great time where many of the Ascended Masters and Angelic Hosts gather to prepare their plans for the upcoming year on Earth and their service that they give willingly to Beloved Babajeran, the Mother Earth, and also to humanity.

"IS THERE ANOTHER WAY?"

There have been many new changes within the hierarchal structure. That is, it has been decided through the Spiritual Hierarchy that a greater acceleration and use of the Violet Ray is now needed upon the Earth Plane and Planet and to be given to humanity. You see Dear ones, Dear hearts, this is also being activated through Saturn's closest position to the Earth at this time and allowing the Violet Ray to come forward, to open the greater Heart of Compassion within humanity. As you see, there is much turmoil and trouble upon the Earth Plane and Planet. Many are asking, "Will there be another world war upon the planet?" This has been of deep trouble and concern to us, but as you well know, Dear ones, Dear hearts, we are never allowed to interfere with the choices of man. But it is also important that we are here to give our spiritual counsel for those who ask, "Is there another way?"

Dear ones, Dear hearts, indeed there is always another way. For as you know, in this time of convergence and confluence, there is an opportunity to move into a Golden Age within this deeply troubled time. But I have said before in my Prophecies of Change in the I AM America Material, that it will be almost as if there were two worlds existing side by side. This teaching was also brought forward in the Six-Map Scenario, so you can understand, from this Point of Perception, that there are many possibilities that a person or perspective can choose.

It is also important to understand, at this time, that there are those forces that are gathering a great planned holocaust for humanity. Now, it is important, when you understand that this is given only as a perspective or alternative of consciousness, that there are also those who plan a great heavenly celebration. That is the work of the Spiritual Hierarchy and the Angelic Host. That is the focus of Shamballa. How can humanity rise into a greater understanding, into a greater evolution? So Dear ones, Dear hearts, at this time of great feasting, we now issue to humanity this information, which will lay out for you the Six-fold Path for the upcoming year.

PRINCIPLES OF THE SIX-FOLD PATH

**Principle One.** Practice tolerance, love, and kindness towards one another. We know at times that this is very difficult for humanity but tolerance is one of the greater lessons that can come forward, to lead one into the greater Heart of Compassion. Tolerance is important, Dear ones, Dear hearts.

**Principle Two.** Begin to study the Twelve Jurisdictions, for they are a template of Golden Age Consciousness. Know and understand that each one of these principles raises you into a greater understanding and spiritual evolution. Each of these teachings is designed to take the Chakra Centers and move them into a greater acceleration, that is, alignment into the New Times and into the New Age.

**Principle Three**. Practice the Law of Forgiveness. Learn to forgive those who do not understand you. Learn to forgive those who do not walk the same path as you. Learn to forgive those who cross the same path as you. When you develop greater states of detachment within the human heart, you are then able to accelerate at a higher refinement of vibration. This is most important Dear ones, Dear hearts, to accept the new energies that are being flooded upon the Earth through the great Divine Decree of the Spiritual Hierarchy and that mighty Violet Ray.

**Principle Four**. Respect All of Life. That is, develop a kindness towards the Animal Kingdom. Do all that you can do to assist the Animal Kingdom in moving into higher vibration and energy, this is destined. For you see Dear ones, Dear hearts, they too move forward in their evolutionary process. What this does indeed is help to accelerate the energies upon the Earth Plane and Planet. Help all Humane Societies. Help all of those who are assisting the Animal Kingdom to move into a greater harmony, energy, and vibration.

**Principle Five**. Dear ones, Dear hearts, have respect for Mother Earth. Give this respect to your Earth Mother in the same way that you would give respect to your birth mother. Honor and respect Mother Earth, for she gives you life. Honor and respect Mother Earth, for she is an evolved being who has sponsored you into your many vibrations of lifetimes upon the Earth Plane and Planet. And . . .

**Principle Six**. Above all Dear ones, Dear hearts, Dear chelas of mine, live in harmony. Live in harmony in all that you do. Seek this harmony at the level of self, so that love may flow in, through, and around you. Extend this harmony as love to one another, not only in your partnerships, but within your families. Extend this love outward from the family and into your community. You see Dear ones, Dear hearts, as this heart of harmony grows among humanity, an eruption of love, true love, can then manifest for those who have the eyes to see and the ears to hear.

This Six-fold Path is something that I ask all chelas, all students, all light workers to practice throughout the year. For you see Dear ones, this will bring about a greater understanding of the inner working, a greater experience with and within the Spiritual Hierarchy's Plan.

PROPHECY TRANSMUTES PREDICTION

Now, I could at this time give you many predictions that are about to occur, but as we now well know, prophecy has the ability to transmute any dire prediction and take us from the levels of doom and gloom, transcending us into the levels of pure and absolute love and harmony for all of life. It is important then to understand that the direst of predictions that do come forward can always be transmuted and understood in their higher context.

THE LABORATORY OF SELF

Dear ones, in the Six-fold Path, always strive towards higher intelligence and knowledge in working with these six principles. While they are simple indeed, they may at times feel complicated and complex in their undertaking. But I assure you Dear ones, that you will always have, not only my assistance in the Six-fold Path, but the assistance of Beloved El Morya, Beloved Kuthumi, Beloved Mother Mary, Beloved Kuan Yin, and Beloved Dear Lord Sananda. We all come forward in our energies to assist humanity at this time in applying this Six-fold Path. For you see Dear ones, it is a time of peril upon the Earth Plane but it is also during the greatest darkness that light indeed does appear.

It would seem that humanity appears to be teetering upon the precipices of consequence. But know this Dear ones, Dear hearts, for each dual action is also the action of purpose. All that happens upon the Earth Plane and Planet comes forward in Divine Timing and in Divine Purpose. As I have always stated, Dear ones, Dear hearts, Dear chelas of mine, there is no mistake, ever, ever, ever. Take the Six-fold Path unto the laboratory of self. Bring it into your daily activities and into your own experience. So Be It. Questions?

Response: *So Be It. Yes, I have one question.*

Proceed.

Question: *With regard to past lives and the perfection of our world, is everything here something we're just coming back to, to re-perfect?*

LAWS OF PERCEPTION

There are many ways, or shall we say, Points of Perception, for seeing one given situation. Very often, we move from lifetime to lifetime gaining this experience. One may be in a position of being the adored, then they may move into the position of not being adored, then they move to the position of the adorer. Do you see how each one of these, as subtle as they may seem in their context, is also the great application of the law eternal? For every action there is an equal action. As above so below. Everything seeks its equal, its equilibrium. All of these Laws of Perception then take on further definition when they are known in the context of simultaneous realities and embodiments. However, to not confuse this lesson, let us keep this most simple.

## LOVE IS THE LAW OF UNDERSTANDING

It is important to understand that everyone has a multiple of experiences, even within one embodiment. But to go into other embodiments, then one also gets to move into additional experiences. For as you well know Dear ones, Dear hearts, it would appear to humanity, that pain is always the eternal teacher. But in the New Times, it shall be known that love will come forward and open the hearts of those who are ready to receive. This mighty cosmic love, in its vibration and energy, will awaken all to a new Law of Understanding. In this context, one then is prepared to begin to receive the higher knowledge, or shall we say, additional knowledge and instruction that naturally leads one into the Time of an Open Heart. Through the open heart, compassion is then felt through devotion, love, and service. This compassion opens the heart of humanity and moves it into a greater identification with service to God. This service moves one into the desire for liberation. This desire for liberation brings one into a greater contact with the purpose of duality. Questions?

## SPONSORSHIP BY A MASTER TEACHER

Response and question: *Yes. The desire for liberation is great. Do you recommend a specific decree for liberation?*

It is important Dear one, Dear heart, for those who seek liberation to take up, just for this year, as a discipline of self, the Six-fold Path. This will bring, at a vibration and energy level, especially at this time upon the Earth Plane and Planet, a greater alignment with the Spiritual Hierarchy. As you well know Dear ones, Dear hearts, it is always through the time-honored tradition of the relationship between the teacher and the student that leads one into a greater level of liberation. Why is this so?

You see Dear ones, Dear hearts, the Master Teacher, when he or she comes forward to give that sponsorship of the student or chela, takes on a portion of that karma that is difficult at that time for that student or chela to transmute. During this process, the student or chela feels an upliftment, as you have both well noted. This upliftment then brings that student or chela into a greater identification with higher energy and vibration. Little by little, the Master Teacher releases the hold upon the karma being held for the student and little by little, the student then begins to transmute through the laws that are given by the teacher to the student. Is this understood?

Response: *So initially, the Master Teacher helps to mediate the greater karmic burden but as the laws are understood by the student, then it's the student's responsibility to continue on.*

It was never promised to be easy but the reward immeasurable.

"SELF-DISCIPLINE LEADS TO LIBERATION"

Question: *And the Six-fold Path will help in that remediation of the karmic burden?*

You see Dear ones, when we have made requests regarding dietary changes, we make these requests, yes, for energy and vibration purposes, but also, you must understand that bringing about self-discipline is one of the greater arenas that leads to liberation. Also, the process of detachment; learning to detach from outcomes is also extremely important. Now the Master Teacher sometimes, in taking on the karmas of the student or the chela, will mitigate detachment, will mitigate certain circumstances and situations for the student or chela, until they are ready to have their eyes and their ears opened. Do you understand?

Answer: *Yes. I understand.*

VIOLET FLAME FOR DIFFICULTIES

Call upon the Violet Flame if you are having difficulty with any situation or circumstance that I have outlined before you for the year:

Mighty Violet Flame blaze in, through, and around my Astral Body.
Blaze in, through, and around my Causal body,
Blaze in, through, and around my Physical Body.
Mitigate the cause and effect, record and memory, forever,
of any difficult karma or obstacles that keep me
from my Divine Path
and position in the Divine Plan.
So Be It.

Response and question: *So Be It. Does our guest have any questions?*

Guest Response: *I don't know how to ask questions.*

Dear student of mine, never feel a shyness in dealing with me directly, for I am here too to give you assistance. This is my work upon the Earth Plane and Planet as Sanctus Germanus, Beloved Holy Brother. I help those who are ready to receive. Dear one, I shall always assist you. I shall first start by assisting you in the dream state at night and admit you into a series of seven lessons, or classes that you will attend over the next seven nights. It is also important for you, at a physical level, to keep your electrolyte system balanced, which at this time is somewhat depleted. It is suggested that you consider bringing this back into balance. It will assist your memory function to a greater degree.

Guest Question: *How do I bring it back?*

[*Saint Germain is scanning her body.*]

I would suggest, first, the use of Chromium within this system to accelerate metabolic rate. This will allow vibration to come to a higher level. Also, I would add almonds to the diet, no less than six per day. Also, limit the intake of salt in this system, for you see there is a problem in the assimilation of certain important minerals that run the finer bodies. If possible, curtail the use of dairy products and meat products within the system. Now, I know at times it is difficult for chelas to begin this discipline of moving into a more vegetarian diet, but as you move into this, it will also help to bring a greater assimilation of the vibrational forces within the body. Call upon me and there I am. Questions?

Guest Question: *How do I call upon you?*

Ask in your prayers and there I shall be.

Guest Response: *Thank you.*

Unless if there are further questions, then I shall take my leave from your density.

Response: *I have no further questions and I will do my best to follow the discipline of the Six-fold Path, as you've requested. Thank you.*

Om Manaya Pitaya Hitaka.

Response: *Hitaka and Shamballa.*

# 11

## Golden City Prayer
*Saint Germain*

Greetings Beloved chelas, stalwart students, friends of mine. I AM Saint Germain and I stream forth on that Mighty Violet Ray of Mercy, Transmutation, and Forgiveness. As usual Dear ones, Dear hearts, I request permission to come forward?

Response: *Please Saint Germain, come forward. You are most welcome.*

"I AM THERE"

There is much work for us still to complete, Dear ones, Dear hearts. For you see, the I AM America Material was brought forward to bring spiritual teaching, not only on the topics and subjects of Earth Changes and the Golden City Vortices, but also to give spiritual teaching for those whose eyes are open and whose ears are ready to hear this message. Dear ones, Dear hearts, we must never forget the work of the mighty Violet Flame and its transmuting effect. Dear ones, Dear chelas, Dear students, this mighty Violet Flame brings forth an ultimate transformation and transmutation of all energy bodies and brings you into a different resonance or energy, shall I say, for lack of a better word for understanding. This mighty Violet Flame has the ability to erase the cause and effect, record and memory, forever, of any karma that is keeping you from your eternal freedom.

Dear students of mine, those who take on this mighty Violet Flame as a discipline, know that I am there and stand with you. I am always with you in every Violet Flame decree, in every Violet Flame meditation, in every Violet Flame visualization, and every Violet Flame mantra. Any time that you call forth the use of this mighty law in action, I am there. For you see Dear ones, Dear hearts, this is my work that I have brought to the Earth Plane and Planet and this mighty Violet Flame indeed is through my sponsorship.

LIGHT THROUGH THE VIOLET FLAME

Now do not confuse this with the history of the Violet Flame. For you see Dear ones, Dear hearts, the Violet Flame has been in use upon the Earth Plane and Planet for many, many eons. But at this most certain time, the Golden Age, I shall sponsor this Violet Flame to come forth for all those who have the eyes to see, the ears to hear, and all who want to put this mighty law into action.

> Mighty Violet Flame stream forth from
> the Heart of the Great Central Sun.
> Charge all of my lower bodies, all of my light bodies,
> all of my energy bodies.
> Dissolve the karmas of the past
> and move me in to the greater Plan Divine,
> Almighty I AM.

Just the use alone of this one Violet Flame decree will bring forth a most remarkable effect. You will feel a lightening of your light bodies when you use this Violet Flame decree. Use it for any situation that you find to be difficult or if you're feeling any discomfort with any situation or circumstance that you may be experiencing.

## A CROSSROADS

Dear ones, Dear hearts, today we shall continue our discourse, not only upon the work of Shamballa, but also upon the work of the Southern Doors of the Golden City Vortices. You see Dear ones, it was decided in this most recent Shamballa that we would begin the process of sending our, shall we call them, Sergeants and Lieutenants at Arms, those who are our most stalwart followers. They are to move forward into the Earth Plane and Planet at this time to ready the Golden City Vortices and to also bring the great assistance that the Earth needs at this most perilous time. For you see Dear ones, Dear hearts, you have known for some time, that the Earth Plane is at a crossroads where a choice must be made.

## MIGHTY LOVE AND LIGHT

There has been much talk about the peril of war upon your Earth Plane and Planet and this indeed, in its threat, causes a great source of the energy of fear. This fear energy, you see, then is used for even a greater purpose, is used to bring about economic ruin, not only upon people as individuals, but also upon nations. For you see Dear ones, Dear hearts, fear itself grows in its own momentum. Now, it is important to understand that also the energy of love grows in even greater momentum. As I have said so many, many times, Dear ones, Dear hearts, the mighty Light of God, Never, Never Faileth.

## THE FREED CHELA

Now I shall like to explain some of the inner working of the hierarchy. It is important that you have always understood that the Master Teacher and chela relationship works on the premise of energy for energy. And you know Dear ones, Dear hearts, as you move ahead in your own spiritual understanding and evolution, that at sometime, in this process, you will achieve your Ascension and glory in that mighty Light of God that Never Fails. Where upon that fact, you shall then no longer require physical incarnation. Yet there may still be at that time, requirements that will be made of you in the Astral Body and also requirements that will be made of you in the causal fields. You will then again go through a type of reincarnation process, although not to confuse this with physical reincarnation. These will take place in those fields, shall we say, or dimensions of experience.

Those beings that have freed themselves from the need to reincarnate on the physical plane, take upon a higher service. They are still under the auspice of their Master Teacher, an Ascended Master, who has freed himself also from astral and causal influence. The Master Teacher, under this auspice, still gives their sponsorship to the freed chela. This freed chela then is able to operate at a greater level of service for the Earth Plane and Planet. These are the Master Teachers that are now entering into the Adjutant Points of the Southern Doors of all Golden City Vortices. They are Masters indeed and come under the service of the hierarchy. Many of them are Angels, Brothers and Sisters of Peace. It is true that a few of them will seek embodiment, so that they can bring forward the greater teachings at this time. They will be known as the "Indigo Children" or the "Children of the Seventh Manu." These are the new children, finding great popularity, as your Earth Plane and Planet are now understanding.

SERVICE IN THE SOUTHERN DOORS

It is now important to understand that there will come forward these Master Teachers in their great service within the Southern Doors. It was no mistake Dear one, Dear heart, that I sent you to activate Adjutant Points in the Southern Door of Gobean. I sent you for the purpose primarily so that you could perform the service of a Step-down Transformer in these specific Adjutant Points. This brought forth a necessary influx of energy; for you see, as above, so below. All energy, when it is sustained upon the Earth Plane and Planet, is under these types of applicable laws.

## TEACHERS OF THE FOURTH DIMENSION

Now, so that you can gain further understanding into this process, many of these servants are coming forward, each of them of course through different Master Teachers. As the Gobean Vortex is sponsored by Master El Morya, there are many Master Teachers working for the influence of Master El Morya and coming forward now to assist this great influence of energy. It is true too that some of these Master Teachers will keep their residence in the higher level, that is, in the Fourth and the Fifth Dimension. Those Master Teachers who retain an influence of the Fourth Dimension have a more Elemental or Deva type energy. They shall serve the cause of influencing weather patterns, also the Earth energy itself, and allowing an imbuing of the energies of that mighty Blue Ray to come forward for the true healing of the nations.

## TEACHERS OF THE FIFTH DIMENSION

Those Master Teachers who choose to remain at a Fifth Dimensional level of each of the Adjutant Points, will then retain an energy that will be more influential upon the mass consciousness of humanity. This will allow the opening of greater classes at night, for those who wish to travel to receive such teaching. But let us put our focus upon the work at hand and the appearance of the Master Teachers in physical bodies; for you see, much preparation is needed for this to occur.

## THE TEACHERS APPEAR

You see Dear ones, Dear hearts, the hierarchy has planned this out, one step at a time, and we will tell you as much as we feel that you can understand with your present state of consciousness. We shall also ask for your assistance in these certain locations, so that you can bring forth the necessary energies as a Step-down Transformer. There will also be, from time to time, certain ceremonies that will be carried out, not only by the hierarchy, but also in the Earth Plane and Planet, for those who choose to give this loving service. Dear ones, these Master Teachers that are taking their physical bodies are manifesting at the Adjutant Points.

Now, just so you have some clarity over this, there are a few who will appear in the public and give their teachings. However, you must know and understand that their teachings will always be given on a one-on-one basis. Perhaps some day you shall be hiking along a trail and thereupon, you meet your Brother of the Light. A few words are given to you. Those words connect with you at a deep level of understanding. Indeed, at that moment, you have been touched by the purpose of the Golden City Vortices. But is this the moment that you build a Temple and form a religion around this teacher? I say, in this moment, all is choice, Dear ones, Dear hearts. But remember the intention behind such teaching.

We are here to lift the hearts of men, to shed light where ignorance and despair abound. We come forward, Dear ones, Dear hearts, to uplift your consciousness, to help set you free by the practice of the laws. Listen and pay attention. Heed the voice always within. Know that at these times indeed, you shall always be tested, but you know Dear ones, Dear hearts, that there is never a test given that you are not prepared and ready for. It is also important to know and understand, that each of these points, in their service and activity, relate and serve to that mighty Light of God that Never, Never Faileth.

THOUSANDS FLOOD THE EARTH

All in all, there will be thousands and thousands of Master Teachers that will flood the Earth in the next twenty years. Some of them, yes, making their physical and apparent appearance, but many will retain, shall we say, the status of the silent watcher, who will imbue an area geophysically with the energies necessary to raise humanity in vibration. Gobean right now is serving this greater purpose. For you see Dear ones, Dear hearts, it is the first Golden City and its location has been placed in certain motion so that it can move consciousness into the beginning days of a Golden Age.

All Southern Doors will be activated for this purpose in all of the five Golden Cities of the United States. Also included in the sequence will be one Golden City that is now currently activated in Canada. There will be another Golden City that will come into its full activation process in the next year and, if need be, Master Teachers will also be making their appearance in these Southern Doors. It is important to understand the process of the Step-down Transformer. And now I would like to give a small lesson upon this.

## SERVICE OF THE STEP-DOWN TRANSFORMER

You see Dear ones, Dear hearts, when one travels forward to these Adjutant Points, with only the intent of service, that is enough to be given. That is the great sacrifice. It is important to not get yourself bogged down in religious ceremonies and also, to not get yourself too bogged down in religious symbols. But know that the religious ceremonies and symbols that have been given to you are given to you to teach you the continuity of consciousness that carries over from one age into the next. This is to show you that time is an illusion and that you are never separated in conscious activity from the intention of your desires. The chela who wishes to grow in spiritual service, in sacrificing their time and their energy to help a greater Cause Divine, is perfect to serve as a Step-down Transformer. This service may happen at any time and at any place, as you all well know Dear ones, Dear hearts. In that instance, ask:

Mighty I AM Presence, come forward
and let me serve the Cause Divine of the Spiritual Hierarchy,
the Great White Brotherhood and Sisterhood
of Breath, Sound, and Light.
I now call forth my perfect service in alignment to the Divine Plan.

"A GREAT OUTPOURING"

Such a simple, humble prayer comes forward as an offering to the great Divine Plan and the Ascended Master who knows and understands the law then pours the radiance into this individual. During this time upon the Earth Plane and Planet, Mother Earth, Beloved Babajeran, has offered herself to be of service and when this prayer is offered, along side the influence of the Master Teacher at the geomantic Adjutant Points, a great service then is Co-created. The Step-down Transformer then is allowed to activate an Adjutant Point. Energy from the Third Dimension intersperses with energy of the Fourth and the Fifth Dimension. For you see Dear ones, Dear hearts, all is connected as ONE and that mighty Unana, unity of consciousness, at this moment then, opens a great portal of light into the Fifth Dimension. This allows a great outpouring of influence from the Fifth Dimension into the Earth Plane and Planet.

AT THE ADJUTANT POINTS

Now, as you well understand, the great Sergeant-At-Arms Masters then reside at the Fifth Dimension, the Fourth Dimension, and yes indeed, there are those who reside at the Third Dimension, protecting these Adjutant Points. Remember that the Master Teacher who comes into the Third Dimension has a greater Mastery, that is, over the physical realm and has the ability to become invisible or to take on a body at will. So these points are kept in their ever-present protection. But know Dear hearts, Dear ones, that indeed they do exist. This great appearance serves, not only to raise the overall vibration of the Earth, but it also serves a greater plan in the system of the ages or Yugas, if you will. This brings forward a greater vibration and harmony and raises consciousness into a sub-period similar to Dvapara Yuga, a Bronze Age of Consciousness. However, Dear ones, Dear hearts, let us not get too confused, but just understand that the Golden Age will bring a greater influx and understanding of the Ray Forces and their energies in raising consciousness to a greater understanding, levels of compassion, and ultimate Ascension in that mighty Light of God.

## CONTRAST

Now as each of these Adjutant Points are brought forward in their greater cooperation and harmony, a greater vibration comes upon the Earth, not only in that particular Golden City Vortex, but also within the first layer of the field of the atmosphere of the Earth. And so you will see, as these appearances occur, one after another at the Adjutant Points, that a stabilizing effect will happen also with the weather in that area. You will also see that for every energy, there is another energy; as a stabilizing effect occurs in one area, you will see likewise, outside of that area, a destabilizing effect. That is why we have always spoken of the Golden City Vortices as safe places. As the vibration is raised, while you will see an overall vibratory effect, you will also see a more contrasting or lessening effect in areas outside of Golden City Vortices. I can give more supplementary teaching on this in the future if you require or ask. And now, Dear one, I shall open the floor for questions, for I see that you have many.

## ENERGY ADJUSTMENT

Question: *Is it necessary to continually strive to maintain the balance of the planet because there's so much energy being focused through the Golden Cities that it then depletes other areas?*

It is important to understand that the Earth Plane and Planet is a place for teaching and learning. It is still a plane of duality and it is a critical balance indeed, as we move into these higher fields of energy as consciousness. As this vibration rises, for lack of a better word, in electromagnetic consciousness, it is important to understand that there is a dual expression of this. This is why you will see increasing weather patterns of greater intensities, high temperatures and low temperatures, but you will see and experience more medium temperatures in Golden City Vortices, particularly those of the Southern Doors. For you see right now, we are working to bring this great adjustment of energies to the Earth Plane and Planet. We are working directly with the Ray Forces as they arc from that Great Central Sun to the core of this Earth from your own Solar Sun. Do you understand?

INTEGRATION OF LIGHT

Answer and question: *Yes I do. Since we have just returned from working at the Northern Door of Gobean, do you wish us to continue on in the Eastern and Western doors?*

This would be wonderful work to achieve. For you see Dear ones, Dear hearts, this activation brings about much more integration into your own light bodies. This also brings much more integration into your service and work for the Golden City Vortex that you serve. When you activate a Western Door, you bring about a higher knowledge, not only for yourself, but for all of humanity who then travel into the Golden City of Gobean. I know that I am speaking now in much more metaphoric and mystic terms, but again, do not underestimate the work and the use of the Step-down Transformer. The same for activation of Eastern Doors, this will bring greater harmony into your own family structure, into your one-on-one and personal relationships. But this too brings a greater energy for all families of the world. Do you know of what I speak?

Response: *Yes, I know exactly of what you speak. Then we shall complete that as soon as possible.*

So Be It. And know Dear ones, Dear hearts, I shall personally guide and assist you in your journey.

Response and question: *So Be It and thank you. Is there more discourse before we continue on with questions?*

Please continue with your questions. I know that I have given you much to think about today and if indeed you have more questions for the next session, I shall be available.

A MIGRATORY SEQUENCE

Question: *I understand. What is the best sequence through the Doorways?*

It is always best to work in a clockwise fashion. That is, start with the Northern Door, move to the Eastern, then to the Southern, and complete with the West. In this way, the energies are greater in their integration process for you at an individual level. This also enhances the clockwise motion of the Vortex. Now you remember from the early teachings, that a Golden City Vortex can move backwards, that is counterclockwise, to remove toxic energies. If you are working to remove a toxic energy from your light fields, that is a purification process, then this can be done in a reverse order. Do you understand?

Question: *Yes I do, so I would assume then, for our immediate purposes, the next step is to go the Eastern Door. Do you wish us to revisit the Southern Door?*

The Southern Door, in its activations to bring forward the Sergeant-At-Arms servants, is complete for Gobean. However, there will come a time where you may be called upon to bring this service into other Golden City Vortices. We shall move then of course to Malton.

"OF SERVICE"

Question: *I understand. For the completion of Gobean then, are we to go to the Eastern Door and then complete at the Western Door?*

So Be It. If this is the service that you choose Dear one.

*We will be happy to do this.*

As you well know Dear one, Dear heart, it is rare that I would ask you to do anything. It is rare that I would tell you what to do. But when you ask to be of service, then I shall give direction.

Response: *I understand but unless we complete the service, then the experience does not allow us to continue to grow and to be educated.*

This is so Dear one.

Response: *Then that is all that I need to know for the moment to complete this work for Gobean. We have questions from others who need your assistance and your guidance.*

Proceed.

FOLLOW THE JOY

Question: *We have a question from a gentleman from Connecticut: "Beloved Saint Germain, I am trying to understand why I keep having these feelings of such anxiety at work. I find it difficult to smile, my face tightens up, I get nervous because I cannot communicate. My heart races, my palms get sweaty, etc. It's been going on and off for the last few years now. I have a very public job and these last two weeks have been the worst yet. I do some Violet Flame decrees on my way to work, in the car, and try to find some answers. Beloved Saint Germain please help me to understand and overcome this problem that has burdened my heart for so long. With much love."*

Dear one, Dear heart, the Violet Flame will indeed set you free. Continue in your use and application and know Dear one, that I shall stand forward, and help, guide, and assist you. In many of the teachings that I have brought forward, I have always addressed that of the heart's desire, that it is always important to follow the inner longing within the heart. Sometimes it is difficult to identify what we are longing or searching for. This causes confusion and brings about conflict within the self. These small blockages then erupt, you see Dear one, from the light fields into the emotional body and finally into the field of activity.

As it has always been said Dear one, "Follow your bliss." Follow the joy in your life and see if this does not lessen the tension that you feel in your life. Follow the longing within your heart, for it would appear that there are some decisions that you have recently made that are not in alignment with what you truly desire. Now again, I shall not tell you what to do, I will only make this as a suggestion. It is also important for you to spend time in meditation and clear your mind from the stresses of this job. Experiences sometime stay with you day after day, week after week, and this builds its own subjective energy within. I always recommend to my chelas, the use of the Violet Flame in the salt-water bath. Use approximately two cups of salt within the tub. This will bring about a greater soothing of the light fields. You can use any Violet Flame decree that you prefer, but I would suggest:

> Mighty Violet Flame blaze in through and around me.
> Harmonize all of my energy fields
> and bring forth your soothing Ray.
> So Be It.

THE WATERS OF THE DIMENSIONS

Question: *So Be It. Thank you. I have another question from someone in Pennsylvania: "For many years, I have awoken with fleeting remembrances of having been in the presence of a person or persons imparting great knowledge. I used to call it "Soul School." I assumed I was out-of-body, studying with others. I also am aware of being lifted from my bed, rolled over, having a net of golden electrified energy passed through my body, beginning with my feet. I was then lifted toward the ceiling. I was awake and fully cognizant until it sped up and I felt like I was passing through water. From that point on, I don't remember anything. I have awoken feeling energy coursing through my energy system and on one or more occasions heard a voice say clearly: '4-9-1-0.' Can you give me insight on what is occurring with me regarding these events?"*

You're passing through the waters of the Dimensions. You are moving from the Fourth Dimension into the Fifth Dimension. Of course, this happens when you sleep, for you naturally then leave the body. It is true, as I've stated before, many chelas and students move into these classes of the Fifth Dimension. You, Dear one, Dear heart, have studied with Master Serapis Bey in many other lifetimes and are well acquainted with the Egyptian Initiatory Rites. You've studied the work of Akhenaton and Dear one, this is what is coming forward as a type of past-life recall. However, it is coming through at a Fifth Dimensional level. You see, it is brought into your conscious memory and now is being used to awaken you to another level of service, working to bring this into your conscious activity. You see Dear one, Dear heart, there will be lessons and teachings that will come to you soon regarding what I speak. The "4-9-1-0" has been given to you as a message to watch for. It will be associated with the teachings that will be given to you soon.

## A STUDENT'S PAST LIFE

Question: *Thank you. I have two more questions. "Does Saint Germain have any suggestions for those involved in my overseas project that will enhance the probability of success?"*

It is important to understand Dear one, Dear heart, to keep all within balance in your life. To not only take the time out to serve justice but also to take time into your life to feel the joy of life that life does indeed bring. The suggestion that I have is to practice the visualization of the Violet Flame upon all of your documents every day. This is a work that you can achieve through the Violet Flame mudra, as I have taught many of my students. Place the left hand over your heart and the right hand projecting energies of the mighty Violet Flame in, through, and around all documents that you have prepared and have sent:

> Mighty Violet Flame, surround all of my documents,
> imbuing them with the Golden Light of Justice.
> So Be It.

You see Dear one, Dear heart, you are calling forth that beloved Law of Justice, that all shall be in balance, that all shall seek its equal status. This Dear one, Dear heart, is work that you have brought forward from another embodiment you had during the Civil War. During that time, you worked closely in the governmental cabinets, hoping to achieve a greater balance in the economic status of the United States. Of course, you felt somewhat reluctant and a failure in that lifetime and so now in this lifetime, you are seeking to serve at yet another level. Know Dear one and Dear heart, that I stand behind your work of justice. Call upon Beloved Portia, for she too shall bring her assistance.

## A HEALING PROCESS

Question: *Thank you and he has one more question: "One year ago, Saint Germain suggested that I use rose tea for assistance with gastro-esophageal reflux. I have been using the tea. How many times a day is recommended? I have been using the decree that he gave me. Does he have any other suggestions for this condition, to help me cure it?"*

This was brought as a suggestion, not only to bring healing of certain molds and bacteria that reside in the stomach lining, but to also bring forward an opening of the chakra. For you see Dear ones, we are dealing with vibration. Now you can indeed bring an intensity, by raising this vibration just through rose oil. One or two drops applied upon the wrist on a daily basis. This vibration will assist the healing process. But it is also important to address, at a spiritual cause, the reason for this. This comes from stress and tension. Again, I shall address, living the life with joy, finding that which brings the smile upon the face is always so important, is it not Dear one, Dear heart? Live with this balance of joy always in your life. Know too, that time does not press upon you. Time is only an illusion, like the waters that separate one dimension from the next. All is united as ONE, Dear heart. Know this truth.

Response: *Thank you. I have no further questions.*

Then I shall take me leave and return to give more discourse.

Response: *Thank you.*

I AM the Light of God that Never Fails. Om Manaya Pitaya, Hitaka.

Response: *Hitaka*

# 12

## Time and the Violet Flame
*Saint Germain*

Greetings Beloved students, chelas of mine, in that Mighty Violet Flame. I AM Saint Germain and I stream forth on that mighty Violet Ray of Mercy, Transmutation, and ultimate Forgiveness. As usual Dear hearts, I request permission to come forward?

Response: *Please Saint Germain, you are most welcome. Please come forward.*

TRANSMUTE FEAR

May the Mighty Violet Flame blaze forth, in, through, and around all of your energy bodies, Dear ones, Dear hearts. The mighty Violet Flame, you see Dear ones, at this time has been brought forward to bring a complete transmutation of the obstacles, that is, karmic obstacles of the past. Sometimes these karmic obstacles present themselves in just a small way. They may be just through an attitude. They may be through a slight feeling of ingratitude. Sometimes, this small obstacle comes forward in a word that you speak, an unkind thought, a judgment of another. But you see Dear ones, Dear hearts, each of these obstacles, when they come across your path, is an element of fear that is harboring in your energy bodies. When I call forth the mighty Violet Flame, it comes forward to transmute fear at many levels. You see, it is the purpose and the intention of the Violet Flame, brought forward at this time, to bring an acceleration to humanity's collective Heart of Love.

## THE LIGHTED STANCE

This collective consciousness exists in a higher concept, in a higher will, for lack of a better term. When it is given its complete unfoldment towards and among humanity, it will bring humanity into a New Time, a new state of consciousness, that of the Golden Age. The Golden Age will be a time upon the Earth Plane and Planet where we will see love in its highest and finest vibration, expressing among all of humanity. We will see suffering drop to the side. Obstacles once perceived, now will be seen as mere stepping stones into a greater understanding and realization of lighted consciousness. You see, the Violet Flame, as I've explained before in many other discourses, also brings about a lighted stance within the physical body. The Violet Flame, when it's called upon, begins to invigorate the light bodies, removing obstacles, so they can be seen at a different perception, a different point of understanding. The lighted stance then comes through this influence of the light bodies and brings about a higher revolution within the metabolic rate. This allows the body, you see Dear ones, Dear hearts, to merge in a more collective operating position with the light bodies.

Now as you know Dear ones, Dear hearts, there has always been a direct correlation between the disease process, the human aura, and the physical body. In the same way, there is also a direct correlation between the mighty Violet Ray, the use of the Violet Flame decree, the light bodies of the human aura, and the physical body. It brings about, not only an inner marriage within the heart and the ability to express love in its greater capacity, but it also brings about a merging into a more unified field of experience. This allows the body to raise, not only in vibration, but also to move at a higher rate. To begin to understand the lighted stance is to begin to understand the Ascension process. Indeed Dear ones, students of mine, the Violet Flame prepares the body and the light bodies for the process of the Ascension. This indeed begins the process of spiritual liberation.

## DETACHMENT

Now, it is important to understand that when one begins to use the Violet Flame, that yes indeed, many obstacles seem to drop by the way side. Things are seen from a more whole perspective. As I have always stated before, Dear ones, Dear hearts, there is no mistake, ever, ever, ever. When one begins to use the Violet Flame, one also sees how one situation is a result of many other situations. As I have stated so many times before, things do not happen *to* a person, but indeed, things happen *with* a person. Through the use of the Violet Flame, one is then able to see through their whole perspective of experiences and events and how they are held as one whole unified experience. It is not just one experience that is plucked among these many experiences and labeled as bad or good but it is seen from a more detached state of understanding, that all experiences are serving the Greater ONE, the unified field of all experience.

## PURIFICATION AND ACCELERATION

In terms of the physical body, it can and will bring about a purification process. Now sometimes, with advanced use of the Violet Flame, one is brought into a purifying process where one may feel instantly the effect of a disease that it normally would have not felt. Now this may seem a bit confusing to you, but let me explain. The diseased process, as you know, is held first within the light bodies and as it works through each layer of the field of the human aura, it then manifests in physical activity, in the physical body. Sometimes this may be felt first as a discomfort, as a small cold, or the aches and pains of the flu. Now, it is the same with disease and the use of the Violet Flame. When you are working to bring about a purification process, you will still feel the aches and the pains of this as a energy vibration; however, the Violet Flame will allow you to feel this effect much, much sooner. So for instance, if it was within your karmic path to have the experience of a dreaded disease, instead of that dreaded disease being extended for a three to six year process, you may be able to enhance this process. You see Dear ones, Dear hearts, all is given to nature.

Now when I say enhance, what I am explaining to you is a process through which there is an acceleration of the karma. This may bring about the effects of a dreaded disease in a twenty-four hour period. So you see, it is brought through in that twenty-four hour period and the body may feel some of the effects, as well as the emotional strain and the ensuing strains on the other energy bodies. This has been brought forward to bring a greater acceleration for chelas, students, and light workers who are ready to serve the Cause Divine and move into a greater understanding of the Golden Age.

Yes indeed, it would be so great, would it not Dear ones, if disease, famine, pestilence, and all could be wiped away from this planet? But you see, know, and understand, through your eyes and ears, that are well opened to the light of wisdom, that all upon the Earth Plane is brought forward, yes, for your complete total Mastery. This of course is being presented to you through the dual forces; that which is left, that which is right, that which is hot, that which is cold. Those two extreme differences meet somewhere within the middle and seek forever balance. It is indeed only an experience and this is what is being taught through the Violet Flame. When you use this higher law and this energy is set into motion, there occurs within the energy fields, which do indeed have their effect upon the physical body, a greater movement towards balance. Because it is being sponsored, not only by me but also by many other members of this hierarchy, you are brought into a greater acceleration, especially at this time.

## VIOLET FLAME AND VIBRATION

These Beloved Beings of Light are coming forward in their sponsorship, to allow a greater momentum of the energy through that the mighty Violet Ray, the mighty Violet Flame that has been brought forward to help and assist humanity and mankind at this time. The Violet Flame is brought forward to collectively raise humanity into a greater vibration. Now this greater vibration functions within the Law of Attraction and Duality. So you see, Dear ones, Dear hearts, it allows also for a greater influx of souls then to be born upon the Earth Plane and Planet. These greater souls, as I have talked about in many past discourses as that Seventh Manu, they come forward and raise the Earth into an even greater vibration and onward and onward this goes.

GOLDEN SPIRAL DECREE

So you see Dear ones, not only is there a greater use for the Violet Flame at an individual level but there is also this great use of the Violet Flame to serve the world in a greater harmonizing effect. Indeed, the Violet Flame can transmute many types of personal diseases of the body. But you know, Dear ones, Dear hearts, that the Violet Flame harmonizes the light fields first and this indeed carries the influence upon the physical body. So, all is inner connected as ONE. There indeed is no separation. It is but the process of involution and evolution, both connected to the Golden Spiral of Life, all connected as ONE in one unified field.

> Mighty Violet Flame blaze in, through, and around
> all of my energy bodies.
> Transmute all obstacles, all discord, any disease
> within my physical body,
> uniting and raising me within the Golden Path.
> So Be It.

Response: *So Be It.*

Now Dear ones, Dear hearts, any questions upon the Violet Flame?

## LIGHT BODIES AND ASCENSION

Question: *As I understand the light bodies, each light body relates to a specific Ray. Is this true?*

It is true, Dear one, but it is also important to understand that there are three distinct bodies that are dealt with in the Ascension process: the physical body, the Astral Body, and the Causal body. Now, when we speak specifically of the light fields, there are indeed seven light bodies and each of these seven light bodies correspond to the chakras.

Response and question: *Yes, so each of the light bodies is part of the refractory process of the Central Sun to our Solar Sun and then reflecting off of our local planets. Is this true?*

It is true Dear one. For instance, to bring this into greater clarity and understanding, there are seven light bodies for the physical body; there are seven light bodies for the Astral Body; and there are seven light bodies for the Causal body. Does this give clarity?

Response and question: *Yes and so essentially, there is Ascension for the physical realm, the astral realm, and the causal realm. Is that true?*

That is true Dear one and the use of the Violet Flame at this time brings about the Ascension of the physical body, uniting the physical body in the light bodies with the astral light bodies and also with the causal light bodies. Does this clarify?

Question: *Yes, so in your state of consciousness as an Ascended Master, you have ascended through the physical, the astral, and the causal. Is this true?*

It is true Dear one, Dear heart. However, let us keep our focus upon the work in front of you, that which must be achieved in this moment, and can be achieved in this ever- present now, Almighty I AM.

"THE VEIL IS LIFTED"

Response and question: *I understand. We'll focus on the physical body, as you have directed. In the disease state, or potential disease state, before it becomes a reality, it will show up in all of the light bodies of the physical plane first?*

It is true Dear one. Of course, it is held first within the Astral Body. For you see, it has also been held as a cause in the Causal body, so all is inner connected as ONE. This is why, when a student or chela begins to pursue the science of spiritual liberation, they must also then begin in their pursuit and knowledge of light and sound. For you see, all is inner connected as ONE. It is also very important, when one begins to make their attempt in understanding this science and decides upon that ultimate choice that is engendered in the Divine Plan, they must then attract a Master Teacher who is versed in such knowledge, who can lift certain karmic burdens and obstacles from their path. Then they are able to understand and comprehend the work at hand. Questions?

Response and question: *Yes. In the physical realm, in dealing with the harmonization of all of these light bodies, does the use of the Violet Flame transmutes and transforms all of those disharmonious karmic records?*

It is true Dear chela. What might be a better word of understanding is "karmic pattern." Yes indeed, there is the record that is created of lifetime after lifetime after lifetime and where one is still stuck within the same pattern of perception. The Master Teacher, lifting a karmic burden from the student's eyes and ears, is what is meant by "the veil is lifted." The Master Teacher comes in and lifts away the clouds of perception, so one then begins to view in the clearest form, the possibility and potential that lies within life. That is why we say there is no mistake, ever, ever, ever and that all is connected to the mighty ONE. But this understanding is not given in its greatest clarity until that veil is lifted, is it not so?

Answer: *That has been my experience.*

TIME AND THE VIOLET FLAME

But once it is lifted, one then begins to see, not only the karmic record of past lives, but also, one then begins to clearly see the karmic patterns that one is playing out in their day-to-day experience of life eternal. It is also important, in this perception, to see the role of time and that, within this ever present *now*, there is only one experience. That is why, when we say, "Call upon that mighty Violet Flame," one then begins to feel and vibrate at a level of timelessness. One is then vibrating through the essence of that mighty transmuting fire into the ever present *now*. Seamlessly, past, present, and future become as ONE. This is the experience that is brought about as relief, as hope from despair, as light from darkness, that you feel after you have completed your decree session of the Violet Flame. You see Dear ones, Dear hearts, it is not just the word but it is the spoken word, with the will of your intention aligning with the Master Teachers who serve this mighty Violet Ray. When one comes forward with the intention to seek their spiritual liberation, that light is enough to call forth the attraction of the law. This is the premise of the Violet Flame. Questions?

Question: *In a specific disease state, the Violet Flame can be called into action to mitigate or lessen the severity?*

Yes Dear ones, Dear hearts, and sometimes the Violet Flame comes forward and brings spontaneous remission from disease. Also, it may bring an acceleration of the disease process and a transmutation involved in that. You see, this principle is best understood when one understands time compaction. The disease, you see, no longer becomes subject to the Law of Time. Therefore, past, present, and future become as ONE with that disease process. So within that use of the mighty Violet Flame, one may transcend or transmute a disease process that was scheduled to occur within the regular human body for perhaps a ten or twenty year period. But through the use of the Violet Flame, that can be reduced significantly. It also depends how the chela or the student adheres to the practice of the mighty Violet Flame. But know this Dear ones, Dear hearts, that the continuous application of this mighty law in action will always bring one into a higher and more perfected state of consciousness and from this higher and more perfected state of consciousness, would not then the physical body follow?

Answer and question: *Yes, it would. In that schedule of the disease state, we're referring to the causal coming through the astral then to the physical, are we not?*

Yes.

Response and question: *And then its manifestation would occur in the physical, assuming that it is untreated by the Violet Flame or some other remediation means. Is that also true?*

There are these sad experiences.

## THE VIOLET FLAME OPENS DOORS

Question: *And so, the application of the Violet Flame is an intervention that the individual chooses to mediate all of that suffering?*

And in this joyous choosing, doors begin to open where one had never before imagined. One begins to see what led to the process the physical body is now experiencing. What are all the key components happening *with* the physical body, not *to* the physical body? You see Dear ones, Dear hearts, often in the disease process, people enter into a war with the disease, where they fight an ensuing attack. As you can see Dear one, Dear heart, in this same premise, nothing happens *to*, but happens *with*. It is important then to understand each component, how it has been set up from "A to B" and onward unto the final letter of the alphabet, to see the whole process as it unfolds in the law eternal.

When one uses the Violet Flame, doorways begin to open. A different perception is given upon the disease process. We also see an acceleration that happens within the light bodies; the light bodies of the causal, the light bodies of the astral, the light bodies of the physical, all of these uniting and harmonizing, vibrating to higher planes of understanding and realities. This is indeed what happens. But it is also through the assistance of the Ascended Masters, the Master Teacher pulling forward to remove karmic obstacles from the light bodies, so that one may move into the greater harmonization process. Now it is true, that sometimes the disease process becomes a most educative experience. But in this understanding, it is not through the decay of the body that one then becomes enlightened. One becomes enlightened when they realize the reason for the decay of the body. Is this clear to you?

## VIOLET FLAME DECREE FOR HEALING

Answer and question: *Oh yes. This rings clear. When we're dealing with a diseased part of the body, is there a more refined and focused type of Violet Flame decree to deal just with diseases?*

What we are inducing is a state of healing, not only for the body, the physical body, but for the Astral Body and the Causal body. That is why we call forth the Violet Flame in this way:

Mighty Violet Flame blaze in, through, and around my Causal body,
my Astral Body, and my physical body.
Induce the state of healing and harmonize all light bodies.
Bring me to the Divine Plan supreme.
So Be It.

Response and question: *So Be It. So, a similar type of decree can also be used for our finances or for our strained relationships?*

## STAGES OF THE VIOLET FLAME

For any situation where you perceive there to be a problem or an obstacle, you may bring this into a greater harmonizing process. This brings about each level of these light bodies into their greater harmony for each experience, that of the physical body, that of the Astral Body, that of the Causal body. When you use the Violet Flame to induce these states of healing, you may notice in the beginning an unraveling effect. You may feel at that one juncture in time, "it's not getting better; it's getting worse." But indeed, Dear one, at that moment, call with a stalwart victory in mind, that the Violet Flame will come forward and bring its healing and soothing vibration to all light and sound within your body. For you see, very often what happens in this process is very similar to the cleansing of a wound.

You see, before you can properly bandage the wound and allow it to come forward for healing, one must then properly cleanse the wound. And this is what happens through the use and stages of the Violet Flame.

## TIME COMPACTION: QUICK AND INTENSE

It is important to understand that sometimes, depending on the karma that is involved, there is spontaneous healing, spontaneous remission. Sometimes there is also more of an instant karmic reaction to situations and circumstances where the law has been called forth, that there will be an experience of such karma within the physical plane. But what you will notice is, when you call upon this law, that there is an acceleration of these experiences, that the karma is experienced very quickly, even though it is experienced very deeply. This I have explained before in the Principle of Time Compaction, for again, the law demands what the law demands. But through the use of the Violet Flame and with the assistance and the generous help of your Master Teacher, you see, some of the karmic burden is lifted.

Do you not remember the story of the chela who was thrown into the fire by the Master Teacher? As soon as he was thrown into the fire and taken out, he was instantly healed. He had balanced a karma that had been demanded by the Law of Nature. Now you can see that when you call upon that mighty Violet Flame, you feel some soothing effect, but there is also indeed, an intense purification process. Questions?

## USE AT SUNRISE AND SUNSET

Response and question: *Yes, I recall that story of that student. I think that was actually your teacher who had performed such an action. When the unraveling does occur, what if one becomes discouraged or overwhelmed, should the use of the Violet Flame then be intensified?*

It is best always to use it at sunrise or sunset. For you see, when you use it at sunrise, it is the application of this law bringing its continuous vibration throughout all of your daily activities. When it is used at sunset, it settles the day and brings you into a more restful peace for your nighttime studies. For you see Dear ones, Dear hearts, all chelas who use the mighty Violet Flame are then admitted into the Violet Flame classes at night. This is where they are given many experiences and are able to transmute karmas at the astral level. Do you understand?

Answer: *Yes, these classes at night are at the astral level.*

It is true, in the same way that you attend your classes in your waking time on the physical Earth Plane. All is brought forth in the great balance of the mighty I AM. So Be It.

Response: *So Be It. At sunrise and sunset, it has been my observation, that blue and pink can be seen clearly in the light and also their combination of the violet. Using the Violet Flame at the beginning of the day gives me the sense that I can go forward, no matter what will occur, and gives me a soothing peace at the end of the day.*

At dawn and dusk are the moments of transcendence, where the day is beginning or where the evening begins. These induce a point of movement within the light fields and bring about a greater and higher preparation through the use of that mighty Violet Flame in action. That is why, in all of our teachings, this is the preferred time to use this mighty law in action. However, the Violet Flame, in its law and ability to bring healing to humanity, can work at anytime, any place. So Be It.

Response: *So Be It. I have no further questions, but we have some questions that have been sent forward, if you are available.*

I am available, as this is a service that I bring to the Earth Plane.

## REMOVING FINANCIAL OBSTACLES

Question: *There are two questions, the first is: "I am trying desperately to find a job. At this point, I'm not looking for my right and perfect job. I'm looking to meet my financial obligations. What direction can I take that will help me find any job to meet my financial needs?"*

Let us handle the first section of this question. This Beloved Being of Light has worked in many past embodiments as a healer, with a great knowledge, not only of herbs, but of energy and how energy can be used in its highest or higher state to bring about a total healing of body, mind, and spirit. However, to just work for money, there are many possibilities and opportunities that could open. Through the use of the Violet Flame, Dear one, many obstacles can be removed.

> Mighty Violet Flame blaze in, through, and around
> my financial condition.
> Align and harmonize all of my light bodies.
> So Be It.

## LIVE WITH INTENTION AND PURPOSE

It is that simple, to call upon the Violet Flame to bring the essential abundance and money forward. Also, it is important to understand, through the use of the Violet Flame, why this situation is being brought into its greater purifying fire. For you see, for this Dear one, it is much, much, more than just money. It is important to live a life of this higher intent of a purpose for which this person is born to be lived. When one is not living with the intention and the purpose for which they were born, it becomes much more difficult. The obstacles seem to pile on top of each other, one after the other. I would suggest to begin to study healing through the human aura first. This will open many doors. Through the process of understanding your great dharmic path, then a suitable job will come forward.

## A CONSCIOUSNESS PORTAL

Question: *The second question is: "There seems to be a lot of spiritual minded people congregating in the Las Vegas area. A few friends who live there and myself, in California, are wondering what the draw might be?"*

Well indeed, there is a great magnetization process that is occurring in the Las Vegas area. For you see Dear ones, Dear hearts, this area has attracted great negativity to it. It also is an area where there has been an underground base of great alien influence; however, this has since been moved more to the Midwest and the inner part of the United States. But it is important to understand the healing processes that are now taking place within the Earth. As you see, as Mother Earth is moving forward in her own evolution, a great transcendence of past karmas is now taking place. Indeed, there is a portal that opens up into this area, which travels into the inner Earth. Now when this is stated, you must understand that these portals are to a consciousness of inner Earth. It does not travel at a physical level but it must be obtained through consciousness. For you see, the two are related as ONE. This is the energy that this group is following.

There was an ancient city in the time of Atlantis known as Taleos and many of these individuals remember Taleos and the Temple of Inner Earth that many of them were working towards at that time. Not only did it bring forth an Ascension process, but first, it brought forth a harmonizing effect, a healing to the body, through the touching of a type of lighted mineral that came from the inner Earth at that time. However, we are now living in a different time upon the Earth Plane and Planet and this Golden City of the Inner

Earth is no longer available for those who are learning in this time period. The Golden Cities have now been brought forward in their activation process on the outer Earth, so those who have the eyes to see and the ears to hear may move into this vibration and energy. This too will bring about a great healing process.

This group is working with this point upon the Earth and bringing it into a greater alignment. This will come into a greater understanding in the beginning of Dvapara Yuga, of course this is almost 400,000 years from now in your time span, but we also know Dear ones, Dear hearts, that when one moves into the accelerated understanding of time, it does not even exist. Do you understand?

## GOLDEN CITIES OF THE INNER EARTH

Response and question: *Yes, I do understand. I have another question, "Aloha Saint Germain. My question is this: we live in the black hills of South Dakota. Our being here has been a mission and vision quest of extraordinary proportions and now it seems our portal/vortex is ready to open. Is this the magnetic reversal of what was once the portal of the Lakota's butte? Will we be entering middle Earth with the true Lakota through this portal in the near future, to finish our lessons during the Earth Changes? Thank you for your time and consideration."*

There is no mistake, ever, ever, ever, is there Dear ones, Dear hearts?

Response: *There is no mistake.*

This too is another opening into the inner Earth. It was also part of another Golden City within the Inner Earth that existed in another time upon the Earth Plane and Planet. As you see, it is of no coincidence that this too is opening in its preparation, at the same time as the group working in the Las Vegas area. They are both inner connected and there are many other portals that are inner connected at this level of consciousness and the entering into the Golden Light of the Inner Earth. This is another grid that will emerge in greater understanding at another time upon the Earth Plane and Planet. However, there are those who are working with it right now and are of a finer, crystalline type of consciousness, that can understand and access its knowledge. This is also being brought forward in conjunction with the Golden City network upon the Earth Plane and Planet.

However, it is important to understand that the focus and energy is to be placed for those in that location who have the eyes to see and the ears to hear. What I mean by this is, that there will be those who will be drawn to the Golden Network of the Inner Earth. There will be those who will be drawn to the Golden City Network that exists upon the Earth Plane and Planet; each of these, in their Divine Order and Intention.

GOLDEN CITY NETWORK

The Golden City Network that exists now and the Golden City Vortices that have been brought forward for the Golden Age will exist in this Time of Kali upon the Earth Plane and Planet and will bring this greater acceleration forward for those who desire a spiritual liberation and Ascension, to be set free in the breath, sound, and light. The Golden City Network will also bring a finer vibration and consciousness to those who have the consciousness to access it. You see, all is within a choice. All is within a training. But many of these souls who are being drawn to these types of Inner Earth networks—and this is but one of many—are being brought forward, because you see Dear ones, Dear hearts, they have done this in past lifetimes.

Now, it is important to understand that this particular portal is connected to the Shalahah Vortex; that it plays a special role in balancing and transmuting the energies of the Shalahah Vortex. Even though they would appear to be separate networks, they do ideally all work together as ONE. For you see, one works on the outer, the other works in the inner. There are all levels of understanding and preparation, all levels that are connected to an initiatory process. Questions?

"REMOVE THE VEIL OF IGNORANCE"

Question: *Yes, I have another question, "Dear Saint Germain, help me understand that we do not have to suffer any more in this world, that the time of war and suffering will stop for all."*

Dearest one, all is always within choice. For you see, upon the Earth Plane and Planet, one is brought forward here to learn and learn indeed we do. Sometimes such lessons are given with pain. Sometimes such lessons are given with love. But know and understand, that within your choice is the heart of understanding. When one begins to see with one thousand eyes, they begin to see, know, and understand, why there is suffering. You see Dearest one, it is important to remove the veil of ignorance and then one begins to see that nothing happens *to* any individual upon the Earth Plane and Planet; all happens *with* a person. For instance, it is no mistake that the United States, at this time in its evolution in history, stands as a leader and a light bearer unto the world. That is why at times, yes indeed, it is ridiculed and it is looked upon with deep suspicion and intolerance. But it is also looked upon as someone who can lend that helping hand, who can give that right demonstration of light and law simultaneously.

When one decides that they have learned all that they can upon this Earth Plane and Planet, they make the choice to liberate themselves, to free themselves from the endless and sometimes needless rounds of birth, death, and rebirth. It is all within a choice, Dear one, Dear heart. It is also how you wish to see a situation. There are those penniless beggars who lay beside the road in such endless rounds of bliss and there are those who live in a castle, with so much material comfort, in the pit and despairs of hell. It is how you wish to see things, Dear ones, Dear hearts. It is all within the choice of the experience. Questions?

## CONSCIOUSNESS AND CATASTROPHE

Question: *We have another question, "I would like to know more about Planet X or Nibiru, which relates to the Sumerians and the Second Coming, according to the many facts about this. All of the other ancient prophecies and supernatural events spoken of by all great beings are upon us. Please, if you could enlighten us with your clear vision?"*

It is true that such a planet does exist. And it is true that it will make its pass above the atmosphere of the planet Earth. But it is important to understand how one would see such an event. It is important to understand that, yes indeed, in the past such an event has brought about global catastrophes. Now, it is also important to understand consciousness and the time period that the Earth is entering into. All is directed in course and time by the Galactic Center in this stream of consciousness. As you will note, there are two luminaries that serve the Earth Plane and Planet, the Sun and the moon, and they direct this life stream upon the Earth Plane and Planet, one, influencing Light Rays, the other, influencing Sound Rays. It is important to see that the Earth is a schoolroom that has been brought forward time after time, again to forge an education to one of the physical planes. This serves a great purpose indeed and one thinks that there will come about an ending of this schoolroom. This is not so.

There will be physical life upon the Earth Plane and Planet and it will continue through this Time of the Golden Age of Kali Yuga. This will bring a heightening effect upon the Earth Plane and Planet. Yes, it is true that this planet is associated with other Brothers and Sisters and there are many stories about these more evolved beings and their place in your history. As I have stated before, some of them are entirely true and some of them are entirely false. Not to understate the position of the history, but it is important to understand that the appearance of this planet will bring a heightening of consciousness. For even now, there are many who are exploring the reaches of consciousness through examining this probable and possible event.

## THE FIELD OF PROTECTION

It is important to understand each layer of the field of the Earth and how it is sensitive to the collective thought. For you see Dear one, Dear student, thoughts indeed do create and they are held, not only in your own energy fields, but in the energy fields of Earth. Now it is also important to understand, that there are indeed Master Teachers who are working with many different chelas and students upon the Earth Plane and Planet. This event that is prophesied and perhaps predicted to happen is also an event that may be seen with much doom and gloom. However, it is important to understand that it is also a time where one must then begin to live their life in alignment to their Divine Plan, where one begins to ask the questions, "How can I live my life on Earth with greater purpose?" or, "Should I live my life for the ending of this Earth as we know it?" You see, all works together in that greater ONE, all works together to bring a greater heightening, especially at this time upon the Earth Plane and Planet.

This planet will bring about, in the greater scheme of things, a heightening of consciousness upon the Earth Plane and Planet. It will bring a greater awareness, not only of Earth Changes themselves, but it also brings a greater understanding of the Earth as an environment, in position in the overall scheme. Know this quite clearly and quite well, that indeed, at one time there was such a high possibility for nuclear disaster and a total annihilation of the Earth Plane and Planet. I, myself, wove a golden band of energy above this Earth so that it would hold the consciousness intact, so that such an event would not happen. Now as we enter into this New Time through the Golden City Vortices, the Ascended Masters are weaving a network of Golden energy above the Earth to bring a higher Field of Protection for such type of activity. This is our purpose and our intention. However, it is not the only purpose and intention of the Golden City Vortices, as I have so carefully laid down in so many prior discourses. But know indeed Dear one, Dear heart, that this is one of their Purposes Divine. Questions?

A QUICKENING

Question: *Yes. We have had many, many people call or write, saying, "Is Planet X coming by and is it the big change to our planet?"*

It is already instigating change, just in its vibration and energy. For you see, it is brought as an instigator of change, not only in its physical presence but in consciousness. And this is being felt by many upon the Earth Plane and Planet. Of course, the hierarchy has been aware of this planet always, for it comes in its Divine Timing and Intent to bring about a quickening, a raising of consciousness upon the Earth Plane and Planet. It is possible, as has been predicted, for such a catastrophe to occur. Yes indeed, in the same way that it was possible forty years ago for the world to be entirely annihilated by nuclear bombs. Now you must place this in the context of your own action. So Be It.

ADJUSTMENT OF EARTH'S VIBRATION

Response and question: *I see. That's very interesting. Does the Spiritual Hierarchy have an estimation of the distance in kilometers or light years it is from the influence of our Earth?*

It is a difficult estimation to give, primarily because we are also dealing with causal, astral, and physical affects of this type of occurrence. You see, it was about fifteen years ago that your own Earth was nearly missed by another type of asteroid. This was diverted, you see, through the work of the hierarchy. It is brought about on the conscious planes, as I have just admitted, through causal light bodies and astral light bodies. We are now in the process of this finer and higher adjustment. Each day that you use the Violet Flame and you work towards your freedom in light and sound, brings the Earth into a higher vibration and energy. This is our work. This is our purpose. Do you understand the direct correlation?

PROPHECIES OF THE WHITE STAR

Question: *Yes. Do you wish us to announce that the Planet X is actually coming?*

It has always been coming. It is no announcement. It travels in a circular motion from the nine o'clock position to its opposite side, you see, from the Galactic Center. It comes in a timing and an intention, which always brings about a heightening of awareness and consciousness. It is not a dark star. It is indeed the great white star that ushers in a new twenty-year period. It comes to bring a greater understanding of the spiritual essence of the Earth and how all life is inner connected as ONE. It will also bring about a greater understanding and heightening of the Golden City Vortices. It indeed comes, not as a death star. It is the white star. So Be It.

Response and question: *So Be It. So from your perception, it is coming by in its normal timing and other events have been arranged so that its reception is then welcome?*

Its reception is brought in Divine Order, for again things do not happen *to*, but happen *with*. Now you must also consider that we are constantly readjusting and rearranging, working to mitigate disaster and to bring about a greater effect for the entry into the Golden Age. Do you understand?

Answer: *Yes, I do.*

It is important to not live with fear. It is important to live with life and above all, the Law of Love.

Question: *In addition to our regular work and the work we are continuing with the Doorways for Gobean, is there anything else that you wish us to be doing at this time?*

THE TIME IS NOW

Let us bring about full activation of all of the Golden Cities of the United States. Now when I speak this, you know the Golden Cities themselves are activating in their own timing and intention through the work of the Beloved Ascended Masters and the work of Beloved Babajeran. But when I say, to bring it into a conscious activation, you would be serving, in essence, as a Step-down Transformer to allow the new Master Teachers to come forward in this twenty-year period to heighten the Earth's conscious energy.

Response and question: *I will be happy to do that and to go forward and to complete that as soon as possible. Do we have time to complete all the Golden Cities?*

The time is *now*, as I have always stated Dear one, Dear heart.

Response: *Yes.*

Always live within the time is *now*.

## LOVE OF LIVING

Response and question: *And So Be It, it will be done. I have one other question, 'Greetings and Salutations from your chela. I have a question regarding my health. A doctor recently told me I may be dying from an inoperably damaged, weak, and enlarged heart. I am sixty-two years old and feel well, although I am taking medicine for the affliction. Was this diagnosis accurate? Another doctor disagrees with the first one.'*

Now, it is important to understand that these are diagnosis that are based upon a certain system and only you, yourself, may be able to judge that system. But Dear one, Dear heart, as you well know, the Law of Love is the Law Supreme. It is always important to live your life within this Law of Love. Are you doing the things that you love to do? This is always the most important question I ask the one when they begin to enter the path of healing. Schedule the things that you like to do into your life and do them on a daily basis. This is ever so important. It is also important to understand that life is always eternal, that there is really, in essence, no such thing as death. There is only the Law of Change. Know too that this change would be your choice, if you would choose to leave at any time, you see Dear one. It is important to study the information that I have given on this discourse. For you see Dear one, there is much information that I have given regarding the Violet Flame and disease. And I would suggest that you adhere and use the Violet Flame always at sunrise and sunset. In less than one week, you will begin to notice a difference in your overall health.

Question: *There is more to his question. 'Lori's Jyotish astrologer sees me living a long life. What is your diagnosis? If my heart is damaged and I suspect it is, what caused this condition and what is the cure? I would like to stay, although I occasionally dream of returning to the Great Round, but I do not feel I have accomplished what I am here to do.'*

You have come forward in this lifetime to share the work of spiritual knowledge with humanity at large and to bring this information forward in a greater understanding. You have begun to do some of this work, as it has been shown to you. However, in the next twenty years, you will complete this greater part of your work. This is what is laid out for you, as work within the Earth Plane and Planet. But it is also important to understand, as you begin within this work of sharing this spiritual message with humanity, that you must not ever forget your own spiritual work, the joy of the heart, the love of living. It is important for you to keep your focus upon the Violet Flame and always upon your spiritual liberation. Yes, how nice it would be to return, when we are challenged, to that Great Round. But you are living right now at a time that is a challenge for you, but with my help and assistance. Dear one, take my hand and we shall cross this threshold.

Response: *There are no further questions from anyone.*

I shall now take my leave, and will return at the appointed time. So Be It!

Response: *So Be It and thank you.*

# Appendix A

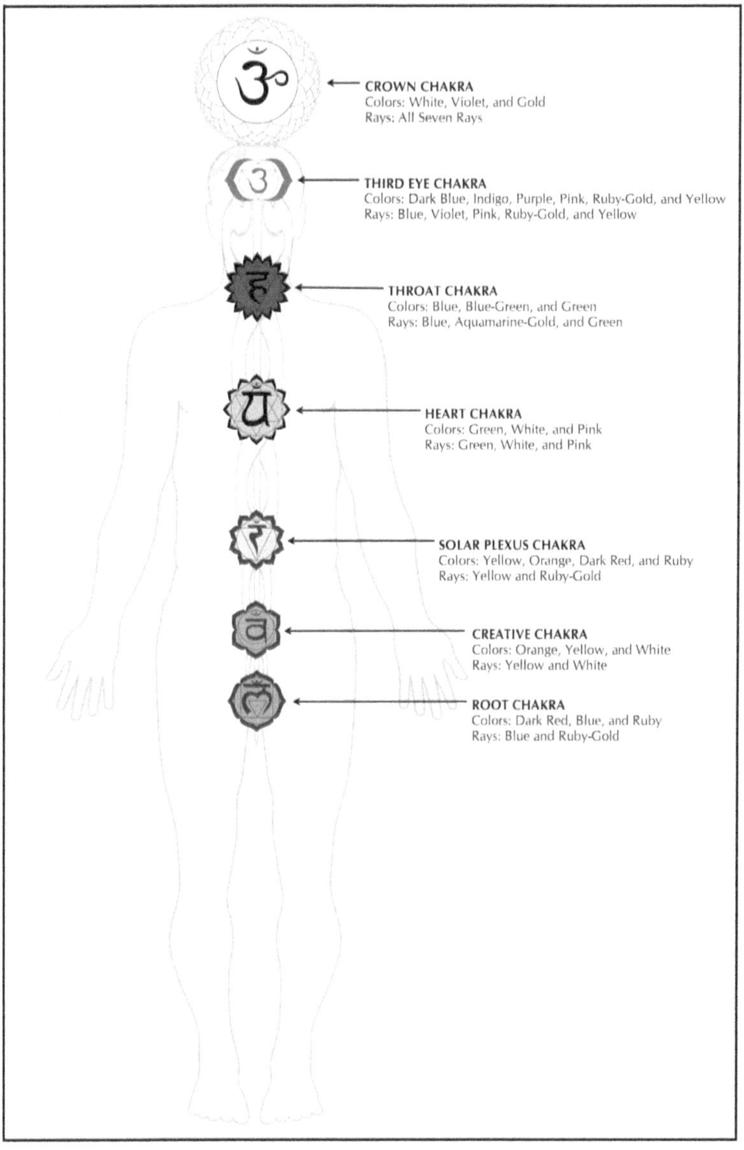

**CROWN CHAKRA**
Colors: White, Violet, and Gold
Rays: All Seven Rays

**THIRD EYE CHAKRA**
Colors: Dark Blue, Indigo, Purple, Pink, Ruby-Gold, and Yellow
Rays: Blue, Violet, Pink, Ruby-Gold, and Yellow

**THROAT CHAKRA**
Colors: Blue, Blue-Green, and Green
Rays: Blue, Aquamarine-Gold, and Green

**HEART CHAKRA**
Colors: Green, White, and Pink
Rays: Green, White, and Pink

**SOLAR PLEXUS CHAKRA**
Colors: Yellow, Orange, Dark Red, and Ruby
Rays: Yellow and Ruby-Gold

**CREATIVE CHAKRA**
Colors: Orange, Yellow, and White
Rays: Yellow and White

**ROOT CHAKRA**
Colors: Dark Red, Blue, and Ruby
Rays: Blue and Ruby-Gold

*Kundalini System*
The *Kundalini System* and the Seven Major
Chakras; the Ancient Caduceus

# Appendix B

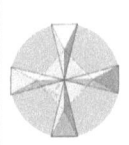 Golden Cities Through the Dimensions

| | THIRD DIMENSION | FOURTH DIMENSION | FIFTH DIMENSION |
|---|---|---|---|
| EVOLUTIONARY ARCHETYPE | The awakened, conscious human. | The HU-man Nature Beings | Ascended Masters Elohim Archangels Evolutionary Archetypes |
| COMMUNITY | Golden City Community. Harmonious connection to Mother Earth. Stewardship | Elemental Kingdom Mineral Kingdom Plant Kingdom Animal Kingdoms Nature Kingdoms | Shamballa (Spiritually perfected community.) |
| ACTIVITY | Longevity Slower aging process. Greater healing and recovery ability. Physical Regeneration (Cell replication) | Telepathic Ability Psychic Ability Development of the Super Senses. Lucid Dreaming Multi-dimensional awareness. | Unana Consciousness of the ONE. Fellowship through the ONE and Oneship. |
| PLANE | Physical | Astral | Causal |
| TIME | Duality Linear Time Continuous time is a series of transactions. | Time Compaction Time Warp Deja Vue *Peak* or *Zone* Experience | Timelessness The Abiding *Presence* Ever Present Now Continuous Flow |
| SOCIAL | Human Rights Civil Rights Twelve Jurisdictions | Group Mind Collective Consciousness Brotherhood and Sisterhood | Unity |
| CULTURE | Cultivation of the Four Pillars: Arts, Languages, Sciences, Ancient Religions and History, Philosophy | Beauty, Harmony, Cooperation | Grace Peace |

*Golden Cities through the Dimensions*

# Appendix C

*DAHL Universe:*
The DAHL Universe, also known as the DAL Universe, is mentioned by Billy Meier as a twin parallel universe created simultaneously with our DERN Universe. Meier is a well-known contactee of the *Plejaren Federation*, from the Pleiades. The early 1970's Pleiadians' mission shared life-enhancing information for humans, such as our true origin and essential laws of creation. Saint Germain affirms many of Meier's disclosures throughout the *I AM America Teachings*, and asserts that evolved, spiritual beings from both the Pleiades and the DAHL have played significant roles tending to the spiritual needs of humanity at timely junctures. According to Meier's spiritual teachers, the DAL means, "Creation as second born."[1]

Saint Germain suggests that evolved Masters from the DAHL assisted civilizations on the Pleiades through critical junctures of spiritual growth and evolution. Today, cosmic Masters from both the DAHL and the Pleiades support the Golden Age on Earth and the creation of the Golden City Network on Earth's surface. According to Meier's Pleiadian advisors, the DAL "nudges the seventh outer belt of our DERN Universe."[2]

Members from both the DAHL Universe and Pleiades Star system allege advanced technology includes both time and travel portals between the parallel creations.

---

1. DAL Universe." http://futureofmankind.co.uk 21 Aug. 2010. Web. 1 Jan. 2019.

2. Ibid.

# Appendix D

*Eight-sided Cell of Perfection within the Human Heart*

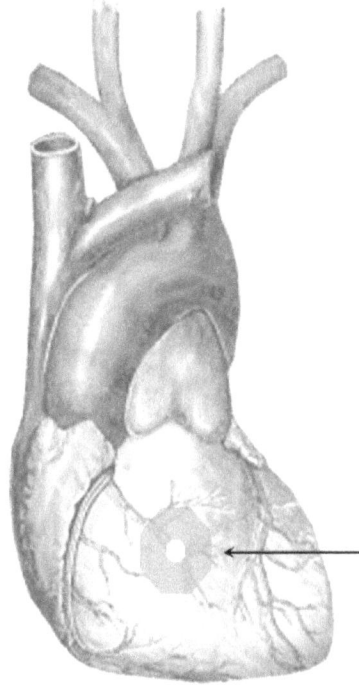

The Eight-sided Cell of Perfection holds the Flame within the Heart
*(not to scale)*

*Eight-Sided Cell of Perfection within the Human Heart*
(Above) According to the Ascended Masters, the Eight-Sided Cell of Perfection is an atomic cell located within the human heart. The cell holds the Unfed Flame, which matures and grows with spiritual development and evolution. The Eight-Sided Cell carries each individual's Divinity.[1]

---

1. Häggström, Mikael. "File:Human Heart.png." Wikimedia Commons. 13 Apr. 2010. Web. 27 Jan. 2011. <http://commons.wikimedia.org/wiki/File:Human_heart.png>.

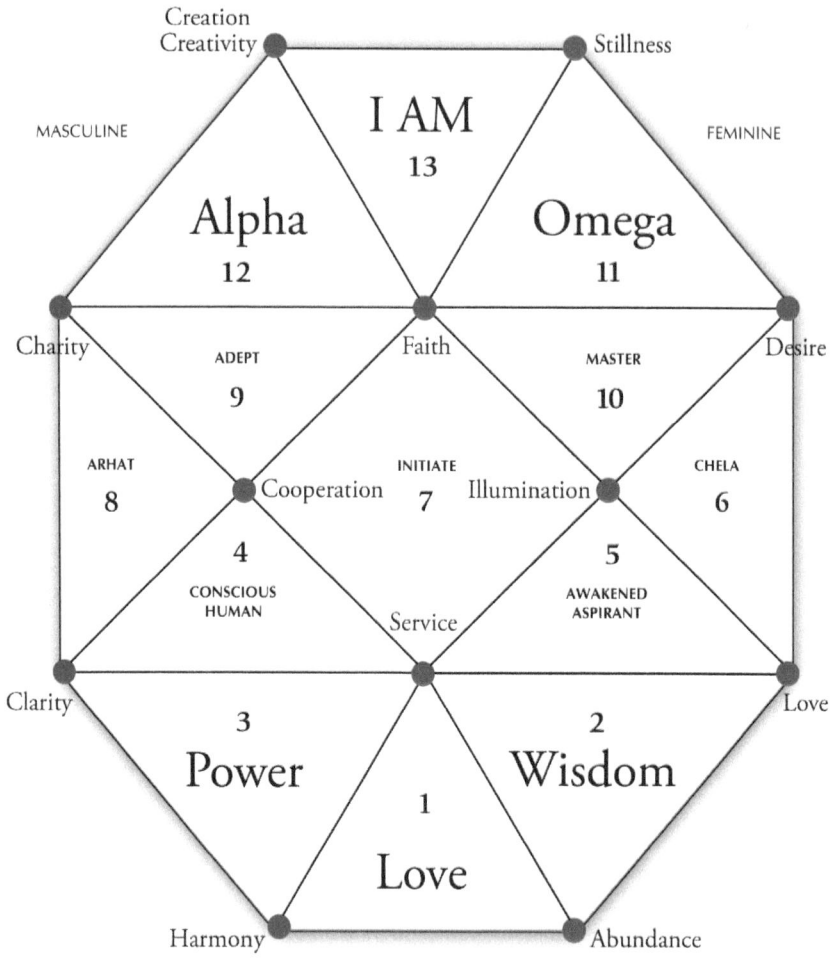

*The Thirteen Pyramids and Twelve Evolution Points of the Eight-Sided Cell of Perfection*
The Thirteen Initiatory Pyramids (stages) of the growth of the HU-man and their states of consciousness depicted in the geometry of the Eight-Sided Cell of Perfection. Also shown are the Twelve Evolution Points (Twelve Jurisdictions).

# Appendix E

*The Violet Flame:*
Simply stated, the Violet Flame stabilizes past karmas through Transmutation, Forgiveness, and Mercy. This leads to the opening of the spiritual heart and the development of bhakti—the unconditional love and compassion for others. Our Co-creative ability is activated through the Ascended Master's gift of the Unfed Flame in adjunct with the practice of the Law of Love, and the Power of Intention. But the Violet Flame, capable of engendering our greatest spiritual growth and evolution, is spiritual velocity pure and simple.

Invoking the flame's force often produces feelings of peace, tranquility, and inner harmony—its ability to lift the low-vibrating energy fields of blame, despair, and fear into forgiveness and understanding, paves the path to love.

The history of the Violet Flame reaches back thousands of years before the Time of Christ. According to Ascended Master legend, the Lords of Venus transmitted the Violet Flame as a spiritual consciousness during the final days of the pre-Atlantis civilization Lemuria. As one society perished and another bloomed, the power of the Violet Flame shifted, opening the way for Atlantean religiosity. This transfer of power initiated a clearing of the Earth's etheric and psychic realms, and purged the lower physical atmosphere of negative forces and energies. Recorded narratives of Atlantis claim that Seven Temples of Purification sat atop visible materializations of the Violet Flame. The archangels Zadkiel and Amethyst, representing freedom, forgiveness and joy, presided over an Atlantean Brotherhood known as the Order of Zadkiel, also associated with Saint Germain. These Violet Flame Temples still exist today in the celestial realm over Cuba.

The Violet Flame benefits humans and divinities equally. During spiritual visualizations, meditations, prayers, decrees, and mantras, many disciples seek the Violet Flame for serenity and wisdom. Meanwhile, the Ascended Masters always use it in inner retreats—even Saint Germain taps into its power to perfect and apply its force with chelas and students

The Violet Flame, rooted in Alchemic powers, is sometimes identified as a higher energy of Saturn and the Blue Ray, a force leavened with justice, love, and wisdom. Ascended-Master lore explains the

Violet Flame's ability to release a person from temporal concerns: Saturn's detachment from emotions and low-lying energies sever worldly connections. That's why the scientific properties of violet light are so important in metaphysical terms. The shortness of its wavelength and the high vibration of its frequency induce a point of transition to the next octave of light and into a keener consciousness.

# *Appendix F*

*The Law of Love:*
In previous teachings the Ascended Masters have affirmed, "If you live love, you will create love." This is foundational to understanding the Law of Love. In further teachings, the Master Teachers expand this concept and explain the concept of love in depth and dimension and declare that through practicing the Law of Love, one experiences acceptance and understanding; tolerance, alongside detachment. Saint Germain elaborates: "The Law of Love brings a sense of detachment. The Law of Love, at times, allows you to turn your back in a trying situation, but yet this Law of Love moves the soul onward and upward in complete understanding of the dual forces." Metaphysically, the Law of Love *allows* different and varied perceptions of ONE experience, situation, or circumstance to exist simultaneously. From this viewpoint the Law of Love is the practice of tolerance. To synthesize Saint Germain's teachings on this venerated yet highly misunderstood spiritual precept: Love + Tolerance = Alchemy (Transformation). This is the philosophical basis of the activity of the Violet Flame.

# Appendix G

## Golden City Vortex Activation Dates

| GOLDEN CITY | VORTEX ACTIVATION (Year) | STAR ACTIVATION (Year) | MASTER TEACHER | COUNTRY |
|---|---|---|---|---|
| GOBEAN | 1981 | 1998 | El Morya | United States |
| MALTON | 1994 | 2011 | Kuthumi | United States |
| WAHANEE | 1996 | 2013 | Saint Germain | United States |
| SHALAHAH | 1998 | 2015 | Sananda | United States |
| KLEHMA | 2000 | 2017 | Serapis Bey | United States |
| PASHACINO | 2002 | 2019 | Soltec | Canada |
| EABRA | 2004 | 2021 | Portia | Unites States, Canada |
| JEAFRAY | 2006 | 2023 | Archangel Zadkiel, Amethyst | Canada |
| UVERNO | 2008 | 2025 | Paul the Venetian | Canada |
| YUTHOR | 2010 | 2027 | Hilarion | Greenland |
| STIENTA | 2012 | 2027 | Archangel Michael | Iceland |
| DENASHA | 2014 | 2031 | Nada | Scotland |
| AMERIGO | 2016 | 2033 | Godfre | Spain |
| GRUECHA | 2018 | 2035 | Hercules | Norway, Sweden |
| BRAUN | 2020 | 2037 | Victory | Germany, Poland Czechoslovakia |
| AFROM | 2022 | 2039 | Claire and Se Ray | Hungary, Romania |
| GANAKRA | 2024 | 2041 | Vista | Turkey |
| MESOTAMP | 2026 | 2043 | Mohammed | Turkey, Iran, Iraq |
| SHEHEZ | 2028 | 2045 | Tranquility | Iran, Afghanistan |
| ADJATAL | 2030 | 2047 | Lord Himalaya | Afghanistan, Pakistan, India |
| PURENSK | 2032 | 2049 | Faith, Hope, and Charity | Russia, China |
| PRANA | 2034 | 2051 | Archangel Chamuel | India |
| GANDAWAN | 2036 | 2053 | Kuthumi | Algeria |
| KRESHE | 2038 | 2055 | Lord of Nature, Amaryllis | Botswana, Namibia |
| PEARLANU | 2040 | 2057 | Lotus | Madagascar |

| GOLDEN CITY | VORTEX ACTIVATION (Year) | STAR ACTIVATION (Year) | MASTER TEACHER | COUNTRY |
| --- | --- | --- | --- | --- |
| UNTE | 2042 | 2059 | Donna Grace | Tanzania, Kenya |
| LARAITO | 2044 | 2061 | Lanto and Laura | Ethiopia |
| MARNERO | 2046 | 2063 | Mary | Mexico |
| ASONEA | 2048 | 2065 | Peter the Everlasting | Cuba |
| ANDEO | 2050 | 2067 | First Sister, Constance, Goddess Meru | Peru, Brazil |
| BRAHAM | 2052 | 2069 | Second Sister | Brazil |
| TEHEKOA | 2054 | 2071 | Third Sister | Argentina |
| CROTESE | 2056 | 2073 | Paul the Devoted | Costa Rica, Panama |
| JEHOA | 2058 | 2075 | Kuan Yin | New Atlantis |
| ZASKAR | 2060 | 2079 | Reya | China |
| GOBI | 2062 | 2079 | Lord Meru | China |
| ARCTURA | 2064 | 2081 | Arcturus | China |
| NOMAKING | 2066 | 2083 | Cassiopea and Minerva | China |
| PRESCHING | 2068 | 2085 | Archangel Jophiel | China, North Korea |
| KANTAN | 2070 | 2087 | Great Divine Mother and Archangel Raphael | China, Russia |
| HUE | 2072 | 2089 | Lord Guatama | Russia |
| SIRCALWE | 2074 | 2091 | Group of Twelve | Russia |
| ARKANA | 2076 | 2093 | Archangel Gabriel | Russia |
| MOUSSE | 2078 | 2095 | Kona | New Lemuria |
| DONJAKEY | 2080 | 2097 | Pacifica | New Lemuria |
| GREIN | 2082 | 2099 | Viseria | New Zealand |
| CLAYJE | 2084 | 2101 | Orion | Australia |
| ANGELICA | 2086 | 2103 | Angelica | Australia |
| SHEAHAH | 2088 | 2105 | Astrea | Australia |
| FRON | 2090 | 2107 | Desiree | Australia |
| CRESTA | 2092 | 2109 | Archangel Crystiel | Antarctica |

# Appendix H

*Golden City Activation:*

A full comprehension of the word "activate" is key to understanding this spiritual phenomena. The following dictionary definitions describe its usage: "to make active;" "to make more active;" "to hasten reactions by various means"; and "to place in active status." So, the term *Golden City Activation* includes several meanings and applications to illustrate the four types of Golden City activations.

1. Ascended Master Activation: *Made Active*

The Spiritual Hierarchy first conceptualized the idea of the Golden Cities by the perfect out-picturing of these spiritual centers. Certain Master Teachers, Archangels, and Elohim—in cooperation with Mother Earth Babajeran—sponsor specific Golden Cities. Their task: to gather the energies of each divine municipality. The grid structure of Earth—in tandem with the focus of the appropriate Ray—is held in immaculate concept by each steward and coalesces the energies of each Golden City. And as consciousness increases, members of mankind seek its Fifth Dimension power as spiritual retreats.

2. Geophysical Activation: *More Active*

The interaction of Mother Earth and the Golden Cities—Fifth Dimensional structures—produces Third and Fourth Dimensional characteristics. This phenomenon creates a more active activation. The significance of Third Dimensional activation lies in its ability to generate a Vortex at the intersection of lei-lines. When eight of these invisible coordinates crisscross, a Vortex emerges, including the formation of Golden City Vortices. Vortices move in a clockwise/counterclockwise motion. Geophysically activated Golden Cities have a profound effect on humans: they experience longevity, greater healing abilities, and physical regeneration. In the Fourth Dimension, Nature Kingdoms begin to interact with Vortex energies; human visitors experience telepathic and psychic abilities, and lucid dreaming. [Lei-lines are magnetic lines of detectable energy.]

3. Ceremonial Activation: *To Hasten Reactions by Various Means*

Ceremonial activations, inspired by humans who seek an intense result from a Golden City, occur on an emotional-astral level in areas throughout these sacred Vortices. Similar to pujas or yagyas—known in Hindu as sacrifices—fire or water-driven ceremonies neutralize difficult karmas and enhance beneficial human qualities.

4. Great Central Sun Activation: *To Place in Active Status*

Produced by a greater timing or origin, this type of activation relies on the energies that emanate from the Great Central Sun or Galactic Center (our universe rotates around a larger Sun). Some theosophical scholars say power from the Galactic Center sends subtle energies to our solar system via the planetary fire triplicity: Jupiter, Mars, and the Sun.

# Appendix I

***Golden City Structure, Perspective:*** Golden Cities are 400 kilometers or 248.5 miles high.

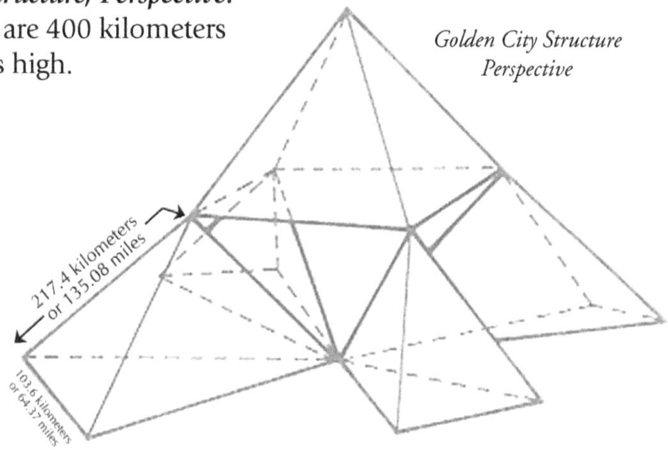

*Golden City Structure Perspective*

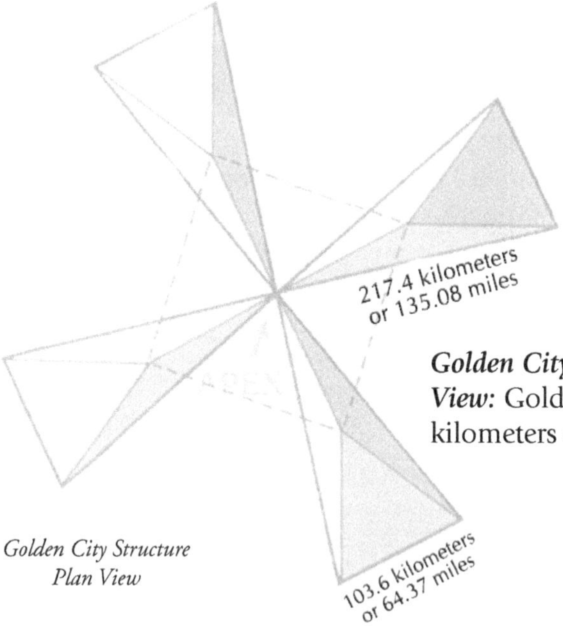

217.4 kilometers or 135.08 miles

103.6 kilometers or 64.37 miles

217.4 kilometers or 135.08 miles

***Golden City Structure, Plan View:*** Golden Cities are 434.8 kilometers or 270 miles across.

*Golden City Structure Plan View*

103.6 kilometers or 64.37 miles

Golden City Series: Book Six

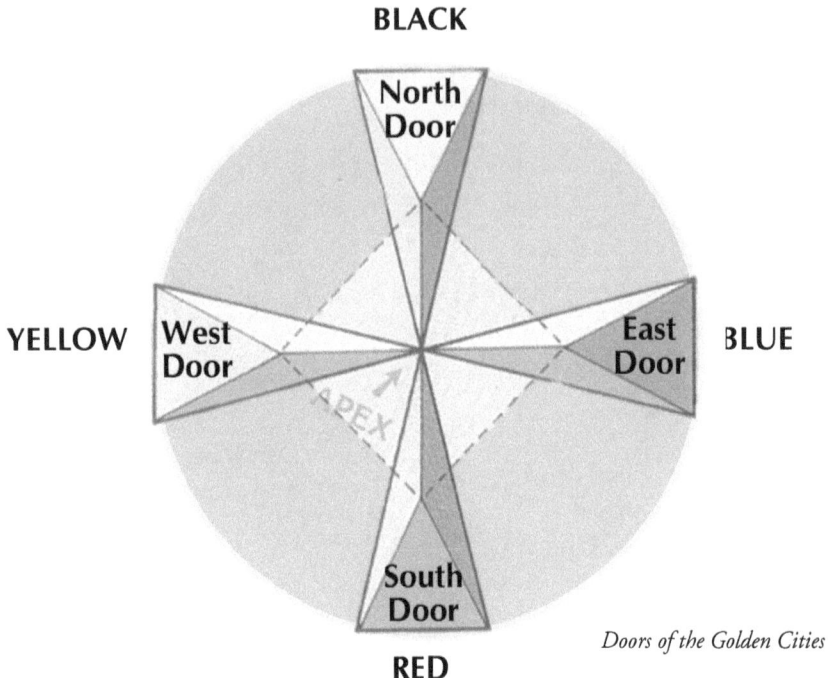

*Doors of the Golden Cities*

*Doors (gateways) of the Golden Cities:*
The four doors of the Golden Cities signify the four directions, and each represents certain attributes and characteristics. They also represent four spiritual pathways or spiritual initiations.

*The Seven Adjutant Points of a Golden City Doorway:*

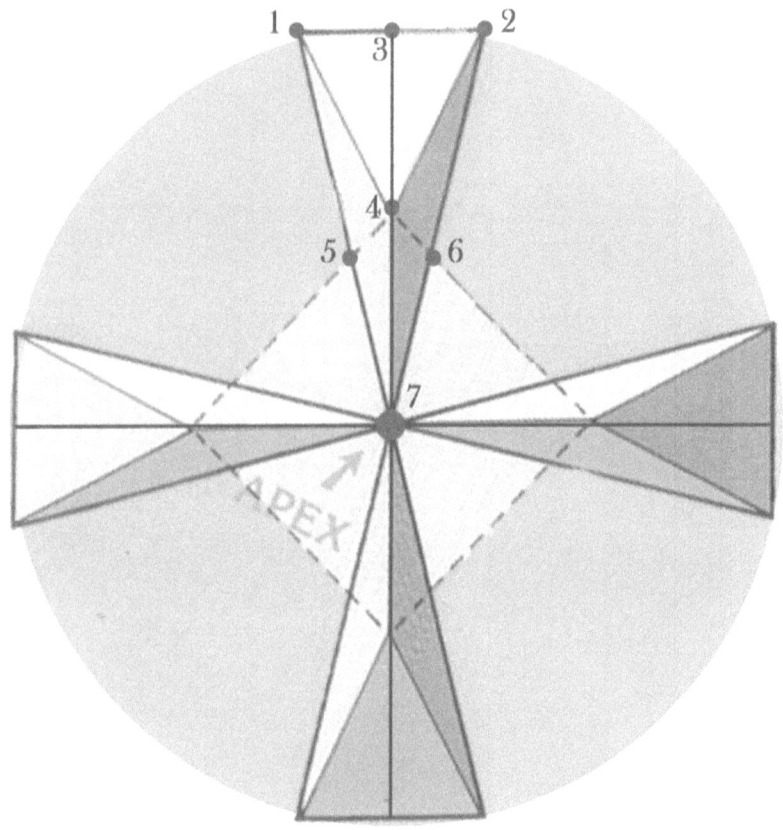

# Appendix J

*Sananda's Sunday Peace Meditation*
In this turbulent Time of Change, Lord Sananda suggests a weekly Sunday Peace Meditation. He instructs:

> "It is important at this time for those who seek the Christ within to find it through inner meditation. First, it is important to silence the mind. This may be done with several decrees, that the individual may choose. But bring within, an inner silence. Sit in contemplation. Gently close the eyes. Focus all energy upon the heart. In that moment of the focus of energy upon the heart, feel within the connection to all of life. Feel, as this heart is connected to all of life, the radiating pulse that is in all living creatures, that is in all living consciousness. This consciousness that permeates all living things is the consciousness of the ONE, Unana. Meditate upon this pulse. Work to hear this pulse within the inner ear. In this inner hearing comes a radiation. This radiation is the growth of a new energy body. This energy source is carried with you throughout the day. Bless all that you come in contact with throughout the day. Carry the radiance of this loving Christ throughout your day. This I encourage all to do."

Unana, or Unity Consciousness, is another name for the unified field of human consciousness. Major General Kulwant Singh of India explains, "This field of consciousness—termed the unified field in the language of quantum physics—is millions of times more fundamental and powerful than nuclear force." Major Singh, a 35-year career army veteran who helped to assemble thousands of meditation experts for peaceful defense explains, "This will produce an indomitable influence of peace and coherence, in the country. No nation will ever be moved to attack India, as it becomes a lighthouse of peace and coherence to its neighbors and the world."

The Stars of Golden City Vortices function with a unique similarity to a technique developed by the late Dr. David Hawkins whose research mapped states of human consciousness known as critical-point analysis. In his book "Power Versus Force," Hawkins explains his process: "Critical point analysis is a technique derived from the fact that in any highly complex system there is a specific critical point at which the smallest input will result in the greatest change. The great gears of a windmill can be halted by lightly touching the right escape mechanism; it is possible to paralyze a giant locomotive if you know exactly where to put your finger."

All spiritual practice, especially prayer and meditation, is extremely effective while one is located in any Star area of a Golden City Vortex for World Peace. The Ascended Masters' instruction focuses on Lord Sananda's Heart Meditation and recommends that a group of seven individuals focused on this meditation can effect personal change for global peace. In essence, this technique is a force field of light, especially when applied within the Star of a Golden City Vortex, where the least amount of energy exerts the greatest effect.

A partial list of towns and cities located in the United States Golden City Stars follows. [Editor's Note: For more information see *I AM America Atlas* and *I AM America United States Golden City Map.*]

*Golden City Star of Gobean*
Pinetop, AZ
Lakeside, AZ
Springerville, AZ
Eagar, AZ

*Golden City Star of Malton*
Mattoon, IL
Charleston, IL
Shelbyville, IL
Sullivan, IL
Humboldt, IL

*Golden City Star of Wahanee*
Augusta, GA
Grovetown, GA
Appling, GA
Harlem, GA
Gracewood, GA
Thompson, GA
Modeo, GA
North Augusta, SC

Trenton, SC
Eureka, SC
Parksville, SC
Kitchings Mill, SC
Williston, SC

*Golden City Star of Shalahah*
Lolo Pass, MT
Lolo, MT
Missoula, MT
Stevensville, MT

*Golden City Star of Klehma*
Cope, CO

# Appendix K

*The Gold Ray*

The Ascended Masters Kuthumi and Saint Germain both prophesy that the Gold Ray is the most important energy force currently present on Earth. While its presence catalyzes the spiritual growth of the HU-man, it is also associated with Karmic Justice and will instigate change at all levels: Earth Changes, economic and social change.

The Master Teachers prophesy that its appearance fosters the dawn of a New Consciousness for humanity, which ends the turbulence of Kali Yuga and ushers in a 10,000-year time of spiritual potential and opportunity for all—the Golden Age of Kali Yuga.

Saint Germain gives this decree to initiate the stream of the New Consciousness within:

> Mighty Golden Ray, stream forth now,
> into the heart of the consciousness of humanity.
> Mighty Golden Ray, bring forth new understanding.
> Bring forth a new Spiritual Awakening.
> Bring forth complete and total Divinity
> In the name of I AM THAT I AM.
> So be it.

This decree allows the Brotherhood to give further aid and contact to individuals who desire the Masters' help and assistance for spiritual development.

The Gold Ray initiates and transforms through the spiritual principles of balance and harmony. Working through the Hermetic Principle of vibration, Saint Germain claims that the Gold Ray creates, "Absolute Harmony." This sublime Ray of Consciousness also helps the chela to shape and form the will and align our emotions and inevitably our actions to the Divine Will. It enters into the Seventh Chakra and its current flows alongside the Golden Thread Axis (Medullar Shushumna). The ideal of Unana—the ONE—is initiated and inevitably created through the presence of the Gold Ray. Saint Germain suggests this decree for the Violet Flame to prepare spiritual consciousness to receive and apply the influence of the Gold Ray.

> Mighty Violet Ray,
> Come forth in all transmuting action.
> Mighty Violet Ray,
> Come forth now and dissolve all discord
> and the cause and effect of all that is holding me
> from understanding and moving forward into the new Golden Age.
> I call this forth in the name of
> That mighty Christ I AM.
> So be it.

The Gold Ray assists humanity's evolution at this important time. This process is calibrated by the premise of vibration and is a developmental step associated with the use of the Violet Flame. Those who apply this teaching may notice a golden tinge in their light bodies, hear a high-pitch sound, or celestial music (the Harmony of the Spheres) before falling asleep or upon awakening. As the Gold Ray floods the Earth with energies to evolve human consciousness this energy is controlled by both the Galactic Center and further calibrated by the Spiritual Hierarchy for humanity.

# *Appendix L*

*Golden Ray Mantra:*

Mantras are alchemical sounds that are chanted for protection or for enhancement of specific Ray Forces. The Golden Ray Mantra provokes the presence of the Golden Ray in our aura, or enhances the affect of the Ray throughout our lightfields. The structure of the mantra is: "Om Banandra, (2x), Om Hunana, (1x), and Om Sunana, (1x)." Its language is *Owaspee*, the divine language of the Angels, often used by the Master Teachers for specific spiritual phrases and Golden City Names.

The etymology of the Golden Ray Mantra breaks down like this:

*Om*: Invokes the presence of our solar Sun that step-downs the sublime energy of the Great Central Sun, the Galactic Center.

*Bunandra*: Means "delight," or "of the light."

*Hunana*: A melodic version of the "HU," a bija-seed mantra that invokes the presence of all of the Rays, and primarily the transformative Violet Ray.

*Sunana*: Invokes the presence of Sanat Kumara, the ancestral Ascended Master who now resides in the higher dimensions of Venus. Sanat Kumara was the venerated leader and master planner of Shamballa that serves as the formative template of all Golden Cities.

# Appendix M

*"Why should I listen to channeled tapes?"*

The Spiritual Lessons from the Master Teachers are voice-received trance channeling (clairaudient) and every effort is made to keep the recordings in their authentic, original condition. There are no alterations to the sound quality so each listener may receive full benefit of the vibrational energy through this unique type of trance-work and its transformational healing effect. We keep this information on cassette tape, as digital conversion will destroy the natural magnetism that is also conveyed and recorded throughout each individual trance session. The unique combination of the Teacher's magnetism and their consciousness-expanding wisdom transmits an essential, yet precious Alchemy that is rarely achieved through conventional spiritual pursuit.

Listening to authentic I AM America trance-work has many benefits, including:

- Access to the subconscious mind, (astral state), while simultaneously connecting to the conscious mind, (physical state).
- Circumvents the ego state and activates the spiritual self—the I AM.
- Provides vital spiritual experience of varied states of consciousness.
- Creates unity with the I AM—the God state of consciousness.
- Initiates Oneness and Unity Consciousness.
- Opens the God Mind through the use of metaphor and active, flowing imagery.
- Transforms negative beliefs and establishes positive, life-affirming knowledge.
- Reduces stress and emotional pain.
- Helps to release and lessen difficult karmas and spiritual blockages.
- Balances energy fields, (aura), and produces harmony, peace, and well-being.

- Awakens our spiritual potential and innate Divinity.
- Can produce spiritual ecstatic states or peak experiences, described in the works of Abraham Maslow.

Listening to trance-work can evoke a similar state of trance-consciousness. It is suggested to listen to channeled tapes when you are awake, calm, and receptive to personal spiritual growth and experience.

# Appendix N

*Saint Germain, the Holy Brother:*
The Lord of the Seventh Ray and the Master of the Violet Flame, Saint Germain lived numerous noteworthy lifetimes, dating back thousands of years, before incarnating as the Comte de Saint Germain during Renaissance Europe. He lived as the Englishman Sir Francis Bacon, the sixteenth-century philosopher, essayist, and Utopian who greatly influenced the philosophy of inductive science. His most profound and well-known work on the restoration of humanity, the *Instauratio Magna* (Great Restoration), defined him as an icon of the Elizabethan era. Research also shows his co-authoring of many Shakespearean sonnets.

According to Esoteric historians, Queen Elizabeth I of England—The Virgin Queen—was his biological mother. Before Bacon's birth, the queen married Earl of Leicester, quieting ideas of illegitimacy. Elizabeth's lady in waiting, Lady Ann Bacon, wife of the Lord High Chancellor of England, adopted him following the stillbirth of her baby. Bacon was, therefore, the true heir to the crown and England's rightful king.[1] But his cousin James I of Scotland succeeded the throne. Sir Bacon described this turn of events in his book, Novum Organo, published in 1620: "It is an immense ocean that surrounds the island of Truth." And Saint Germain often reminds us to this day "there are no mistakes, ever, ever, ever."

Bacon's philosophies also helped define the principles of Free Masonry and democracy. As an adept leader of the Rosicrucians (a secret society of that time), he set out to reveal the obsolescence and oppression of European monarchies.

Eventually, Bacon's destiny morphed. He shed his physical form and sought the greatest gift of all: immortality. And that's what placed him in the most extraordinary circumstances throughout history. Even his death (or lack of) evokes controversy. Some say Bacon faked his demise in 1626—the coffin contained the carcass of a dog.

---

1. Marie Bauer Hall, *Foundations Unearthed*, originally issued as *Francis Bacon's Great Virginia Vault*, Fourth Edition (Los Angeles: Veritas Press), page 9.

According to the author, ADK Luk, Saint Germain ascended on May 1, 1684 in Transylvania at the Rakoczy mansion. He was 123 years old. Some say Saint Germain spent the lost years—from 1626 to 1684—in Tibet. During this time he took (or may have been given) the name *Kajaeshra*. Interpreted as *God's helper of life* and *wisdom*, it was possibly a secret name and rarely used. Kaja has several interpretations: in Greek it means *pure*; Balinese, *toward the mountain*; early Latin (Estonian), *echo*; Hopi, *wise child*; Polish, *of the Gods*; and Hebrew, *life*. The second part of the name—Eshra (Ezra)—translates into *help* or *aid*.

Indeed, Bacon's work would impact centuries to follow. During his time in Tibet, tucked away in silent monasteries, Germain designed a society that eventually created a United Brotherhood of the Earth: Solomon's Temple of the Future. It's a metaphor used to describe the raising of consciousness as the greater work of democracy. Author Marie Bauer Hall studied the life of Francis Bacon. In her book, *Foundations Unearthed*, she described the legendary edifice: "This great temple was to be supported by the four mighty pillars of history, science, philosophy, and religion, which were to bear the lofty dome of Universal Fellowship and Peace."[2]

But Germain embraced an even deeper passion: the people and nation of America, christening it *New Atlantis*. He envisioned this land—present-day United States, Canada, Mexico, and South America—as part of the United Democracies of Europe and the People of the World. America, this growing society, held his hope for a future guided by a Democratic Brotherhood.

The Comte de Saint Germain emerged years later in the courts of pre-revolutionary France—his appearance, intelligence, and worldliness baffled members of the Court of Versailles. This gentleman carried the essence of eternal youth: he was a skilled artist and musician; he spoke fluent German, English, French, Italian, Portuguese, Spanish, Greek, Latin, Sanskrit, Arabic, and Chinese; and he was a proficient chemist. Meanwhile, literary, philosophic, and political aristocracy of the time sought his company. French philosophers Jean-Jacque Rousseau and Voltaire; the Italian adventurer Giacomo Casanova; and the Earl of Chatham and statesman Sir Robert Walpole of Britain were among his friends.

---

2. Marie Bauer Hall, *Foundations Unearthed*, originally issued as *Francis Bacon's Great Virginia Vault*, Fourth Edition (Los Angeles: Veritas Press), page 13.

In courts throughout Europe, he dazzled royalty with his Mastery of Alchemy, removing flaws from gems and turning lead into Gold. And the extent of Germain's ken reached well into the theosophical realm. A guru of yogic and tantric disciplines, he possessed highly developed telepathic and psychic abilities. This preternatural knowledge led to the development of a cartographic Prophecy—the Map of Changes. This uncanny blueprint, now in the hands of the scion of Russian aristocracy, detailed an imminent restructuring of the political and social boundaries of Europe.[3]

But few grasped Germain's true purpose during this time of historic critical mass: not even the king and queen of France could comprehend his tragic forewarnings. The Great White Brotherhood—a fellowship of enlightened luminaries—sent the astute diplomat Saint Germain to orchestrate the development of the United States of Europe. Not only a harbinger of European diplomacy, he made his presence in America during the germinal days of this country. Esoteric scholars say he urged the signing of the Declaration of Independence in a moment of collective fear—a fear of treason and ultimately death. Urging the forefathers to proceed, a shadowed figure in the back of the room shouted: *Sign that document!*

To this day, the ironclad identity of this person remains a mystery, though some mystics believe it was Saint Germain. Nevertheless, his avid support spurred the flurry of signatures, sealing the fate of America—and the beginning of Sir Francis Bacon's democratic experiment.

The Comte de Saint Germain never could shape a congealed Europe, but he did form a lasting and profound relationship with America. Germain's present-day participation in U.S. politics reaches the Oval Office. Some theosophical mystics say Germain visits the president of the United States the day after the leader's inauguration; others suggest he's the fabled patriot Uncle Sam.

Saint Germain identifies with the qualities of Brotherhood and freedom. He is the sponsor of humanity and serves as a conduit of Violet Light—a force some claim is powerful enough to propel one into Ascension.

---

3. K. Paul Johnson, *The Masters Revealed: Madame Blavatsky and the Myth of the Great White Lodge (Suny Series in Western Esoteric Traditions)* (Albany, NY: State University of New York Press), page 19.

# *Appendix O*

*The Twelve Jurisdictions:*
Twelve Laws (virtues) for the New Times that guide consciousness to Co-create the Golden Age. The Twelve Jurisdictions in sequence are:

1. **Harmony:** The first virtue of the Twelve Jurisdictions based on the principle of the Law of Agreement.

2. **Abundance:** The second of the Twelve Jurisdictions is the principle of overflowing fullness in all situations and circumstances based on the Law of Choice.

3. **Clarity:** The third of the Twelve Jurisdictions lends lucidity to our perceptions through the Law of Non-Judgment.

4. **Love:** "Light in action." The fourth of the Twelve Jurisdictions evolves our understanding of love as the Law of Allowing, Maintaining, and Sustainability.

5. **Service:** The fifth of Twelve Jurisdictions is a helpful act based upon the Law of Love.

6. **Illumination:** The sixth of the Twelve Jurisdictions gives light to our life without fear or judgment.

7. **Cooperation:** The seventh of the Twelve Jurisdictions advises joint actions, work, and assistance to faithfully adhere with fairness, honesty, and the acknowledgment of the Divine Presence.

8. **Charity:** The eighth of the Twelve Jurisdictions deems the generous actions of Charity as the everyday habit of living with love and equity.

9. **Desire:** Of the source; the ninth of Twelve Jurisdictions states the heart's desire is the source of creation.

10. **Faith:** The tenth of the Twelve Jurisdictions places confidence and trust in our innate creative birthright.

11. **Stillness:** The eleventh of the Twelve Jurisdictions produces motionless quiet as the foundation of the Law of Alignment.

12. **Creation-Creativity:** The final spiritual precept of the Twelve Jurisdictions is best understood as the engendered Law of Divine Order.

Through the application and practice of the Twelve Jurisdictions, a refined state of higher consciousness develops, known as the *Sea of Consciousness*. This allows one to enter into a state of Unity Consciousness, or the ONE. This entrance marks the development of faculties that in the ordinary human are dormant, and this awakening hones the mind, its perceptions, and development of the Will and the ability to make effective choices and decisions. This mindful discernment parallels the development of the Super Senses and the transcendent reunion with the I AM Presence. The entrance into the state of universal consciousness results in personal tranquility and peace, and produces a sharpened and attentive awareness that pierces illusion and the mental phenomenon of both the Physical and Astral Planes. It is the acclaimed level of consciousness attained by Buddha and the frequent domain of mystics, enlightened spiritual teachers, and those on the Path of Ascension.

# *Spiritual Lineage of the Violet Flame*

The teachings of the Violet Flame, as taught in the work of I AM America, come through the Goddess of Compassion and Mercy Kuan Yin. She holds the feminine aspects of the flame, which are Compassion, Mercy, Forgiveness, and Peace. Her work with the Violet Flame is well documented in the history of Ascended Master teachings, and it is said that the altar of the etheric Temple of Mercy holds the flame in a Lotus Cup. She became Saint Germain's teacher of the Sacred Fire in the inner realms, and he carried the masculine aspect of the flame into human activity through Purification, Alchemy, and Transmutation. One of the best means to attract the beneficent activities of the Violet Flame is through the use of decrees and invocation. However, you can meditate on the flame, visualize the flame, and receive its transmuting energies like "the light of a thousand Suns," radiant and vibrant as the first day that the Elohim Arcturus and Diana drew it forth from our solar Sun at the creation of the Earth. Whatever form, each time you use the Violet Flame, these two Master Teachers hold you in the loving arms of its action and power.

The following is an invocation for the Violet Flame to be used at sunrise or sunset. It is utilized while experiencing the visible change of night to day, and day to night. In fact, if you observe the horizon at these times, you will witness light transitioning from pinks to blues, and then a subtle violet strip adorning the sky. We have used this invocation for years in varying scenes and circumstances, overlooking lakes, rivers, mountaintops, deserts, and prairies; in huddled traffic and busy streets; with groups of students or sitting with a friend; but more commonly alone in our home or office, with a glint of soft light streaming from a window. The result is always the same: a calm, centering force of stillness. We call it *the Space*.

**Invocation of the Violet Flame for Sunrise and Sunset**
I invoke the Violet Flame to come forth in the name of I AM that I AM,

To the Creative Force of all the realms of all the Universes, the Alpha, the Omega, the Beginning, and the End,
To the Great Cosmic Beings and Torch Bearers of all the realms of all the Universes,
And the Brotherhoods and Sisterhoods of Breath, Sound, and Light, who honor this Violet Flame that comes forth from the Ray of Divine Love—the Pink Ray, and the Ray of Divine Will—the Blue Ray of all Eternal Truths.

I invoke the Violet Flame to come forth in the name of I AM that I AM!
Mighty Violet Flame, stream forth from the Heart of the Central Logos, the Mighty Great Central Sun! Stream in, through, and around me.

(Then insert other prayers and/or decrees for the Violet Flame.)

# Glossary

**Abundance**: The second of the Twelve Jurisdictions is the principle of overflowing fullness in all situations and circumstances based on the Law of Choice.

**Acceleration:** A rapid rate of change of velocity, especially with respect to Spiritual Development and the perception of time.

**Adjutant Point**: Power points that form where the lei-lines of the geometric Maltese cross formation of a Golden City traverse or intersect. Adjutant points support the infrastructure of a Golden City, both geometrically and spiritually, and assist and disburse the unique energies held by Babajeran, the Ascended Masters, and the Golden City's Ray Force.

**Akashic Record**: Timeless, immortal records of all created things, especially souls and their many lifetimes.

**Alchemy**: The process of transmutation.

**Alignment**: Convergence or adjustment.

**Ancestral Planet:** A hidden planet, whose view is obscured by the dark, twin Sun. Its inhabitants are highly evolved Spiritual Beings who assist humanity during times of evolutionary darkness.

**Archangels** (the Seven): The seven principal angels of creation are: Michael, the Blue Ray; Jophiel, the Yellow Ray; Chamuel, the Pink Ray; Gabriel, the White Ray; Raphael, the Green Ray; Uriel, the Ruby Ray; and Zadkiel, the Violet Ray.

**Ascended Masters**: Once an ordinary human, an Ascended Master has undergone a spiritual transformation over many lifetimes. He or she has Mastered the lower planes—mental, emotional, and physical—to unite with his or her God-Self or I AM Presence. An Ascended Master is freed from the Wheel of Karma. He or she moves forward in spiritual evolution beyond this planet; however, an Ascended Master remains attentive to the spiritual well-being of humanity, inspiring and serving the Earth's spiritual growth and evolution.

**Ascension**: A process of Mastering thoughts, feelings, and actions that balance positive and negative karmas. It allows entry to a higher state of consciousness and frees a person from the need to reincarnate on the lower Earthly planes or lokas of experience. Ascension is the process of spiritual liberation, also known as moksha.

**Ascension Process**: The Ascension Process, according to Saint Germain, gathers the energies of the individual chakras and expands their energy through the heart. The Law of Love calibrates the energy fields (aura) to Zero Point—a physical and philosophical viewpoint of neutrality. From there, the subtle and fine tuning of the light bodies is effectuated through the higher chakras, sequentially including the Throat Chakra, the Third Eye Chakra, and finally the Crown Chakra. Zero Point is crucial in this process and it is here that the energies of all past lives are brought to psychological and physical (karmic) balance. Then the initiate is able to withdraw their light bodies from the physical plane into the Astral Light of the Fourth Dimension. The Ascension Process may take several lifetimes to complete and the beginning stages are defined through the arduous process of obtaining self-knowledge, the acceptance of the conscious immortality of the soul, and the use of Alchemy through the Violet Flame. Intermediate stages may manifest the anomalies of Dimensional Acceleration, Vibrational Shifting, Cellular Awakening and Acceleration, and contact with the Fourth Dimension. Use of the Gold Ray at this level accelerates the liberation process and unites the individual with soul mates and their beloved Twin Ray. Later stages of Ascension include the transfiguration of light bodies and Fifth Dimensional contact through the super-senses as the magnificent Seamless Garment manifests its light. It is claimed that the Golden Cities assist the Ascension Process at every stage of development. According to the Master Teachers diet and fasting will also aid the Ascension Process at various phases.

**Astral Body or Plane**: The subtle light body that contains our feelings, desires, and emotions. It exists as an intermediate light body between the physical body and the Causal body (Mental Body). According to the Master Teachers, we enter the Astral Plane through our Astral Body when we sleep, and many dreams and visions are experiences in this Plane of vibrant color and sensation. Through spiritual development, the Astral Body strengthens, and the luminosity of its light is often detected in the physical plane. Spiritual adepts may have the ability to consciously leave their physical bodies while traveling in their Astral Bodies. The Astral Body or Astral Plane has various levels of evolution and is the heavenly abode where the soul resides after the disintegration of the physical body. The Astral Body is also known as the Body Double, the Desire Body, and the Emotional Body.

**Atlantis**: An ancient civilization of Earth, whose mythological genesis was the last Puranic Dvapara Yuga—the Bronze Age of the Yugas, and its demise occurred around the year 9628 BC. The legends of Atlantis claim the great empire co-existed with Ameru, Lemuria, and the Lands of Rama. According to Theosophical thought, Atlantis's evolving humanity brought about an evolutionary epoch of the Pink Ray on Earth, and the development of the Astral-Emotional bodies and the Heart Chakra. Ascended Master provenance claims the Els—now the Mighty Elohim of the Seven Rays—were the original Master Teachers to the spiritual seekers of Atlantis. Esoteric historians suggest three phases of political and geophysical boundaries best describe its ancient record: the Toltec Nation of Atlantis (Ameru); the Turian Nation of Atlantis (the invaders of the Land of Rama); and Poseid, the Island Nation of the present-day Atlantic Ocean. The early civilizations of Atlantis were ruled by the spiritually evolved Toltec and their spiritual teachings, ceremonies, and temples were dedicated to the worship of the sun. Atlantean culture later deteriorated into the use of nuclear weapons and cruelty towards other nations, including the use of genetic engineering. The demise of Atlantis was inevitable; however, modern-day geologists, archaeologists, and occultists all disagree to its factual timing. Ascended Master teachings affirm that Atlantis—a continent whose geophysical and political existence probably spanned well over 100,000 years—experienced several phases of traumatic Earth Change. This same belief is held by occult historians who allege Earth repeatedly cycles through periods of massive Earth Change and cataclysmic pole-shifts that activate tectonic plates which subsequently submerge whole continents and create vital new lands for Earth's successors.

**Aura**: The subtle energy field of luminous light that surrounds the human body.

**Babajeran**: A name for the Earth Mother that means, "Grandmother rejoicing."

**Balance**: "Put into proper order."

**Belief:** An opinion, conviction, or doctrine based upon insufficient grounds, or proof.

**Blue Ray**: A Ray is a perceptible light and sound frequency, and the Blue Ray not only resonates with the color blue, but is identified with the qualities of steadiness, calm, perseverance, transformation, harmony, diligence, determination, austerity, protection, humility, truthfulness, and self-negation. It forms one-third of the Unfed Flame within the heart—the Blue Ray of God Power, which nourishes the spiritual unfoldment of the human into the HU-man. Use of the Violet Flame evokes the Blue Ray into action throughout the light bodies, where the Blue Ray clarifies intentions and assists the alignment of the Will. In Ascended Master teachings the Blue

Ray is alleged to have played a major role in the physical manifestation of the Earth's first Golden City—Shamballa and six of fifty-one Golden Cities emanate the Blue Ray's peaceful, yet piercing frequencies. The Blue Ray is esoterically linked to the planet Saturn, the development of the Will, the ancient Lemurian Civilization, the Archangel Michael, the Elohim Hercules, the Master Teacher El Morya, and the Eastern Doors of all Golden Cities.

**Cause and effect**: Every action causes an event, which is the consequence or result of the first. This law is often referred to as karma—or the sixth Hermetic Law.

**Chakra(s)**: Sanskrit for wheel. Seven spinning wheels of human-bioenergy centers stacked from the base of the spine to the top of the head.

**Chela**: Disciple

**Choice**: Will

**Christ, the or Christ Consciousness**: The highest energy or frequency attainable on Earth. The Christ is a Step-down Transformer of the I AM energies, which enlighten, heal, and transform all human conditions of degradation and death.

**Co-creation**: Creating with the God-Source.

**Collective Consciousness**: The higher interactive structure of consciousness as two or more.

**Compassion**: Sensitivity and understanding for another's suffering and the desire to give aid to relieve human pain, distress, and anguish.

**Consciousness**: Awakening to one's own existence, sensations, and cognitions.

**Decree**: Statements of intent and power, similar to prayers and mantras, which are often integrated with the use of the I AM and requests to the I AM Presence.

**Desire**: Of the Source.

**Divine Inheritor**: Successor and progeny of the inner God-Source.

**Divine Plan**: The outcome of creative and Co-creative processes that provoke spiritual growth and evolution. From a traditional viewpoint, the will of God.

**Divine Will**: The idea of God's plan for humanity; however, from the perspective of the HU-man, the Divine Will is "choice."

**Duality**: An understanding that the world is divided into two perceptible categories.

**Dvapara Yuga:** The Age of Bronze, both equal in sin and virtue, when Earth receives twenty-five to fifty percent of light from the Galactic Center.

**Earth Changes**: A prophesied Time of Change on the Earth, including geophysical, political, and social changes, alongside the opportunity for spiritual and personal transformation.

**Earth's Grids**: Geometrical patterns that cover the Earth and follow symmetrical links to sacred geometry and crystalline shapes.

**Eastern Door**: The East side of a Golden City gateway, also known as the Blue Door.

**Eighth Light Body:** Known as the *Buddha Body* or the *Field of Awakening*, this energy body is initially three to four feet from the human body. It begins by developing two visible grid-like spheres of light that form in the front and in the back of the Human Aura. The front sphere is located three to four feet in front of and between the Heart and Solar Plexus Chakras. The back sphere is located in front of and between the Will-to-Love and Solar Will Chakras. These spheres activate an ovoid of light that surrounds the entire human body; an energy field associated with harmonizing and perfecting the Ascension Process. This is the first step toward Mastery. Once developed and sustained, this energy body grants physical longevity and is associated with immortality. It is known as the first level of Co-creation, and is developed through control of the diet and disciplined breath techniques. Once this light body reaches full development, the spheres dissipate and dissolve into a refined energy field, resembling a metallic armor. The mature Eighth Light Body then contracts and condenses, to reside within several inches of the physical body where it emits a silver-blue sheen.

**Eight-sided Cell of Perfection**: An atomic cell located in the human heart. It is associated with all aspects of perfection, and contains and maintains a visceral connection with the Godhead.

**Elemental**: A nature being.

**Elemental Kingdom**: A kingdom comprising an invisible, subhuman group of creatures who act as counterparts to visible nature on Earth.

**El Morya**: Ascended Master of the Blue Ray, associated with the development of the will.

**Emotional Body**: A subtle body of light that exists alongside the physical body. It comprises desires, emotions, and feelings.

**Energy Field**: Distinct and definable layers of energy that exist around all forms of physical life: mineral, plant, animal, and human.

**Energy for energy**: The transfer of energies. To understand this spiritual principle, one must remember Isaac Newton's Third Law of Motion: "for every action there is an equal and opposite reaction." However, while energies may be equal, their forms often vary. The Ascended Masters often use this phrase to remind chelas to properly compensate others to avoid karmic retribution, and repayment may take many different forms.

**Feng-shui twenty-year cycles**: According to Taoist understanding, the Earth undergoes a cyclic series of nine twenty-year segments. This is known as the *Nine Cycles*, a total of one hundred and eighty years. A further division of the one-hundred and eighty years is the *Three Eras*—sixty years each, comprised of upper, middle, and lower. Universal energy is said to change during each of the Three Eras, and Earth is currently in the Lower Era which started in 1984. Each era contains three cycles of twenty years each, hence the Nine Cycles. According to Taoist philosophy small changes occur between cycles; considerable changes occur between eras. Currently Earth is in the eighth cycle that began in 2004. The ninth cycle begins in 2024. The flow of universal energy significantly changes between each of the Nine Cycles, or every twenty years. The Ascended Masters often refer to the twenty-year cycles of the Earth, and their influence on culture, societies, and individuals. They prophesy a twenty-year period that is likely the Ninth Cycle, in the year 2024, or the Beginning of the Upper Era (first cycle) in 2044, when the spiritual Masters appear on Earth, in physical bodies to teach and heal the masses.

**Fifth Dimension**: A spiritual dimension of cause, associated with thoughts, visions, and aspirations. This is the dimension of the Ascended Masters and the Archetypes of Evolution, the city of Shamballa, and the templates of all Golden Cities.

**Fourth Dimension**: A dimension of vibration associated with telepathy, psychic ability, and the dream world. This is the dimension of the Elemental Kingdom and the development of the super senses.

**Gateway Adjutant Points**: Two Golden City power points that are located on either side of each directional gateway of a Golden City Vortex and are situated to the outer perimeter of the Vortex.

**Gobean**: The first United States Golden City located in the states of Arizona and New Mexico. Its qualities are cooperation, harmony, and peace. Its Ray Force is blue, and its Master Teacher is El Morya.

**Gobi**: Steps-down the energies of Shamballa into the entire Golden City Network. This Golden City is located in the Gobi Desert. It is known as the City of Balance, and means Across the Star; its Master Teachers are Lord Meru and Archangel Uriel.

**Golden Age**: A peaceful time on Earth prophesied to occur after the Time of Change. It is also prophesied that during this age human life spans are increased and sacred knowledge is revered. During this time the societies, cultures, and the governments of Earth reflect spiritual enlightenment through worldwide cooperation, compassion, charity, and love. Ascended Master teachings often refer to the Golden Age as the Golden-Crystal Age and the Age of Grace.

**Golden Age of Kali Yuga**: According to the classic Puranic timing of the Yugas, Earth is in a Kali-Yuga period that started around the year 3102 BCE the year that Krishna allegedly left the Earth. During this time period, which according to this Puranic timing lasts a total of 432,000 years—the ten-thousand year Golden Age period, also known as the Golden Age of Kali Yuga, is not in full force. Instead, it is a sub-cycle of higher light frequencies within an overall larger phase of less light energy.

    This Golden Age is prophesied to raise the energy of Earth as additional light from the Galactic Center streams to our planet. This type of light is a non-visible, quasar-type light that is said to expand life spans and memory function, and nourish human consciousness, especially spiritual development. There are many theories as to when this prescient light energy began to flow to our planet. Some say it started about a thousand years ago, and others claim it began at the end of the nineteenth century. No doubt its influence has changed life on Earth for the better, and according to the I AM America Teachings, its effect began to encourage and guide human spiritual evolution around the year 2000 CE.

    The Spiritual Teachers say that living in Golden Cities can magnify Galactic Energies and at their height, the energies will light the Earth between 45 to 48 percent—nearly reaching the light energies of a full-spectrum

Treta Yuga or Silver Age on Earth. The Spiritual Teachers state, "The Golden Age is the period of time where harmony and peace shall be sustained."

**Golden City Doorway**: The four gateways of the Golden City Vortex based on the cardinal directions of North, East, South, and West. They comprise the North Door (or the Black Door); the East Door (or the Blue Door); the South Door (or the Red Door); the West Door (or the Yellow Door). The center of a Golden City is known as the "Star" and is affiliated with the color white.

**Golden City Grid**: The matrix comprised of all Golden Cities covering the Earth.

**Golden City Vortex**: A Golden City Vortex—based on the Ascended Masters' I AM America material—are prophesied areas of safety and spiritual energies during the Times of Changes. Covering an expanse of land and air space, these sacred energy sites span more than 400 kilometers (270 miles) in diameter, with a vertical height of 400 kilometers (250 miles). Golden City Vortices, more importantly, reach beyond terrestrial significance and into the ethereal realm. This system of safe harbors acts as a group or universal mind within our galaxy, connecting information seamlessly and instantly with other beings. Fifty-one Golden City Vortices are stationed throughout the world, and each carries a different meaning, a combination of Ray Forces, and a Divine Purpose. A Golden City Vortex works on the principles of electromagnetism and geology. Vortices tend to appear near fault lines, possibly serving as conduits of inner-earth movement to terra firma. Golden Cities are symbolized by a Maltese Cross, whose sacred geometry determine their doorways, lei-lines, adjutant points, and coalescing Star energies. Since their energies intensify experiences with both the Fourth and Fifth Dimensions, Golden City Vortices play a vital role with the Ascension Process. The clockwise motion of the Vortex absorbs energy from its Ray Force, Ascended Master Hierarch, the Great Central Sun, and Mother Earth—Babajeran. Its counterclockwise motion releases energy. The spin of the Vortex creates a torsion field.

**Gold(en) Ray**: The Ray of Brotherhood, Cooperation, and Peace. The Gold Ray produces the qualities of perception, honesty, confidence, courage, and responsibility. It is also associated with leadership, independence, authority, ministration, and justice. The Gold Ray is currently influencing the spiritual growth and evolution of the divine HU-man. It is also associated with karmic justice and will instigate many changes throughout our planet including Earth Changes and social and economic change.

**Golden Thread Axis**: Also known as the Vertical Power Current. The Golden Thread Axis physically consists of the Medullar Shushumna, a life-giving nadi comprising one-third of the human Kundalini system. Two vital currents intertwine around the Golden Thread Axis: the lunar Ida Current, and the solar Pingala Current. According to the Master Teachers, the flow of the Golden Thread Axis begins with the I AM Presence, enters the Crown Chakra, and descends through the spinal system. It descends beyond the Base Chakra and travels to the core of the Earth. Esoteric scholars often refer to the axis as the Rod of Power, and it is symbolized by two spheres connected by an elongated rod. Ascended Master students and chelas frequently draw upon the energy of the Earth through the Golden Thread Axis for healing and renewal using meditation, visualization, and breath. *See Tube of Light*

**Great Central Sun**: The great Sun of our galaxy, around which all of the galaxy's solar systems rotate. The Great Central Sun is also known as the Galactic Center, which is the origin of the Seven Rays of Light and Sound on Earth.

**Great Purification:** Primarily considered a Native American term, the Great Purification signals the end of one period of time for humanity and the beginning of a New Time. The Hopi Prophecies state the Great Purification will occur in several stages with prophesied Earth Changes, global wars, Climate Change, and nuclear devastation. Contemporary prophets view the Great Purification as a time for humanity to heal and transform individually and collectively. These actions create an opportunity for the Brotherhood of Man and a new society built on the ideals of cooperation rather than competition.

**Great Silence**: The Master Teachings encourage a contemplative period of quiet and stillness to intensely apply spiritual energies in certain circumstances and situations. This period of tranquil power is often referred to as the Great Silence.

**Great White Brotherhood and Sisterhood (Lodge)**: This fraternity of ascended and unascended men and women is dedicated to the universal uplifting of humanity. Its main objective includes the preservation of the lost spirit, and the teachings of the ancient religions and philosophies of the world. Its Mission: to reawaken the dormant ethical and spiritual spark among the masses. In addition to fulfilling spiritual aims, the Great White Lodge has pledged to protect mankind against the systematic assaults—which inhibit self-knowledge and personal growth—on individual and group freedoms.

**Green Ray**: The Ray of Active Intelligence is associated with education, thoughtfulness, communication, organization, the intellect, science, objectivity, and discrimination. It is also adaptable, rational, healing, and awakened. The Green Ray is affiliated with the planet Mercury.

**Guru**: Another name for teacher.

**Harmony**: The first virtue of the Twelve Jurisdictions based on the principle of agreement.

**Heart Chakra**: Known in Sanskrit as the Anahata. The location is in the center of the chest. Its main aspect is Love and Relationships, and includes our ability to feel compassion, forgiveness, and hold our own Divine Purpose.

**Hermetic Law**: Philosophical beliefs and principles based on the writings of Hermes Trismegistus, the Greek sage who is analogous to the Egyptian God Thoth.

**HU, the:** In Tibetan dialects, the word *hue* or *hu* means breath; however, the HU is a sacred sound and when chanted or meditated upon is said to represent the entire spectrum of the Seven Rays. Because of this, the HU powerfully invokes the presence of the Violet Flame, which is the activity of the Violet Ray and its inherent ability to transform and transmit energies to the next octave. HU is also considered an ancient name for God, and it is sung for spiritual enlightenment.

**HU-man**: The God-Man.

**I AM**: The presence of God.

**I AM Presence**: The individualized presence of God.

**I AM THAT I AM**: A term from Hebrew that translates to, "I Will Be What I Will Be." "I AM" is also derived from the Sanskrit Om (pronounced: A-U-M), whose three letters signify the three aspects of God as beginning, duration, and dissolution—Brahma, Vishnu, and Shiva. The AUM syllable is known as the omkara and translates to "I AM Existence," the name for God. "Soham," is yet another mystical Sanskrit name for God, which means "It is I," or "He is I." In Vedic philosophy, it is claimed that when a child cries, "Who am I?" the universe replies, "Soham—you are the same as I AM." The I AM teachings also use the name "Soham" in place of "I AM."

**Initiation**: Admission, especially into secret, advanced spiritual knowledge.

**Immortality**: Everlasting and deathless. Spiritual immortality embraces the idea of the eternal, unending existence of the soul. Physical immortality includes the notion of the timeless, deathless, and birthless body.

**Inner Earth**: Below the Earth's Crust lie many magnificent cities and cultures of various break-away races of humans, evolved HU-mans, and extraterrestrials. The Inner Earth is filled with reservoirs, streams, rivers, lakes, and oceans. According to metaphysical researchers the Earth is honey-combed with pervasive caves and subterranean caverns measuring hundreds of miles in diameter. This viewpoint is held by the Ascended Masters and shared throughout their Earth Changes Prophecies and historical narratives.

**Jiva**: The immortal essence of a living thing that survives death.

**Judgment**: The act of forming negative assumptions and critical opinions, primarily of fellow human beings.

**Kali Yuga**: The Age of Iron, or Age of Quarrel, when Earth receives twenty-five percent or less galactic light from the Great Central Sun.

**Karma**: Laws of Cause and Effect.

**Klehma**: The fifth United States Golden City located primarily in the states of Colorado and Kansas. Its qualities are continuity, balance, and harmony; its Ray Force is White; and its Master Teacher is Serapis Bey.

**Kuan Yin**: The Bodhisattva of Compassion and teacher of Saint Germain. She is associated with all the Rays and the principle of femininity.

**Kundalini**: The coiled energy located at the base of the spine, often established in the lower Base and Sacral Chakras. In Sanskrit, Kundalini literally means coiled, and Kundalini Shatki (shatki means energy) is claimed to initiate spiritual development, wisdom, knowledge, and enlightenment.

**Kuthumi**: An Ascended Master of the Pink, Ruby, and Gold Rays. He is a gentle and patient teacher who works closely with the Nature Kingdoms.

**Law of Attraction and Repulsion**: Like charges repel; unlike charges attract.

**Law of Correspondence:** "As above, so below."

**Law of Love**: Perhaps every religion on Earth is founded upon the Law of Love, as the notion to "treat others as you would like to be treated."

The Law of Love, however, from the Ascended Master tradition is simply understood as consciously living without fear, or inflicting fear on others. The Fourth of the Twelve Jurisdictions instructs Love is the Law of Allowing, Maintaining, and Sustainability. All of these precepts distinguishes love from an emotion or feeling, and observes Love as action, will, or choice. The Ascended Masters affirm, "If you live love, you will create love." This premise is fundamental to understand the esoteric underpinnings of the Law of Love. The Master Teachers declare that through practicing the Law of Love one experiences acceptance and understanding; tolerance, alongside detachment. Metaphysically, the Law of Love allows different and varied perceptions of ONE experience, situation, or circumstance to exist simultaneously. From this viewpoint the Law of Love is the practice of tolerance.

**Law of Nature:** The cycle of reincarnation.

**Law of Opposites:** Sir Isaac Newton's third Law of Motion, "Every action has an equal and opposite reaction." When this is understood according to Hermetic insight, everything has a pair of opposites, (e.g., hot and cold), and their difference is separated only by degrees.

**Law of Reciprocity:** In Biblical texts this is known as, "Give, and it will be given to you." The Master Teachers rephrase this to mean, "Energy flows within, energy flows without."

**Lei-lines**: Lines of energy that exist among geographical places, ancient monuments, megaliths, and strategic points. These energy lines contain electrical or magnetic points.

**Lemuria:** According to Ascended Master Teachings, Lemuria primarily existed in the present Pacific Ocean and esoteric historians theorize the oceanic tectonic Pacific Plate, through periodic geologic upheaval and Earth Changes forms the submerged lost continent of Lemuria. Spiritual teachings claim the evolutionary purpose of the ancient civilization developed humanity's Will (the Blue Ray of Power), and Lemurian culture venerated the *Golden Disk of the Sun* and the *Right-hand Path*. Lemuria, while claimed to be one the earliest cultures of humanity, ultimately integrated with the Lands of Rama, and Sri Lanka is alleged to have been one of the empire's capital cities. Asuramaya is one of the great Manus of Lemuria's Root Race. According to Theosophical history the Lemurian and Atlantean epochs overlap and it is alleged the lands of Lemuria, also known as Shalmali, existed in the Indian and Southern Pacific Oceans, and included the continent of Australia. Lemuria is the remaining culture and civilization of Mu—an expansive continent that once spanned the entire present-day Pacific Ocean. Some esoteric writers place the destruction of Mu around the year 30,000 BCE; others place its demise millions of years ago. The apparent discrepancy of these timelines is likely due to two different interpretations of the Cycle of the Yugas. It is claimed the venerated Elders of Lemuria escaped the global tragedy by moving to an uninhabited plateau in central Asia. This account mirrors Ascended Master teachings and Lord Himalaya's founding of the Retreat of the Blue Lotus. The Lemurian elders re-established their spiritual teachings and massive library as the Thirteenth School. It is claimed these teachings and spiritual records became foundational teachings in the Great White Brotherhood of the mystical lands of *Hsi Wang Mu* (the Abode of the Immortals), and the Kuan Yin Lineage of Gurus. Today, present-day Australia once known by Egyptian gold-miners as the ancient Land of Punt is the remainder of the once great continent of Mu and Lemuria which likely existed in the time period of Dvapara-Yuga, over 800,000 years ago.

**Light**: "Love in action."

**Light Body**: A body of subtle energy surrounding the human body. It survives death, and develops and evolves over lifetimes. Also known as the aura, the light body divides into layers of light energy. These strata are referred to as light bodies or layers of the field of the aura.

**Lighted Stance:** A state of light the body acquires during Ascension or the Ascension Process.

**Lords of Venus**: A group of Ascended Masters who came to serve humanity. They once resided on the planet Venus.

**Love**: "Light in action." The fourth of the Twelve Jurisdictions evolves our understanding of love as the Law of Allowing, Maintaining, and Sustainability.

**Malton**: The second United States Golden City located in the states of Illinois and Indiana. Its qualities are fruition and attainment; its Ray Force is Gold and Ruby; and its Master Teacher is Kuthumi.

**Mantra**: Certain sounds, syllables, and sets of words that are deemed sacred. They often carry the ability to transmute karma, spiritually purify, and transform an individual.

**Master Teacher**: A spiritual teacher from a specific lineage of teachers—gurus. The teacher transmits and emits the energy from that collective lineage.

**Mastery**: Possessing the consummate skill of command and self-realization over thought, feeling, and action.

**Meissner Field:** A magnetic energy field that does not contain polarity. It is produced during a transitory state of superconductivity. Ascended Master teaching associates this type of energy field with HU-man development, Unana, and Christ Consciousness.

**Mental Body**: A subtle light body of the Human Aura comprising thoughts.

**Michael**: The archangel of the Blue Ray. Archangel Michael is the protector of chelas and initiates of the Ascended Master tradition through the activity of the Blue Flame.

**Migratory Sequence:** A Golden City spiritual pilgrimage that travels through a certain progression of Adjutant Points. The progression of each sacred site may vary, dependent on the desired spiritual result for the chela or initiate. Some sequences focus on healing processes; others focus on integration of Golden City Energies, especially certain Golden City Doorways.

**Monad:** From an Ascended Master viewpoint, the Monad is the spark or flame of life of spiritual consciousness and it is also the Awakened Flame that is growing, evolving, and ultimately on the path to Ascension. Because of its presence of self-awareness and purpose, the Monad represents our dynamic will and the individualized presence of the Divine Father. Ultimately, the Monad is the spark of consciousness that is self-determining, spiritually awake, and drives the growth of human consciousness. The Monad is the indivisible, whole, divine life center of an evolving soul that is immortal and contains the momentum within itself to drive consciousness to learn, grow, and perfect itself in its evolutionary journey.

**Mother Mary:** Ascended Goddess of the Feminine who was originally of the Angelic evolution. She is associated with the Green Ray of Healing, Truth, and Science, and the Pink Ray of Love.

**Mudra:** A symbolic ceremonial or spiritual gesture, mostly expressed by the hands and fingers. It is often used by evolved spiritual beings and Ascended Masters to signify or emit spiritual energies.

**New Times, or New Age:** Prophesied by Utopian Francis Bacon, the New Age would herald a United Brotherhood of the Earth. This Brotherhood and Sisterhood would be built as Solomon's Temple, and supported by the Four Pillars of history, science, philosophy, and religion. These four teachings would synergize the consciousness of humanity to Universal Fellowship and Peace.

**Northern Door**: The North side of a Golden City gateway, also known as the Black Door.

**Om Manaya Pitaya or Om Manaaya Patiya**: This Ascended Master statement has several meanings. Two spiritual translations are: "I AM the Light of God" and "I AM the Seer of the Lord." The Sanskrit translation means: "Amen, honored Lord."

**ONE**: Indivisible, whole, harmonious Unity.

**Oneness**: A combination of two or more, which creates the whole.

**Oneship**: A group or group mind that is based on the notion of whole, harmonious Unity.

**Oral Tradition:** According to the Master Teachers and many indigenous teachers, the Oral Tradition, or learning through oral instruction, is the preferred medium to receive spiritual knowledge. This method requires the use of memory and memorization and also instigates the recognition of vital, yet subtle nuances that engender spiritual comprehension and may include the Master Teacher's use of telepathy, clairaudience, and clairvoyance.

**Perception**: Awareness and intuitive recognition.

**Pleiades:** A seven-star cluster that exists in the same Orion Arm of the Milky Way Galaxy near Earth. Also known as the Seven Sisters, the Pleiades is located in the Taurus Constellation. Its seven stars are: Sterope, Merope, Electra, Maia, Taygeta, Celaeno, and Alcyone.

**Point of Perception:** A certain position of understanding that allows for immediate or intuitive recognition.

**Prophecy**: A spiritual teaching given simultaneously with a warning. It's designed to change, alter, lessen, or mitigate the prophesied warning. This caveat may be literal or metaphoric; the outcome of these events are contingent on the choices and the consciousness of those willing to apply the teachings.

**Protective Grid:** The world-wide network of Golden Cities that exist on the Earth's surface, and within the inner Earth. As the Protective Grid expands into space it is known as the Galactic Web.

**Purification**: A clearing process, especially in spiritual practice, which frees consciousness from cumbersome or objectionable elements.

**Ray**: A force containing a purpose, which divides its efforts into two measurable and perceptible powers, light and sound.

**River of Life**: The thoughtful, conscious experience of life. It is also recognized as a silver-white current of high-frequency energy that separates the Third Dimension and the Fourth Dimension. It is alleged as the soul passes from this life that it travels upon this sublime river of effervescent, flowing energy of light to the heavenly levels of the Astral Plane.

**Ruby Ray**: The Ruby Ray is the energy of the Divine Masculine and Spiritual Warrior. It is associated with these qualities: energetic; passionate; devoted; determination; dutiful; dependable; direct; insightful; inventive; technical; skilled; forceful. This Ray Force is astrologically affiliated with the planet Mars and the Archangel Uriel, Lord Sananda, and Master Kuthumi. The Ruby Ray is often paired with the Gold Ray, which symbolizes Divine Father. The Ruby Ray is the evolutionary Ray Force of both the base and solar chakras of the HU-man; and the Gold and Ruby Rays step-down and radiate sublime energies into six Golden Cities.

**Sacred Fire**: The Unfed Flame of Divine Consciousness within the human heart. Often the term "Sacred Fire" is used to signify the Violet Fire.

**Sacrifice**: The spiritual ideal that through giving selflessly, or taking a short-term loss, that a greater long-term return for others is created.

**Saint Germain**: Ascended Master of the Seventh Ray, Saint Germain is known for his work with the Violet Flame of Mercy, Transmutation, Alchemy, and Forgiveness. He is the sponsor of the Americas and the I AM America material. Many other teachers and Masters affiliated with the Great White Brotherhood help his endeavors.

**Salt Bath:** A spiritual healing technique that cleanses the human aura. Its formula is two cups of any type of salt, used in the bath water with essential oils such as lavender or other floral scents.

**Sananda**: The name used by Master Jesus in his ascended state of consciousness. Sananda means joy and bliss, and his teachings focus on revealing the savior and heavenly kingdom within.

**Serapis Bey**: An Ascended Master from Venus who works on the White Ray. He is the great disciplinarian—essential for Ascension; and works closely with all unascended humanity who remain focused for its attainment.

**Service**: The fifth of Twelve Jurisdictions is a helpful act based upon the Law of Love.

**Seven Rays**: The traditional Seven Rays of Light and Sound are: the Blue Ray of Truth; the Yellow Ray of Wisdom; the Pink Ray of Love; the White Ray of Purity; the Green Ray of Healing; the Gold and Ruby Ray of Ministration; and the Violet Ray of Transmutation.

**Seventh Manu:** Highly evolved lifestreams prophesied to embody on Earth 1981 to 3650 AD. Their goal is to anchor freedom and the qualities of the Seventh Ray into planetary conscious activity. They are prophesied as the generation of peace and grace for the Golden Age. South America is their forecasted home, though small groups will incarnate in other areas of the globe.

**Shalahah**: The fourth United States Golden City located primarily in the states of Montana and Idaho. Its qualities are abundance, prosperity, and healing; its Ray Force is Green; and its Master Teacher is Sananda.

**Shamballa**: Venusian volunteers, who arrived 900 years before their leader Sanat Kumara, built Earth's first Golden City. Known as the City of White, located in the present-day Gobi Desert, its purpose was to hold conscious light for Earth and to sustain her evolutionary place in the solar system.

**Silicon-based Consciousness:** A level or state of consciousness that humanity is moving toward. Silicon-based consciousness is a form of crystalline consciousness that quickly interconnects with others through compassion, empathy, and telepathy. It is associated with clarity, purity, and is uniquely humanitarian. This level of consciousness evolves from our current state of carbon-based consciousness.

**Southern Door**: The South side of a Golden City gateway, also known as the Red Door.

**Spiritual Hierarchy**: A fellowship of Ascended Masters and their disciples. This group helps humanity function through the mental plane with meditation, decrees, and prayer. The term Spiritual Hierarchy often refers to the Great White Brotherhood and Sisterhood. However, the term also connotes the spiritual-social structure for the organization, its members, and the various states of member evolution. The hierarchy includes the different offices and activities that serve the Cosmic, Solar, Planetary, and Creative Hierarchies.

**Spiritual Migration**: The process of moving to and living in certain geophysical areas to purposely integrate and assimilate Earth's sacred energies for spiritual growth and evolution.

**Star**: The apex, or center of each Golden City.

**Star seed**: Souls and groups whose genetic origins are not from Earth. Many remain linked to one another from one lifetime to the next, as signified by the Atma Karaka, a Sanskrit term meaning "soul indicator." Star-seed consciousness is often referred to by the Spiritual Teachers as a family or soul group whose members have evolved to and share Fifth-Dimensional awareness. Star seeds can also contain members who have not yet evolved to this level, who are still incarnating on Earth.

**Step-down Transformer**: The processes instigated through the Cellular Awakening rapidly advance human light bodies. Synchronized with an Ascended Master's will, the awakened cells of light and love evolve the skills of a Step-down Transformer to efficiently transmit and distribute currents of Ascended Master energy—referred to as an Ascended Master Current (A.M. Current). This metaphysical form of intentional inductive coupling creates an ethereal power grid that can be used for all types of healing.

**Super senses:** Primarily the supernormal powers of telepathy, clairvoyance, and clairaudience, as they naturally unfold through the Law of Love and Unity Consciousness. These are the senses of the developed HU-man.

**Third Dimension**: Thought, feeling, and action.

**Third Eye**: The inner eye, referring to the ajna (brow) chakra.

**Thought, Feeling, and Action**: In Ascended Master teachings and tradition, thought, feeling, and action are the cornerstones of the creation process. Thought represents the mental (causal) body and the Yellow Ray. Feeling represents the emotional (astral) body and the Pink Ray. Action represents the physical body and the Blue Ray.

**Time of Change**: The period of time currently underway. Tremendous changes in our society, cultures, and politics in tandem with individual and collective spiritual awakenings and transformations will abound. These events occur simultaneously with the possibilities of massive global warming, climactic changes, and seismic and volcanic activity—Earth Changes. The Time of Change guides the Earth to a New Time, the Golden Age.

**Time of Testing**: The Time of Testing is a period of seven to twenty years which began around the turn of the twenty-first century, following the time period known as the Time of Transition. According to Saint Germain and other Ascended Masters, the Time of Testing is perhaps one of the most turbulent periods mankind will experience and its first seven years is prophesied as a period of change and strife for many. As its title suggests, the Master Teachers claim this timeframe may challenge students by testing their spiritual acumen and inner strength.

**Time of Transition**: A twelve-year period when humanity experienced tremendous spiritual and intellectual growth, ushering in personal and global changes. In the year 2000 a new era, called the Time of Testing, got underway. It's a seven-year span of time when economies and societies encountered instability and insecurity. These years are also defined by the spiritual growth of humanity; Brotherly love and compassion play a key role in the development of the Earth's civilizations as mankind moves toward the Age of Cooperation.

**Tube of Light**: Light surges from the tributaries of the Human Energy System: Chakras, meridians, and nadis—to create a large pillar of light. Decrees, prayers, and meditation with the Tube of Light increase its force and ability to protect the individual's spiritual growth and evolution. *See Golden Thread Axis*

**Twelve Jurisdictions**: Twelve laws (virtues) for the New Times that guide consciousness to Co-create the Golden Age. They are Harmony, Abundance, Clarity, Love, Service, Illumination, Cooperation, Charity, Desire, Faith, Stillness, Creation/Creativity.

**Unana**: Unity Consciousness.

**Unfed Flame**: The Threefold Flame of Divinity that exists in the heart and becomes larger as it evolves. The three flames represent Love (pink); Wisdom (yellow); and Power (blue).

**Universal Laws**: Laws that apply to the entire universe; considered a fundamental basis of nature and reality.

**Vibration**: The moving, swinging, or oscillation of energy. In Ascended Master teachings, vibration is associated with light's movement during physical and spiritual activities, as well as in the presence of the Masters.

**Violet Flame**: The Violet Flame is the practice of balancing karmas of the past through Transmutation, Forgiveness, and Mercy. The result is an opening of the Spiritual Heart and the development of bhakti—unconditional love and compassion. It came into existence when the Lords of Venus first transmitted the Violet Flame, also knows as Violet Fire, at the end of Lemuria to clear the Earth's etheric and psychic realms, and the lower physical atmosphere of negative forces and energies. This paved the way for the Atlanteans, who used it during religious ceremonies and as a visible marker of temples. The Violet Flame also induces Alchemy. Violet light emits the shortest wavelength and the highest frequency in the spectrum, so it induces a point of transition to the next octave of light.

**Violet Ray**: The Seventh Ray is primarily associated with Freedom and Ordered Service alongside Transmutation, Alchemy, Mercy, Compassion, and Forgiveness. It is served by the Archangel Zadkiel, the Elohim Arcturus, the Ascended Master Saint Germain and Goddess Portia.

**Vortex**: A Vortex is a polarized motion body that creates its own magnetic field, aligning molecular structures with phenomenal accuracy. Vortices are often formed where lei-lines (energy meridians of the Earth) cross. They are often called power spots as the natural electromagnetic field of the Earth is immensely strong in this type of location.

**Wahanee**: The third United States Golden City located primarily in the states of South Carolina and Georgia. Its qualities are justice, liberty, and freedom; its Ray Force is Violet; and its Master Teacher is Saint Germain.

**White Ray**: The Ray of the Divine Feminine is primarily associated with the planet Venus. It is affiliated with beauty, balance, purity, and cooperation. In the I AM America teachings the White Ray is served by the Archangel Gabriel and Archeia Hope; the Elohim Astrea and Claire; and the Ascended Masters Serapis Bey, Paul the Devoted, Reya, the Lady Masters Venus and Se Ray, and the Group of Twelve.

**White Star**: Nibiru, or Planet X. Its appearance ushers in a period of spiritual awareness and spiritual consciousness for humanity.

**Will**: Choice.

**Yuga**: Large recurring periods of time employed in the Hindu timekeeping system.

# *Discography*

*This list provides the recording session date and name of the original selected recordings cited in this work that provide the basis for its original transcriptions.*

**Toye, Lori**

*The Hidden Planet,* I AM America Seventh Ray Publishing International Audiocassette. ℗ No.071201. © July 12, 2001.

*All Is Love,* I AM America Seventh Ray Publishing International, Audiocassette. ℗ No. 072601. © July 26, 2001.

*The Master Within,* I AM America Seventh Ray Publishing International, Audiocassette. ℗ No. 081601, © August 2, 2001.

*The Mighty Violet Flame,* I AM America Seventh Ray Publishing International, Audiocassette. ℗ No. 081601. © August 16, 2001.

*I AM Awareness,* I AM America Seventh Ray Publishing International, Audiocassette. ℗ No. 120601, © December 6, 2001.

*Eternal Balance,* I AM America Seventh Ray Publishing International, Audiocassette ℗ No. 121301. © December 13, 2001.

*Golden Ray Mantra,* I AM America Seventh Ray Publishing International, Audiocassette ℗ No. 010302. © January 3, 2002.

*Path of Mastery,* I AM America Seventh Ray Publishing International, Audiocassette. © May 9, 2002.

*Galactic Energy, Shamballa 2002-2003,* I AM America Seventh Ray Publishing International, Audiocassette. ℗ No. 010603, © January 6, 2003.

*Six-fold Path,* I AM America Seventh Ray Publishing International, Audiocassette. ⓟ No. 011003, © January 10, 2003.

*Golden City Prayer,* I AM America Seventh Ray Publishing International, Audiocassette. ⓟ No. 012403, © January 24, 2003.

*Time and the Violet Flame,* I AM America Seventh Ray Publishing International, Audiocassette. ⓟ No. 013003, © January 30, 2003.

# Index

## A

Abraham Maslow  228
abundance
 *appendix*  233
 *definition*  237
acceleration(s)
 *definition*  237
 *in Southern Doors*  131
 *through the Violet Flame*  173
active intelligence  76
Adjutant Point(s)  140
 *definition*  237
 *Fifth Dimension*  159
 *help to stabalize weather*  163
 *Master Teachers*  162
 *Sergeants and Lieutenants at Arms*  157
 *service*  158
 *traveling to*  161
Africa
 *stabilized by Wahanee*  105
Age of Cooperation  106
Akashic Record(s)
 *and the Meissner Field*  35
 *definition*  237
alchemy
 *and the Violet Flame*  39
 *definition*  237
 *through the Violet Flame*  68
alignment
 *definition*  237
ancestors
 *of the hidden planet*  49
Ancestral Planet
 *behind our Sun*  30
 *definition*  237
 *race of spiritual beings*  34
 *trail of moons*  32
Ancient Builder Races  31
Angelic Kingdom
 *and Shamballa*  144

anger
 *and vibration*  87
animal consciousness
 *and evolution of the emotional body*  61
Animal Kingdom  74
 *and the Golden Age*  129
 *and the I AM Awareness*  92
 *and the Six-fold Path*  147
Antarctica
 *stabilized by Canadian Golden Cities*  105
anxiety  167
Archangel Michael
 *definition*  250
Archangels (the Seven)
 *definition*  237
Ascended Master energy
 *and Adjutant Points*  140
Ascended Master(s)
 *and the Golden Cities*  106
 *consciousness in Golden City*  32
 *definition*  237
 *intervene during Shamballa*  144
 *the Field of Protection*  193
 *their ancestral teachers*  50
Ascension
 *and daily life*  131
 *and galactic energy*  127
 *and light bodies*  178
 *and the Lighted Stance*  174
 *decree for*  134
 *definition*  237
Ascension Process  114
 *definition*  238
 *the freed chela*  158
Asia
 *stabilized by Shalahah*  105
asteroid
 *as a comet trail*  53
 *seven year warning*  54
Astral Body  179, 183
 *definition*  238
Atlantis  187
 *definition*  238

Golden City Series: Book Six                259

aura
  *definition 239*
Australia  105
  *stabilized by Shalahah  105*
Awakening  30

**B**

Babajeran  97, 110, 122, 145
  *and activation of the Golden Cities  106*
  *and prayer  162*
  *and the Earth Planet  74*
  *and the Golden Cities  106*
  *definition  239*
Bacon, Sir Francis  229
balance
  *and duality  176*
  *and non-judgment  88*
  *and the human condition  53*
  *definition  239*
"Before the eyes can see, they must be incapable of tears."  120
belief(s)
  *definition  239*
  *power of  81*
belief systems
  *and choice  36*
Beloved
  *Master I AM within  136*
Bhakti  128
Billy Meier  203
Blue Ray  129
  *definition  239*
brown dwarf star  79
building energy
  *through years of spiritual study and practice  122*

**C**

Canada
  *Golden City of Pashacino  110*
Causal Body  179, 183
cause and effect
  *definition  240*

chakra(s)
  *and Ascension  178*
  *definition  240*
chakra system
  *and Mastery  28*
change
  *and positive growth  43*
channeled sessions
  *appendix  227*
channeling
  *and use of citrus juice  137*
  *and vibration  137*
Charity
  *appendix  233*
chela  118
  *and the necessary sacrifice  139*
  *definition  240*
  *sacrificing time  161*
Children of the Seventh Manu  158
choice
  *and change  43*
  *and liberation  190*
  *and the I AM  89*
  *and thoughts  62*
  *and working with students  121*
  *definition  240*
Christ and Christ Consciousness  42
  *beyond duality  47*
  *birth of Christ Consciousness  39*
  *definition  240*
  *force as a Meissner Field  52*
Christ Plane
  *and Unana  101*
citrus fruits
  *and the Golden Ray  137*
Clarity  98
classes
  *Adjutant Points  159*
Co-creation  61, 95
  *and consciousness  36*
  *and vibration  87*
  *definition  240*
  *process  26, 95*
collective
  *karma  26*

Collective Consciousness
  definition 240
comet trail
  of Nibiru 53
compassion 61, 99
  and the Golden Age 128
  and the Open Heart 150
  and the Six-fold Path 146
  and the Violet Ray 145
  definition 240
  Violet Flame Decree 70
conscious immortality
  decree 71
consciousness 141
  and decrees 133
  and duality 86
  and Earth Changes 191
  and love 47
  and predictable consequences 87
  and prophecy 88
  and spiritual evolution 88
  and spiritual growth 88
  and spiritual practice 101
  and the Earth Plane 74
  and the Violet Flame 73
  and Unified Field Theory 76
  and vibration 85
  continuity of 161
  definition 240
  forms the physical body 36
  moving into silicon-based consciousness 77
  protection from Earth Changes 32
  stewards 33
  the group consciousness of the I AM Awareness 91
  universal 75
creation
  and consciousness 36
Crown Chakra
  and Golden Light 130
Cup
  divine wine 116

cycle(s)
  Galactic Center 141
  Golden Age 129
  twenty-year cycle 130

# D

DAHL Universe 31, 113
  and the Golden Ray 110
  appendix 203
  Master Teachers 110
darkness 99
  overcome through the Six-fold Path 148
decree
  acceleration 133
  before entering sleep 80
  definition 240
  for anxiety and stress 168
  for awareness of the I AM 89
  for drug use 81
  for service 162
  for the I AM Awareness 93
  "I AM eternal life." 71
  "I AM the resurrection." 70
  immortality 71
  Star of Wahanee 103
  to awaken the Master within 63
  to empower the I AM THAT I AM 89
  to out-picture perfection 60
  to raise vibration 86
  Violet Flame for justice 70
  Violet Flame for karmic burden 67
déjà vu 28
DERN Universe 203
desire
  definition 240
  to know God 62
detachment 100, 151
  and the Violet Flame 175
  move beyond duality 100
Deva Kingdom
  Fourth Dimension 159
  healing emotional energy 80

diet
  and Golden Ray  137
  and the schools of light  103
difference
  "Is experience."  94, 99
dimensions
  and the Earth Plane  74
disease
  and the human aura  174
  and the Violet Flame  182
Divine Heritage  63
Divine Inheritor
  definition  240
Divine Intervention
  and the Violet Flame  71
  of the Golden Cities  107
Divine Mission  116
Divine Order
  and disasters  194
Divine Plan
  definition  241
  humanity and the Hidden Planet  68
Divine Will  26, 94
  and change  43
  and choice  28
  and the I AM Awareness  94
  definition  241
  overcoming duality  88
Divinity  94
  and the I AM Awareness  93
doorway(s)  110
doubt  88
dream state
  working in  80
drugs
  "Experience without judgment."  82
dualistic consciousness
  and judging  86
duality  29
  and detachment  100
  and judging  86
  and separation  65
  and the I AM Awareness  92
  and the surrender of the will to the

Divine Will  88
  definition  241
  Earth Plane and Planet  164
Dvapara Yuga
  and the discovery of the hidden planet  51
  civilizations of Inner Earth  188
  definition  241
  development of the mind  77

# E

Eabra  105
  holds the world in balance  105
Earth
  and the kingdoms of creation  74
  astral body  79
  Earth's vibration  193
  Field of Protection  192
  "Is a blessing."  99
  "Is set upon a path of construction and growth."  54
Earth Changes
  and consciousness  191
  and prophecy  26
  and the comet trail of Nibiru  53
  and the Law of Correspondence  97
  collision with planet  32
  consequence  149
  definition  241
  Earth's energy fields  32
  Earth's Grid  32
  healing forces  131
  higher vibration  129
  intense weather  164
  "jumbling and tumbling of energy"  141
  political  109
  protection through higher consciousness  32
  war, famine  128, 157
  White Star  194
Earth Plane and Planet
  defined by Saint Germain  74
  for learning  164

Earth's Grids
 *definition* 241
Eastern Doors
 *definition* 241
economy
 United States 132
Eighth Light Body 113
 *definition* 241
Eight-sided Cell of Perfection 70, 91, 113, 122
 "A mighty transmitter." 35
 and the Fourth Dimension 28
 and the Great I AM 89
 and the I AM 89
 appendix 205
 chakra system 130
 decree for 70
 *definition* 241
 gather energy 133
 illustration 205
 remnant of Ancient Race 34
elemental
 *definition* 242
Elemental Kingdom 74
 *definition* 242
 healing emotional energy 79
El Morya 121, 148, 159
 *definition* 242
emotional body 114
 *definition* 242
 evolution of 61
energy
 and reciprocity 57
energy field
 *definition* 242
 "Energy flows within and without." 62
energy for energy 139, 157
 *definition* 242
enlightenment
 and compassion 61
ethereal schools
 and the Seven Rays 107
 and the Violet Flame 103
 and Wahanee 102

Europe
 stabilized by Malton 105
Ever Present Now 180
evolution 70
 and love 46
 and the Violet Flame 72
expectation
 and illusion 62
experience 89, 94
 "Experience is the guide." 99

# F

Faith
 *appendix* 234
fear 132
 and love 44
 fear energy 157
 transmuting through the Violet Flame 173
Feng-shui twenty-year cycles
 *definition* 242
Field of Protection 192
Fifth Dimension
 *definition* 242
 Master Teachers 159
 opening a portal 162
 waters of 168
financial obstacles
 Violet Flame Decree 186
focus
 and Co-creation 95
"Follow your bliss." 167
food and diet
 taking in of light 130
forgiveness 100
 and perception 105
 and the Six-fold Path 147
 of self 105
Fourth Dimension 29, 33
 and harmony 36
 and the readied heart 33
 *definition* 243
 Master Teachers 159
 waters of 168

freed chela  158
freedom
  *the three spiritual paths*  64

# G

Galactic Center  48, 110
  *and energy*  128
  *and predestination*  27
  *and the White Star*  194
Galactic Energy
  *and Shamballa*  144
  *opens collective heart of humanity*  135
  *Violet Flame*  127
Gateway Adjutant Points
  *definition*  243
genetic codes
  *and spiritual science*  35
global catastrophes
  *and consciousness*  191
Gobean  105
  *affiliated with Gobi*  105
  *and initiations*  121
  *definition*  243
Gobi  105
  *affiliated with Gobean*  105
  *definition*  243
Gobi Desert
  *and Shamballa*  31
God
  *God-like qualities in all things*  98
Golden Age  78, 121, 176, 191
  *definition*  243
  *Golden Spiral Decree*  177
  *in a troubled time*  146
  *influenced through the Galactic Center*  128
  *Saint Germain sponsors the Violet Flame*  156
  *understanding the Ray Forces*  163
Golden Age of Kali Yuga  223
  *definition*  243
Golden City Activation
  *definition*  244

Golden City (Cities)
  *and activation*  106
  *and Babajeran*  106
  *and Inner Earth*  188
  *and meditation*  102
  *and Southern Doors*  131, 161
  *and the White Star*  194
  *Divine Intervention*  107
  *electromagnetism*  110
  *integrating energies*  37
  *interconnectivity*  105
  *many chelas coming forward*  120
  *migratory sequence*  165
  *Protective Field*  32
  *safety and vibration*  163
  *Schools of Light*  107
  *stabilize continents*  105
  *Star, entering*  37
  *the Field of Protection*  192
Golden City Doorway(s)  37
  *activating*  164
  *appendix and illustration*  217
  *definition*  244
  *spiritual pathways*  216
Golden City Energies  37
Golden City Grid
  *definition*  244
Golden City Network  203
  *and Inner Earth*  189
Golden City of
  *Gobean*  121, 161, 166
    *definition*  243
  *Klehma*
    *definition*  247
  *Malton*
    *definition*  249
  *Shalahah*  189
    *definition*  253
  *the first seven*  104
  *Wahanee*  102
    *definition*  256

Golden City Vortex
  *activation*
    Ascended Master 213
    ceremonial 213
    geophysical 213
    Great Central Sun 214
  *Perspective Diagram* 215
  *Plan View Diagram* 215
  *through the dimensions* 201
Golden City Vortex Activation Dates
  *appendix* 211
Golden Ray
  *activates the Golden Thread Axis* 111
  *and diet* 137
Golden Ray Mantra 112
  *appendix* 225
Golden Spiral Decree 177
Golden Thread Axis
  *definition* 244
Gold Ray
  *definition* 244
Great Central Sun 69, 225
  *definition* 245
  *guidance through the ancestors* 50
Great Purification
  *and possibility for humanity* 69
  *definition* 245
Great Silence
  *definition* 245
  *"To do, to dare, and to be silent."* 59
Great White Brotherhood and Sisterhood 120
  *definition* 245
Green Ray
  *definition* 245
group karma 26
Group Mind
  *I AM Awareness* 91
guru
  *and chela relationship* 25
  *definition* 246

# H

Hall, Marie Bauer 230
harmonization of energy 112
harmony 90
  *and cultivation of tolerance* 92
  *and the Six-fold Path* 147
  *appendix* 233
  *definition* 246
  *through the Eight-sided Cell of Perfection* 36
hate
  *and doubt of God within* 87
Hawkins, Dr. David 219
healing
  *and choice* 36
  *and the Violet Flame* 183
  *for the United States* 133
heart
  *opening* 61, 99
Heart Chakra
  *definition* 246
Heart of Compassion 99
Heavenly Lords
  *spiritually liberated* 75
Hermetic Law 76
  *definition* 246
Hidden Planet 51
  *and the Divine Plan of humanity* 68
high-pitched ring 103
holocaust
  *planned by dark forces* 146
HU
  *and Violet Light* 113
  *definition* 246
HU-man
  *definition* 246
human aura
  *and disease* 174
  *definition* 239

# I

I AM 71, 227
  and choice 89
  and God perfection 70
  and the teachings of choice 89
  and Unana 89
  decree for 89
  definition 246
  interconectivity of the I AM
    Awareness 91
I AM America
  purpose of prophecy 88
I AM Awareness 90, 95, 104
  commanding 93
I AM Presence 234
  and the I AM Awareness 92
  and the time of Shamballa 144
  definition 246
I AM THAT I AM 89
  and consciousness 36
ignorance
  "Remove the veil of ignorance." 190
illusion 98
  and expectation 62
  and tests 98
  and the Earth Plane 74
immortality
  decree for 71
  definition 247
India
  stabilized by Shalahah 105
Indigo Children 158
initiation
  definition 246
Inner Earth
  Ascension 187
  definition 247
  portal near Las Vegas, NV 187
intention 161, 186
interconnectivity
  through the I AM Awareness 91

# J

jiva 130
  definition 247
judgment
  and dualistic consciousness 86
  definition 247
  "Is a trap." 82
Jupiter 141

# K

Kali Yuga 31
  and the awakening 77
  and the Golden Age 138
  and use of drugs 81
  definition 247
karma 44
  acceleration through the Violet
    Flame 176
  and duality 129
  and illusion 74
  and the Earth's ancestors 50
  and the Great Central Sun 114
  and the twenty-year cycles 141
  balanced through service 136
  definition 247
  group 26
  Master accepts the student's
    burden 116
  mitigation by Master Teacher 151
  past 207
karmic burden
  and the student 151
karmic pattern(s) 179
  and cycles 129
Klehma 105
  definition 247
  stabilizes North America 105
knowledge
  moves one beyond animal
    behavior 61
  the Path of Knowledge 64
Kuan Yin 148, 235
  definition 247

Kundalini 38, 124
  *and the Galactic Center 128*
  *and the Gold Ray 111*
  *Kundalini System and the Seven Major Chakras 199*
Kuthumi 148
  *definition 247*

# L

laboratory of self 148
Law of Attraction 44, 97
  *"When the student is ready, the Master appears." 98*
Law of Attraction and Duality 177
Law of Attraction and Repulsion
  *definition 248*
Law of Balance
  *and change 130*
Law of Change 196
Law of Correspondence 97
  *and Earth Changes 97*
  *definition 247*
Law of Forgiveness 100
  *and the Six-fold Path 147*
  *and the Violet Flame 101*
Law of Harmony 68
Law of Love 195, 196
  *and spiritual growth 45*
  *and the Earth's ancestors 49*
  *appendix 209*
  *definition 247*
Law of Nature
  *and the Earth Planet 74*
  *and the Violet Flame 72*
  *definition 248*
Law of Non-Judgment 233
Law of Opposites
  *and duality 29*
  *definition 248*
Law of Reciprocity 57
  *definition 248*
Law of Time
  *and the Violet Flame 181*

lei-line(s)
  *definition 248*
Lemuria 105
lessons 98
  *pain and love 190*
light
  *definition 249*
light bodies
  *acceleration through the Violet Flame 182*
  *and the Violet Flame 73*
  *definition 249*
Lighted Stance
  *and the Violet Flame 174*
  *definition 249*
lineage of the Master Teacher 120
Lords of Venus 207
  *and ancestral guidance 52*
  *definition 249*
love
  *and evolution 46*
  *and spiritual growth 100*
  *and the Law of Understanding 150*
  *appendix 233*
  *definition 249*
  *"Love for all." 100*
  *Path of Love 64*
Luk, A. D. K. 230

# M

Malton 105
  *definition 249*
  *stabilizes Europe 105*
mantra(s)
  *definition 249*
  *for the Violet Flame 82*
masses
  *"Led by ignorance." 33*
Master Teacher(s) 25, 119, 131, 182
  *Adjutant Points 162*
  *and Golden Cities 110*
  *and the student's karma 151*
  *appearance 159*
  *as the silent watchers 161*
  *chela and service 166*

lifts obstacles  179
lineage  120
student held in the vibration of  116
"We are here to lift the hearts of men, to shed light where ignorance and despair abound."  160
Mastery  95
 and choices  62
 definition  250
 Seven-Chakra System  28
medicine
 changes through Dvapara Yuga  78
meditation
 and Golden Cities  102
 for stress  167
 for working with students  117
 Golden Light  130
Meissner Field  35, 52
 definition  250
memory  124
Mental Body
 definition  250
messages
 sharing  116
metabolic rate
 and the Lighted Stance  174
Michael
 definition  250
migratory sequence  165
 definition  250
mind
 and the Violet Ray  45
Mineral Kingdom  74
 and the Golden Age  129
Monad  130
 definition  250
Mother Earth
 and the Six-fold Path  147
Mother Mary  148
 definition  250
mudra
 definition  251

# N

Neptune
 and the Golden Age  128
neutrality
 "There is no mistake ever, ever, ever."  88
New Age
 birth of through Earth Changes  32
 definition  250
New Atlantis  230
New Children  158
New Consciousness
 decree for the Gold Ray  223
New Times
 definition  250
 love and the open heart  150
Nibiru  52, 191
North America
 stabilized by Klehma  105
Northern Doors
 definition  251

# O

obstacles
 overcoming through living with intention  186
Om Manaya Pitaya
 definition  251
ONE
 and the I AM Awareness  92
 and the new consciousness  73
 and Unana  101
 definition  251
 overcoming disease  179
 the I AM Presence and the I AM Awareness  92
 "We are always ONE."  65
 with the Master Teacher  25
Oneship  28
 and Fourth Dimension  29, 33
 and the Meissner Field  35
 definition  251

one-world experience
  *not one-world government*  102
Open Heart
  *and compassion*  150
Oral Tradition  124
  *definition*  251
out-picturing  95
  *and the Violet Flame*  86
overtones
  *parallel universes*  28

# P

pain  96
  *"Is often the greatest teacher."*  96
parallel experience  28
parallel universe(s)  26, 203
Pashacino  105
  *stabilizes Antarctica*  105
past life  28, 169
  *reciprocity of mental energies*  58
perception  78, 149
  *and forgiveness*  105, 106
  *and prophecy*  97
  *and the Violet Ray*  41
  *definition*  251
perfection  60, 70
physical body
  *and consciousness*  36
pineal gland  124
Pink Ray  129
Planet X  191
  *a quickening*  193
  *as the White Star*  194
Pleiades
  *and ancient builder race*  31
  *definition*  251
  *Master Teachers*  110
Plejaren Federation  203
Point of Perception  61, 149
  *definition*  251
political changes  109
portal
  *Las Vegas, NV*  187
Portal of Consciousness  187

Portia  105
prayer  38
  *for service*  162
predistination  27
preparation
  *readied to receive*  63
probability
  *and the collective will*  54
prophecy
  *and human consciousness*  88
  *and prediction*  148
  *contains keys to circumventing disasters*  53
  *definition*  251
  *possibility and probability*  54
Protective Field
  *of the Golden Cities*  32
Protective Grid
  *definition*  251
psychedelic drugs
  *use of*  81
purification
  *and the Violet Flame*  175
  *definition*  252

# Q

quality of consciousness
  *and vibration*  85
questions
  *and evolution*  70

# R

race of spiritual beings  34
Ray Forces
  *and Southern Doors*  164
Ray(s)
  *and the ethereal schools*  107
  *definition*  252
reciprocity  57
Red Star  31
respect for all of life
  *and the Six-fold Path*  147

River of Life
  *and Fourth Dimension* 33
  *definition* 252
rose oil
  *for healing* 170
Rosicrucians 229
Ruby Ray
  *definition* 252

## S

sacred architecture 108
Sacred Fire
  *definition* 252
sacred geometry
  *and the Schools of Light* 108
sacrifice
  *definition* 252
Saint Germain
  *and the Violet Flame* 235
  *and the Wahanee School of Light* 104
  *and vibration* 85
  *definition* 252
  *golden band of energy* 192
  *Holy Brother* 152, 229
  *"I give my service."* 137
  *Kajaeshra* 230
  *Map of Political Changes* 231
  *Portia, Twin Flame* 105
  *teachings on the I AM Awareness* 91
  *teachings on vibration* 87
salt bath 117
  *definition* 252
Sananda 99, 111, 148
  *definition* 252
  *Sunday Peace Meditation* 219
Sanat Kumara 225
Sanctus Germanus 152
  *the Holy Brother* 138
Saturn 141, 207
  *and the Golden Age* 128
schools of light 103
science
  *and consciousness* 76

Seamless Garment
  *definition* 253
Sea of Consciousness
  *appendix* 234
self-discipline
  *leads to liberation* 151
self-realization 71
separation
  *and duality* 65
Serapis Bey 168
  *definition* 252
service 166
  *and karma* 136
  *appendix* 233
  *decree* 162
  *definition* 253
  *Path of Service* 64
  *Saint Germain's service to humanity* 139
Seven Rays
  *definition* 253
  *three plus three, plus one* 27
Seventh Manu 177
  *definition* 253
Shalahah 105
  *definition* 253
  *stabilizes India* 105
shaman
  *definition* 253
Shamballa 130, 143, 225
  *and ancient builder race* 31
  *definition* 253
silence 59
silicon-based consciousness 77
  *definition* 253
Singh, Major Kulwant 219
Six-fold Path
  *the principles* 146
Six-Map Scenario
  *teaching* 146
sleep
  *decree of protection* 81
Solomon's Temple 230

Soltec
 *Golden City of Pashacino* 110
soul
 *definition* 253
Southern Doors 131
Spiritual Awakening
 *and Kali Yuga* 77
spiritual growth
 *and Earth Changes* 97
Spiritual Hierarchy 146, 150
 *definition* 253
spiritual liberation
 *and the Heavenly Lords* 75
Spiritual Migration
 *definition* 254
spiritual path
 *and freedom* 64
spiritual practice 101
 *building energy* 122
spiritual stagnation 45, 101
Star of Gobean 123
Star(s)
 *and decrees* 133
 *critical points* 219
 *definition* 254
 *United States cities and towns* 220
Star seed(s)
 *definition* 254
 *groups activate* 130
Step-down Transformer 108, 111, 160, 195
 *activating Adjutant Point* 162
 *and Golden City Doorway activations* 164
 *decree of service* 161
 *definition* 254
stillness
 *appendix* 234
stuck 42
student
 *as a child at a feast* 125
 *Master appears* 135
 *struggle and doubt* 117
subconscious mind 227
subjective energy 167

suffering
 *and the Violet Flame* 73
Sun
 *dual, dead Sun* 30
 *the two Suns* 49, 79
Sunday Peace Meditation
 *and group consciousness* 111
 *appendix* 219
Super Senses 234
 *definition* 254
surrender to God
 *Path of Surrender* 64

# T

teacher
 *and student relationship* 25, 116
teaching
 *recommendations* 119
 *"There is not one soul ever, that we turn away."* 119
 *working with students* 117
telepathy 103
Temple of Mercy 235
Temple of the ONE 70
Temples of Consciousness 103
Third Dimension
 *Akashic Record* 35
 *and Ascended Master Consciousness* 32
 *and personal experience* 145
 *and the Law of Attraction* 44
 *definition* 254
Third Eye 124
 *opening* 42
Thirteen Evolutionary Pyramids
 *growth of the HU-man, illustration* 206
thought, feeling, action 39
 *definition* 254
 *mathematics* 27
time
 *and Fourth Dimension* 29
 *and parallel universes* 29
 *and the Violet Flame* 180

Time Compaction
  *and the Violet Flame* 184
Time is Now 195
Time of Change
  *convergence and confluence* 145
  *definition* 254
  *Dvapara Yuga* 163
  *Las Vegas Portal* 187
  *Master Teachers flood the Earth* 160
  *United States is leader of light* 190
  *weather changes* 164
Time of Testing 98, 101, 132
  *and spiritual stagnation* 101
  *definition* 255
Time of Transition
  *and humanity's potential transformation* 69
  *definition* 255
tolerance 88, 95
  *cultivating tolerance and patience* 92
  *without judgment* 88
transcendence
  *dawn and dusk* 185
transformation 209
transgression 106
truth
  *"Based upon experience."* 37
Tube of Light
  *and the Violet Flame* 72
  *definition* 255
Twelve Jurisdictions 138
  *and the Six-fold Path* 146
  *appendix* 233
  *definition* 255
twenty-year cycles 242
"Two Suns" 48

# U

Unana 65, 69, 89, 111
  *and the Golden City of Wahanee* 102
  *and the I AM* 89
  *as a Meissner Field* 52
  *definition* 255
  *Sunday Peace Meditation* 219

Unfed Flame
  *definition* 255
Unified Field Theory 76
United Brotherhood
  *and Wahanee* 102
United States
  *Declaration of Independence* 231
  *leader of light* 190
Unity Consciousness 227, 234
  *unified field of human consciousness* 219
universal consciousness
  *and the I AM Awareness* 91
Universal Law
  *definition* 255

# V

Vegetable (Plant) Kingdom 74
  *and the Golden Age* 129
vegetarian diet 153
veil
  *"The veil is lifted."* 180
Venus
  *and ancient builder race* 31
vibration
  *and consciousness* 85
  *and listening to channeled tapes* 137
  *and quality of consciousness* 85
  *and the Hidden Planet* 51
  *and the Violet Flame* 73, 176
  *decree to shift vibration* 89
  *definition* 255
  *Earth's* 193
  *"You create your own vibration."* 87
Violet Flame 71, 103
  *acceleration* 175
  *and Ascension* 178
  *and humanity's karmic burden* 67
  *and justice* 69
  *and karma* 44
  *and karmic patterns* 129
  *and Portia* 105
  *and the Law of Forgiveness* 101
  *and the Star of Wahanee* 102

and the use of the I AM  71
and Time Compaction  184
and use of drugs  81
and vibration  176
changes perceptions  182
decree before meditation  103
decree for Ascension  134
decree for difficulties  152
decree for finances  186
decree for healing  183
decree for imbuing documents  169
decree for stress  168
decree for teachers  118
decree for the light bodies  156
definition  207, 255
discipline  155
emotional balance  131
for anxiety  167
for compassion  70
for difficult and trying situations  68
for financial obstacles  186
for health  196
for judgment  86
for the United States economy  133
Golden Spiral Decree  177
healing and disease  181
higher intensity  127
immersion into the divine  82
invocation at sunrise, sunset  235
nighttime studies and classes  185
purification  175
recommendation  117
salt-water bath  167
Spiritual Lineage  235
stages of  183
to eliminate karma  67
to prepare for meditation  103
to raise vibration  86
transmute fear  173
use at sunrise and sunset  184
Violet Flame Mantra  82
Violet Flame Prayer  39
violet light
and the HU  113

Violet Ray  45, 72, 145
and perception  41
definition  256
Vortex (Vortices)
definition  256
Oklahoma  79

## W

Wahanee  105
and the Violet Flame  102
definition  256
Violet Flame Decree  103
waters of the dimensions  168
weather
and Adjutant Points  163
intensities  164
"When the student is ready, the Master then appears."  116
White Ray
definition  256
White Star
definition  256
prophecies  194
will
and choice change situations  26
and non-judgment  88
definition  256
Write and Burn Technique
definition  256

## Y

yuga
definition  256
Yukon Territory  105

## Z

Zadkiel
Order of  207

# *About Lori and Lenard Toye*

**Lori Toye** is not a Prophet of doom and gloom. The fact that she became a Prophet at all is highly unlikely. Reared in a small Idaho farming community as a member of the conservative Missouri Synod Lutheran church, Lori had never heard of meditation, spiritual development, reincarnation, channeling, or clairvoyant sight.

Her unusual spiritual journey began in Washington State, when, as advertising manager of a weekly newspaper, she answered a request to pick up an ad for a local health food store. As she entered, a woman at the counter pointed a finger at her and said, "You have work to do for Master Saint Germain!"

The next several years were filled with spiritual enlightenment that introduced Lori, then only twenty-two years old, to the most exceptional and inspirational information she had ever encountered. Lori became a student of Ascended Master teachings.

Awakened one night by the luminous figure of Saint Germain at the foot of her bed, her work had begun. Later in the same year, an image of a map appeared in her dream. Four teachers clad in white robes were present, pointing out Earth Changes that would shape the future United States.

Five years later, faced with the stress of a painful divorce and rebuilding her life as a single mother, Lori attended spiritual meditation classes. While there, she shared her experience, and encouraged by friends, she began to explore the dream through daily meditation. The four Beings appeared again, and expressed a willingness to share the information. Over a six-month period, they gave over eighty sessions of material, including detailed information that would later become the I AM America Map.

Clearly she had to produce the map. The only means to finance it was to sell her house. She put her home up for sale, and in a depressed market, it sold the first day at full asking price.

She produced the map in 1989, rolled copies of them on her kitchen table, and sold them through word-of-mouth. She then launched a lecture tour of the Northwest and California. Hers was the first Earth Changes Map published, and many others have followed, but the rest is history.

From the tabloids to the *New York Times*, *The Washington Post*, television interviews in the U.S., London, and Europe, Lori's Mission was to honor the material she had received. The material is not hers, she stresses. It belongs to the Masters, and their loving, healing approach is disseminated through the I AM America Publishing Company operated by her husband and spiritual partner, Lenard Toye.

**Lenard Toye,** originally from Philadelphia, PA, was born into a family of professional contractors and builders, and has a remarkable singing voice. Lenard's compelling tenor voice replaced many of the greats at a moment's notice—Pavarotti and Domingo, including many performances throughout Europe. When he retired from music, he joined his family's business yet pursued his personal interests in alternative healing.

He attended *Barbara Brennan's School of Healing* to further develop the gift of auric vision. Working together with his wife Lori, they organized free classes of healing techniques and the channeled teachings. Their instructional pursuits led them to form the *School of the Four Pillars* which includes holistic and energy healing and Ascended Master Teachings. In 1995 and 1996 they sponsored the first Prophecy Conferences in Philadelphia and Phoenix, Arizona. His management and sales background has played a very important role in his partnership with his wife Lori and their publishing company. Other publications include three additional Prophecy maps, thirteen books, a video, and more than sixty audio tapes based on sessions with Master Teacher Saint Germain and other Ascended Masters.

Spiritual in nature, I AM America is not a church, religion, sect, or cult. There is no interest or intent in amassing followers or engaging in any activity other than what Lori and Lenard can do on their own to publicize the materials they have been entrusted with.

They have also been directed to build the first Golden City community. A very positive aspect of the vision is that all the maps include areas called, "Golden Cities." These places hold a high spiritual energy, and are where sustainable communities are to be built using solar energy alongside classical feng shui engineering and infrastructure. The first community, Wenima Village, is currently being planned for development.

Concerned that some might misinterpret the Maps' messages as doom and gloom and miss the metaphor for personal change, or not consider the spiritual teachings attached to the maps, Lori emphasizes that the Masters stressed that this was a Prophecy of choice. Prophecy allows for choice in making informed decisions and promotes the opportunity for cooperation and harmony. Lenard and Lori's vision for I AM America is to share the Ascended Masters' prophecies as spiritual warnings to heal and renew our lives.

## Books and Maps by Lori Toye

### Books:

NEW WORLD WISDOM SERIES: *Book One, Two, and Three*

FREEDOM STAR: *Prophecies that Heal Earth*

THE EVER PRESENT NOW: *A New Understanding of Consciousness and Prophecy*

I AM AMERICA ATLAS: *Based on the Maps, Prophecies, and Teachings of the Ascended Masters*

GOLDEN CITY SERIES
  *Book One: Points of Perception*
  *Book Two: Light of Awakening*
  *Book Three: Divine Destiny*
  *Book Four: Sacred Energies of the Golden Cities*
  *Book Five: Temples of Consciousness*
  *Book Six: Awaken the Master Within*

I AM AMERICA TRILOGY
  *Book One: A Teacher Appears*
  *Book Two: Sisters of the Flame*
  *Book Three: Fields of Light*

I AM AMERICA COLLECTION
  *Building the Seamless Garment: Revealing the Secret Teachings of Ascension and the Golden Cities*

### Maps:
  *I AM America Map*
  *Freedom Star World Map*
  *United States 6-Map Scenario*
  *United States Golden City Map*

I AM AMERICA PUBLISHING & DISTRIBUTING
P.O. Box 2511, Payson, Arizona, 85547, USA. (928) 978-6435
I AM America Online Bookstore:
**www.iamamerica.com**
For More Information:
**www.loritoye.com**

# About I AM America

I AM America is an educational and publishing foundation dedicated to disseminating the Ascended Masters' message of Earth Changes Prophecy and Spiritual Teachings for self-development. Our office is run by the husband and wife team of Lenard and Lori Toye who hand-roll maps, package, and mail information and products with a small staff. Our first publication was the I AM America Map, which was published in September 1989. Since then we have published three more Prophecy maps, thirteen books, and numerous recordings based on the channeled sessions with the Spiritual Teachers.

We are not a church, a religion, a sect, or cult and are not interested in amassing followers or members. Nor do we have any affiliation with a church, religion, political group, or government of any kind. We are not a college or university, research facility, or a mystery school. El Morya told us that the best way to see ourselves is as, "Cosmic Beings, having a human experience."

In 1994, we asked Saint Germain, "How do you see our work at I AM America?" and he answered, "I AM America is to be a clearinghouse for the new humanity." Grabbing a dictionary, we quickly learned that the term "clearinghouse" refers to "an organization or unit within an organization that functions as a central agency for collecting, organizing, storing, and disseminating documents, usually within a specific academic discipline or field." So inarguably, we are this too. But in uncomplicated terms, we publish and share spiritually transformational information because at I AM America there is no doubt that, "A Change of Heart can Change the World."

With Violet Flame Blessings,
*Lori & Lenard Toye*

For more information or to visit our online bookstore, go to:
www.iamamerica.com
www.loritoye.com

To receive a catalog by mail, please write to:
I AM America
P.O. Box 2511
Payson, AZ 85547

# Awaken to the Change Within

FROM THE BESTSELLING AUTHOR OF THE I AM AMERICA MAPS

## THE
## Ever Present Now

A NEW UNDERSTANDING OF
CONSCIOUSNESS AND PROPHECY

LORI ADAILE TOYE

**The Ever Present Now**
ISBN: 9781880050507

loritoye.com
iamamerica.com

Or, call 928-978-6435
or Amazon.com

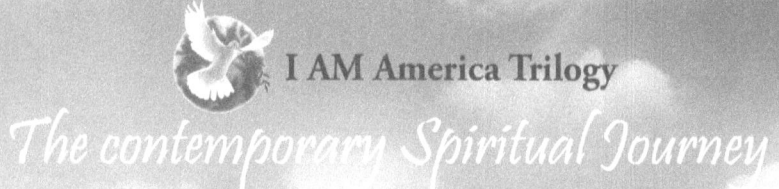

# I AM America Trilogy
## The contemporary Spiritual Journey

**A Teacher Appears**
ISBN: 978180050446
254 pages

**Sisters of the Flame**
ISBN: 978180050262
216 pages

**Fields of Light**
ISBN: 978180050613
310 pages

This series of insightful books, written by the creator of the acclaimed *I AM America Maps* shares a fresh and personal viewpoint of the contemporary spiritual journey. Lori Toye was just twenty-two years old when she first encountered Ascended Master teaching. The *I AM America Trilogy* takes us back to the beginning of her experiences with her spiritual teachers and includes insights that have never been disclosed in any previous books or writings. In "A Teacher Appears," learn how true wisdom and the inner teacher is within all of us. "Sisters of the Flame," continues an initiatory passage into the feminine with the Cellular Awakening. "Fields of Light," explains how to integrate and Master our spiritual light through soul-transcending teachings of Ascension. Lori's personal story is interwoven throughout the *I AM America Trilogy* in a rich tapestry of spiritual techniques, universal wisdom, and knowledge gained through a life-changing spiritual journey.

**I AM America Atlas**

Updated Edition!
Contains all of the
I AM America Maps
Full color
Over 100 Maps
164 pages

**New World Wisdom Series**

Spiritual Teachings from
the Ascended Masters
Books One, Two, and Three

## Spiritual Teaching for the New Times

*For more information:*
loritoye.com
iamamerica.com
*or call* (928) 978-6435

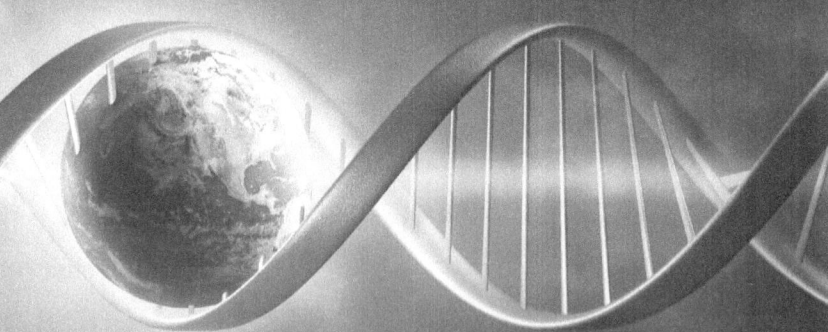

www.ingramcontent.com/pod-product-compliance
Lightning Source LLC
Chambersburg PA
CBHW020108240426
**43661CB00002B/79**